W9-AEE-681

BOOKIE

My Life in Disorganized Crime

by
Gary Mayer

PUBLISHED BY J. P. TARCHER, INC., LOS ANGELES

Distributed by Hawthorn Books, Inc., New York

Library of Congress Catalog Card Number: 74-79507

ISBN: 0-87477-023-8

Manufactured in the United States of America

Published by J. P. Tarcher, Inc.
9110 Sunset Blvd., Los Angeles, Calif. 90069

Published simultaneously in Canada by
Prentice-Hall of Canada, Ltd.
1870 Birchmount Road, Scarborough, Ontario

2 3 4 5 6 7 8 9 0

Contents

To Al, Jeremy, and Jane

Author's Note

The characters, situations and events in this book are factual. In some cases the names, dates, and specific locales have been changed to protect the identity of Mr. Talcum and his customers.

The book contains many words and phrases used in the gambling world. Moreover, it contains many terms used solely by Mr. Talcum, his out-to-lunch customers, and his degennie friends.

If "out-to-lunch" and "degennie" convey nothing to you, if you think a "hedge" is something a gardener trims, "Rikers Island" a resort in the Caribbean, "turkey" what you eat on Thanksgiving, or "tapioca" a pudding, then you would do well to consult Talcum's Terms at the back of this book.

Early morning, Sunday. December 1973. A day of rest for lots of people, just not for bookmakers. Twelve National Football League thrillers, four or five pro basketball games and some NHL hockey. This won't be like spending the day on the beach in Miami.

By 8:30 A.M., I've swallowed a diet pill and two cups of coffee, knowing I'll have to be cooking to contend with the frantic day ahead. By 9 A.M., I'm dressed and outside catching my first and last breath of fresh air—if anybody can consider the air on New York's West 79th Street fresh. I make a quick stop at the corner newsstand to pick up a late *New York Times* and head over to the Mayflower Coffee Shop for some orange juice and final scores. Without that L++ edition of the *Times* my day couldn't start. I have to get a batch of West Coast college football results and, of course, one of those insomnia special Saturday night NBA games (like Seattle at Portland when you can't get a half-time score until 3:30 in the morning).

The late *Times* has all the results, and over breakfast I squeeze them out to get some idea of how much my customers won and lost for the day. I'll do the figures later. I'll have to, because I know from experience that once a Sunday gets rolling during the football season you don't have a chance to breathe, much less think.

After breakfast I walk the twelve blocks to my joint, and by 10 A.M. I'm in the door, dug in at my desk like an offensive tackle, gritting my teeth and waiting for the phones to start ringing.

This is some place for a grown man to spend his time, I think to myself, lighting the first cigarette of a two-pack day. The building I'm in is what Webster had in mind when he defined the word "slum." The glass is broken out of the windows, so they're boarded over, the ceiling's tin, and the only place garbage isn't piled is on the stairway. I don't work here because I like the atmosphere. In my business you sometimes have to sacrifice comfort for cover. For that, this place is perfect.

I work on the fourth floor. My only neighbor is a Spanish man who lives in a two-room apartment with five very large dogs and an equal number of tropical birds. On the rare occasions when I run into Señor Maderos he's always wearing a white tee shirt and a New York Mets baseball cap and is walking two or three of his dogs. He never brings all of them out at once or someone might drag him away. I don't think he speaks any English but I've seen him go into the OTB office in the neighborhood. Maderos probably thinks OTB is an English word like "banana" or "plum." Little does he know that he could save the trip by knocking on my door.

A retired schoolteacher lives below me, and being in the final stages of senility, he's not much of a security risk. At first he made attempts to get friendly, thinking I was a professor (which is what I told the landlord), but I've rebuffed his advances so many times he's given up. If I thought he bet basketball, even once a season, I'd have him up for tea, but I'm sure the guy thinks overtime is when you work late.

The real treat is on the first floor and part of the second: a whorehouse run by someone who calls herself Mrs. Pop. She has the two apartments on the first floor and another on the second in case she gets a standing-room-only crowd. Mrs. Pop thinks I don't know what's going on. To her and the girls I'm Mr. Cohen, a quiet homebody who uses the upstairs apartment to tutor students in the neighborhood. Many times I've seen three or four of the girls walking around the halls buck naked and all they ever say is, "Hi, Cohen." I say, "Good evening, ladies," then walk upstairs mumbling something about being tardy for a geometry lesson. Mrs. Pop tells me they're her daughters. I tell her I went to Harvard. I mean fair is fair, right? It's hard to describe Mrs. Pop. She has legs and arms a lot bigger than Roosevelt Brown's but without any muscle tone whatsoever. She might not even have bones, and with all the makeup she wears her age is hard to figure. Then again, when you're dealing with a woman who resembles a lipsticked hockey puck, who cares?

Her customers all look the same. They wear white shirts and no ties, have huge combs in their back pockets, and come to the house in threes. On Friday and Saturday nights the crowd extends out into the street like guys waiting on a daily double line at Aqueduct. In fact, she does a hell of a business and I have to give Mrs. Pop a lot of the credit. You see, when new johns come to the place and see her fat legs sticking out of a tight mini skirt, the first reaction is panic. Then when she explains to the boys that she's the madam and the girls are inside, the relief is so great the johns forget how bad the girls are and trip over one another racing to the bedrooms.

This early on a Sunday, Mrs. Pop's girls are still asleep, resting from their Saturday night chores. The only sounds I can hear are from Maderos' apartment, where the whine of a muffled bark or the flap of feathers ruffling never stops.

My joint is a wreck. At $50 a month rent I'm still getting beat. It's one big room, and as you walk in, you face a wall with a bricked-up fireplace in its center. To the right there's a corroded bathtub and kitchenette area, and on the left an old mattress lies on the floor, covered by yellowed newspapers I've thrown there in disgust after overdosing on the sports section.

I work seated at an old desk against the near wall. On

the desk are two pillows with a telephone nestled in each. I have the ring on both turned to its lowest level. On a snack table I keep a small portable television along with a transistor radio. These serve two purposes: One, nobody can hear me from the hallway with the TV or radio turned up high; and, two, I can keep up with all the late scores by watching or listening to the games being broadcast while I'm working. I keep a jar full of Bic pens nearby at all times so I can grab a new one in case one runs out of ink and, of course, I never have less than fifteen to twenty yellow legal pads handy so I can record the action. That is, after all, why I spend four to six hours a day in this revolting place.

Sometimes on a Sunday morning the phone is already ringing as I'm coming up the stairs. Any other time of the year my hours are pretty well set between noon and 2 P.M. during the day and 6 P.M. to 8 P.M. at night, but during the football season, when everyone takes a shot, I have to come in this early on Sunday just to handle the ninnies and their action. Ninny action is any bet of $25 or less that I take as an accommodation to my old friends and small bettors who want to get down. As long as I get it done before noon when the heavy numbers start, it's no big deal. All it takes is a little of my time and it's worth it for the goodwill. Sometimes young ninnies grow into hitters later in life. Hell, in five or ten years a twice-a-week $20 bettor might develop into a real monster, so one Talcum Law of Bookmaking is that a BM should be nice to his ninnies. Especially to the ones who have "-$72.50" written in front of their names every Sunday night.

I've been taking action on games all week, and except for a Knick-Chicago Bull puker I got buried by on Thursday, things have been slow. Friday night it began heating up with LSU at Tulane, but until today the action was really preliminary stuff—kind of like the first couple of rounds in a fight when two boxers feel each other out.

Today all the sparring is over. By 11:30, which is the time most BMs are settled in their joints or phone booths around the city, my ninny action is behind me, and I'm waiting for Waldo Dorsohp's call. As always, it comes. (Of course his calls had been coming since Monday when Waldo told me I owed him 1,400 "smackerooskis" in "hedgski" money, and Tuesday when he called to give me the advance betting line on football—adding the comment, "For an early birder it's sharp, but after I get the injury reports I'll start coming in with 'adjustkis.' " But Sunday is always my favorite day to listen to the world's greatest BM. Because on Sundays the action is heaviest, Waldo is most afraid of "heatski," and best of all, my name for the day is always "Flounder." He is also the world's greatest "codeski" maker-upper.)

Well, after Waldo gives me the line to use for the day—arrived at by taking into consideration everything from injuries, to betting patterns, to weather conditions—I wedge my pen between my fingers, brush off a yellow legal pad, and sit back waiting. As usual, it's like getting hit by a tidal wave. The phones start ringing at 11:45, and until 1:10 I don't have five seconds between calls. As each bettor comes in, I write down his bets with one hand and pick up the second phone with the other. "Al, this is Teddy." "Al, this is Max." "Al, this is Abe." "Yeah," I answer each call. "Here they come, Teddy." "Here's what I got, Max." "Okay, Abe." "The Redskins 14 over the Giants, Kansas City 9 over the Bears, Green Bay 6½ over Cincinnati, Oakland pick-em with Cleveland." I like each of my customers to feel he's getting special service, but long before 1:10, I am struggling to sound fresh with any of them.

Most of the early action is on the 2 P.M. TV game, the New York Giants playing at Washington. There are a lot of games being played in the East this afternoon—Baltimore at Jets, San Diego at New England—so the phones are really humming. Even Waldo comments on the amount of early action when he calls in to pick up "hedgskis": "Gimme what you got, Flounder. I'm getting pounded by everybody."

The furious stuff tones down around 2:05, after the Giant game begins. I have time to adjust the fine tuning on the TV and take a bite out of a cheese danish, but before I can swallow the last crumb, the degennies are calling in for the three o'clock games in the Midwest. By 2:10 the phones are like lava, and the insides of my ears are sweating big drops.

At 3:15 I hit the usual midafternoon lull when even the most rabid degennie takes time out for a Budweiser. I get through two cigarettes and a deep breath, but in ten minutes it's banzai time again—the four o'clock TV thriller from the Far West when everyone tries to get even, or if they're having a good week, get even better. (Mainly because Monday is the start of a new cycle when the past week's accounts are settled. Of course, you can get degennies who would like to stay in action right up until midnight by betting Sunday night hockey games like Toronto at Montreal, but since I don't work past 4:00, they're out of luck unless they call me by then.)

Today, the four o'clocker is Dallas at Denver and it is bet like mad. I have more money riding on it than on the Giant or the Jet game and, despite how tired I am, I still have to laugh. I mean, very few people in New York are Bronco or Cowboy fans but they bet the match up like the Rocky Mountain time zone has moved far enough east to put Pike's Peak in the Brooklyn-Battery Tunnel. It's a typical "ironing board job" alright. The losers are pressing, the winners are steam cleaning, and as long as twenty-two guys show up with a pigskin and play ball between Ford Galaxie spots, nothing else matters. Thirty-five minutes and four grand in action later, I am ready to leave the joint, and as the phones stop ringing, I can feel the tension whoosh out of me like air escaping from a deflated balloon. Between the phone calls and flipping the television dial back and forth, moving the line, and writing down who bet what and for how much, I feel like Butkus hit me twice in every game I dealt.

Bookmaking isn't all sweat, but football Sundays make a lot of its good points disappear.

Just a little thing like a customer who wants to chat can make life impossible. Yeah, on a slow Tuesday we can schmooze, but not on Sunday. I don't have time. "The Bears +9, Al—looks like a steal to me." "Steal it, Mel, steal it!" I feel like screaming, "Just let me off the phone so I can breathe." Then there are the guys with four, five, six different bookies, shoppers they're known as, who call every twenty minutes but never bet unless they got an edge. "Larry, I got the Colts, 9½ point favorites," I answer politely, even though it's Larry's ninth call of the day. I have to. Shoppers are as much a part of the game as anything else and, Sunday or not, I have to put up with the fact that some of them had more bookmakers numbers than the police.

And as if the schmoozers and the shoppers aren't enough, I even speak to strangers who get me as a wrong number, wanting to know what time "The Godfather" goes on or if I'll deliver pastrami sandwiches to East 68th Street. "Sure, we deliver," I say every time, "just wait till the Denver game is over."

By 4:15 I pack up my bag of tricks and head for the exits. I put the work in my attaché case, clean up the garbage that accumulated during the week—six or seven *New York Posts*, a couple of *New York Times*, about 400 cigarette butts, and the wrappers of countless half-eaten cheese danishes—check through the peephole for badges, and leave.

I come down the steps with the coast clear, and it's the first time I feel fully relaxed since early that morning, but my Sunday as a BM is hardly finished. When I get home to my West Side apartment, I flick the four o'clock game on the tube, make black coffee, and start going over the work. I almost never make mistakes. When the results of games are embedded in my brain from sitting alone in a one-room dump listening to Ray Scott and Curt Gowdy announce scores for hours, I'm even better than the AP ticker.

My wife and baby girl, having long since given up the hope of ever spending a pleasant autumn Sunday with me, are out for the afternoon, leaving me with Tyrone, my twelve-year-old, twenty-five-pound cat. The work is bearable, but the game on television is a horror (the Cowboys are beating Denver 25 to 14, it's the last quarter, I need the Broncos and they are only +3), and it isn't until past six that I finish Saturday's and Sunday's figures and get to start on the real killer, the work for the week.

By 10:30 I'm wondering why I do something like this for a living. I mean, here I am, a reasonable, fairly intelligent adult, and I won't have sex with my wife until I get a hockey final from Chicago. Luckily, I can ignore her pleas, and I spend the rest of the night hunched over my coffee table doing BM homework. For relaxation, I leave the TV on, with no sound, so Tyrone and I can watch "The Late, Late Show," and with double and triple checking I am finished by 4 A.M.

I take a break to grab a quick slice of roast beef, and too wired from the coffee to sleep, plan my paying and collecting route for the next day. Then I settle down for a wet nap in a hot bath, watching the sun come up through my bathroom window.

By 7:30 I am ready to begin rounds that will take me from the truck-clogged maze of the garment center, down the canyons of Wall Street, in and out of Village brownstones and East Side luxury co-ops. I'll see customers who are cops, butchers, hustlers, talent agents, doctors, stockbrokers, and salesmen. But they all have two things in common—they like to bet and I am their bookie.

You just don't decide to be a bookmaker one day. I mean, let's face it, despite the pride I have in my craft, it's not as if I became a doctor or a lawyer like most of the kids I grew up with. To become a BM you have to be out to lunch to begin with, pay your dues along the way, and pass through life like it's nothing but a long, long ballgame.

When I was growing up, my parents had *one* friend who went by the name of Aristotle J. Feta. Not only was he a family intimate, so close he was chosen to be my godfather, but Aristotle owed his life to my old man. The story was that somewhere in the Argonne Forest during World War I, my father, may he rest in peace, at the very first sound of a whining German artillery shell, grabbed two other soldiers and threw them into a bunker, covering them with his body in the same motion, which you have to admit, was a pretty good move for a man in the ready-to-wear clothing business.

One of the two men he happened to save was the above-mentioned Aristotle J. Feta, and when the war ended they returned to New York and began their lifelong friendship. As it turned out, Aristotle, at the tender age of twenty-three, was already a millionaire. It seemed he had come to this country from Greece, with a family poorer than church mice, and between jobs as a cafeteria dishwasher he perfected the concept of mass producing ready-rolled cigarettes.

What he did with the idea was to get the R. J. Reynolds Tobacco Company interested enough to buy it and agree to pay him a royalty on the cigarettes produced. What evolved from this arrangement was a fortune which went directly to Aristotle and which he kept increasing by the simple method of buying tobacco stock he knew would increase in value thanks to his fertile little Greek mind.

To make a long story short, Aristotle lived a very fine and prosperous life. My father and he were as close as any two men could be, and since Aristotle was a confirmed bachelor with no living relatives, this could have been a very nice thing. Sure enough, one day in March of 1960, when I was twenty years old and in the middle of a hustling trip in West Virginia, I received a telegram from my father:

ARISTOTLE DIED SUDDENLY LAST NIGHT STOP
PLEASE RETURN HOME FOR FUNERAL

Normally, I wouldn't have come home for anything short of a subpoena but this news had possibilities. After all, Aristotle must have accumulated five or ten million dollars in his lifetime and you had to figure his godchild was good for a little taste.

I was so anxious to know the terms of the will that I asked a buddy of mine to go to probate court and find out so when I arrived back in New York I'd get the good news immediately. He found out okay. Not a hello. Everything to "Catholic Church, New York." Everything. What he'd had on his night table, the house in Atlantic Beach, the vegetables in the freezer, everything. I believed it. It was your basic zippo . . . busto . . . blanko time. I went away the day after the funeral, minus the money I'd laid out for plane fare, and pretended to be resigned to my fate. Come on, Al, I said, the

Catholics need the money and, besides, you got plenty of dough. I did, too, close to $45 and I wasn't counting loose change.

I recovered quickly. My values had never been too good, I reasoned, so inheriting big money might have made things worse. In fact, money had done strange things to me since I was a kid jumping checks in luncheonettes while my parents' chauffeured limousine was waiting for me at the curb. Some tykes expressed themselves by drawing pictures; I'd do it by not paying for egg creams.

I was raised in the Colorado Apartments on West 79th Street in a cozy sixteen-room dwelling, and by the time I was five I hated every square foot of it. My routine was to get home from school, call for the limousine, get my dog, and head for a candy store. I'd go in, eat, leave without paying when I could jump back into the car, and be driven to Central Park, where I'd play until it was time to be driven downtown to pick up my parents.

They were your basic penniless, ignorant Jewish immigrants who arrived in New York from Germany in the late 1800s. By the time my father learned a few vowels and my mother memorized the route to Gimbel's, they had formed a thriving ready-to-wear clothing business and had thirty-five people working for them.

Mother was a small, stocky woman with a thick accent. Her first name was Inga, and being an only child, I received all her attention. Unfortunately, it consisted of constant fears that every time I set foot out of the Colorado lobby I was sure to get double kidnapped and polio. Then, again, compared to my father Hymie, she was like having a sky diver for a mother.

Hymie, poor Hymie. If my mother was a museum exhibit, my father was the curator. He was short, squarely built, and always behaved like he was either going or coming from a very close friend's funeral. In fact, I can't remember him ever laughing. Even on days he took off, he wore a three-piece suit and acted like the headmaster of a Prussian military school. At a very early age I felt uncomfortable in his presence, a feeling that never changed, and it was too bad because he was an intelligent, often nice man. I guess you'd say it was a waste, him spending his life sitting erect and looking on edge, but his business was successful, and for many years it kept the man going.

Neither of my parents gambled, or did much of anything, now that I think about it, but their vacations were true classics. Every three years they'd leave for a cruise in the Caribbean and two days later be back home. My mother said she missed her friends, which consisted of Aristotle and our Negro maid, and my father claimed he was restless away from the office.

As dull as my surroundings were, I couldn't do much about it. I was too young to join the Foreign Legion or take my own apartment; so I waited. And I have to admit, it was better growing up with elderly, dull people on Central Park West than it was being raised by an exciting young couple in a cold-water flat. I mean, sixteen rooms is sixteen rooms.

I was no bargain either, a condition I worked hard to maintain. For instance, my mother would have liked me to be nice to her sister, Aunt Mildred, but when she came by I refused to give her a kiss and usually locked myself in the bathroom until she was gone. But when my mother's least favorite relative, Uncle Morris, came by, I always climbed right up on his knee and listened to his foul mouth. He told stories of the fight game he loved, and soon I became fascinated by boxing myself. That was a problem, because in the late forties the Friday night fights came on the radio way past my bedtime and I was never allowed to stay up and listen. I didn't argue. I just did what I've continued to do all my life, which was whatever I wanted. I'd simply go to bed, close the door, and listen to the fights on the radio. When my mother would come to check if I was sleeping, I'd turn the sound off and roll over. It was hell when I missed the knockout, but it beat screaming Yiddish.

Sometimes when the fights would end early, I'd sit up in bed listening for sports results. Everyone I knew rooted for the Yankees, so to be different I rooted for the Boston Red Sox. They were the only team in the American League who could make the "Bombers" sweat, and besides it ticked off every kid on the block.

Enjoying boxing and rooting for the Red Sox were only two of the ways I had to shake things up. Often, I'd say things just to annoy people, and I can still remember one beauty. I was six years old at the time and the Nuremberg trials were being reported nightly over radio. Coming from a Jewish family and living in a Jewish neighborhood, I knew they were *the* big topic of conversation. One night at dinner my parents asked me what I thought of the trials. "They're okay, I guess, but I like to listen to the fights a lot better." This, as you can imagine, got a big round of applause from the folks. They would have sent me to my room, but they knew that's where I wanted to go anyway, so they sat a little more erect and accepted me for what I obviously was—a punishment.

From the age of eight on, I used the people I was surrounded by—my parents, relatives, and business associates— as kind of opposite indicators. When they had no interest in a topic, I'd immediately look into it. On the other hand, I'd automatically feel negative toward almost anything they liked or sanctioned. If they said it was good to eat oranges, I'd want grapefruit; if they demanded I take piano lessons, I'd say drums; to this day I do most of my best learning by using this reverse logic.

Also, as a child I could detect in people, especially the ones I met through my family, a false nicety that made me even less of a delight than I already was. My parents were the wealthiest members of their family, so every weekend a parade of relatives passed through our apartment and I never heard a conversation where someone wasn't asking for money, begging a favor, or making a deal.

It was such a closed, insulated little circle that until I was ten years old I thought the whole world was Jewish, worked in the ready-to-wear clothing business, and had to eat lox to survive.

Thankfully, by that time my family and myself had reached a Mexican standoff. They stopped trying to make me into a combination musician, dancer, child wit and prodigy, and I stopped embarrassing them by asking questions like why my aunt's teeth moved when she talked. It was an uneasy peace at best, but at least it gave my parents hope. As my mother sometimes whispered to my father, just loud enough for me to hear, "Hymie, you know Alfred could be a late bloomer like your brother Leo." I think Hymie knew better.

I wasn't very good at making friends with kids. It wasn't that I was shy or a bully, but I liked being a loner, sort of an eight-year-old Clint Eastwood type. You know, stoic, firm, walking along West 80th Street in shorts pretending not to be with my mother.

Most of my friends were in the Central Park Zoo. A lot of kids liked the zoo, but to me it was more than a place—it was an escape. All I understood was that animals didn't care how much money you made, who you were, or what you gave Uncle Lou for his last birthday. If you were nice to them, they responded in kind, and I never saw that in people. As a result, I spent more and more time at the zoo talking to half-asleep lions and trying not to think about what a pain in the ass school was becoming.

I could get away with plenty of stuff at home, but by the time I hit fifth grade, I had to come up with some new tricks to take care of this education business. It was tough. I was attending a private school in Manhattan called Ethical Culture, which was a great place to spend your formative years if your parents had tons of money and you liked to say, "Yes, Mrs. Techler," a lot. On the other hand, it was a bitch for a pint-sized pagan like myself, and I was hardly a model student. I mean, I was a damned terror. This place kept me away from the zoo too many hours a day, and I didn't think learning 8 + 3 equaled 11 was worth it. The only thing that kept me from getting thrown out was my parents' money, but even that didn't last forever.

My father was selling silk blouses hand over fist, but for every hundred pair sold he had to make another donation to the school's athletic fund to keep me enrolled, and my mother was there so often for meetings with teachers, most people thought she was on the faculty.

With the help of a newly developed interest in baseball, I brought the problem to a head one morning in April that year. I was acting up, and the teachers were threatening to send me home. They didn't know it, but that's exactly what I wanted them to do. Getting out of school was never a punishment to me, and this spring day getting sent home would have been better than ever. It just happened to be the opening day of the baseball season, the Yankees were playing the Red Sox in Boston, and it was going to be carried on television, which in those days was a big thing. Boy, I didn't want to miss Mel Parnell, Ted Williams, and Allie Reynolds; to me that was living, not this crap about hamsters and multiplication tables I was hearing in class.

I couldn't use the pepper-in-the-nose act again. Not even my mother would buy that any longer, so I figured I had to do something drastic to get sent to the principal's office. Suddenly it hit me. All year our class, with the exception of yours truly who was usually home sneezing, had worked on building a papier-mâché castle which was hung on the wall complete with a drawbridge and string attached. I mean this thing took all year, piece by piece, day by day, and with an hour left before game time, it was my ticket out. I took the string from the drawbridge and tied it to the hair bow on the girl (Marilyn Feldstein was her name) who was sitting in front of me. Sure enough, five minutes later the teacher asked the class to get up and go to the back of the room to look at frogs or lizards or something, and boom—Marilyn Feldstein rose and the whole damn castle, an entire year's work by thirty-two little horrors, came crashing down. Of course everyone knew it was my doing. It was always my doing. Even when Michael Shapiro, the other class clown, did something, I was blamed, and this time was no different. I was marched down to the office, by the ear, and sent packing immediately.

I arrived in plenty of time for the game, and it was great. Boston beat the Yankees, I missed a day of school, and the faculty committee decided they were never going to let me attend their school again. My parents suffered, but by the end of the summer they bought my way into another private school, and the next fall I began attending Columbia Grammar, on West 90th Street. One school was just like another to me, so I picked up my reign of preteen terror where I'd left off and behaved worse than ever. There was one change, though, and it was a big one. My interest in boxing had developed to a point where I wanted to participate in it, and after a childhood filled with sleepy lions and telling Nazi jokes to my parents, that was no small thing.

Boxing appealed to me for several reasons. One was that my parents disliked it (the opposite indicator), but more important, I liked the way a boxer could stand alone. A jockey had to have a horse, a basketball team could have four super players and lose with one ninny, a baseball team could have five great hitters and four bad pitchers and be just so-so, but a boxer had only one person to blame if he blew it—himself. It was you and the other guy and no stories. To a kid with my personality that was attractive.

I had my first fight while attending Columbia Grammar, but soon I had to transfer my talents to the local YMCA. The seventy-five-pound gloves the school made me wear slowed me down, but I still kicked ass. I mean I meant business, and in my third fight at school I took those huge gloves and knocked Irving Conklin cold before he was out of his robe. Of course I knocked him out. Irving was there for some light exercise before chemistry class and I wanted to be the next Benny Leonard.

After I was banned from Columbia Grammar's boxing program, I moved on to the "Y," but I was still too tough. Even there, when somebody got hurt, his opponent would stop punching and say, "Oh, are you all right?" I never stopped punching. I boxed to win, and way before my first shave I had a good left-right combination and a hell of an uppercut.

In the summer of 1952 I went away to summer camp, where I was my usual repulsive self but, more importantly, where I suffered the first defeat of my boxing career. I fought a fifteen-year-old kid (I was thirteen at the time) who was only the strongest kid in all of Camp Sagamore. His name was Michael Spindel, and although I was undefeated, I must have been a prefight 30-1 underdog. After all, the kid was fifteen, he had hair on his chest, and I think he might have even been going out with girls.

Naturally, I got smashed, but I did flurry a couple of times, Spindel never knocked me down, and I was still jabbing when the camp director stopped the fight. I was obviously in over my head, but I think he would have let the fight continue if the next weekend wasn't parents' visiting time. There might have been some heavy tipping gone down the drain if Hymie and Inga ever saw me beaten up, and the counselors, much as they would have liked to, weren't about to let that happen for a few thrills. As a matter of fact, the staff scheduled a fight for me that coming Saturday with a kid by the name of Dickey Bradley. Boxing Dickey Bradley was like fighting my leg he was so bad, but the ring was set up, the lights were shining, and my parents were watching. You know I kicked the stuffings out of Dickey, all ninety pounds of him, and the counselors got faked out anyway. My parents never tipped anything except their hats, and Dickey's folks made him leave camp.

I came back to school in the fall and got into trouble immediately. I asked for it. I did everything from putting tacks on chairs to sawing off the leg of a biology teacher's desk, and I'd even begun making some book on the Red Sox, though their best years were behind them. Every time Boston played the Yankees, I'd take my classmates' ten-cent Yankee bets, and once in a while Boston got lucky and actually won. Still, I came out behind every week, no matter what, because in those days I never knew about odds. On a betting line the Yankees would be huge favorites and I was trying to make money letting the sons of textile millionaires bet me lunch money even-up.

Well, somebody put all those bad habits in a report, and I was expelled by midterm. This was a private school, after all—a privilege to attend, not a right, as I was told every day—and I stuck out like a sore thumb. I wondered if it was Marvin Schneider who squealed. Ah, it was my own fault; I never should have thrown that cherry bomb in his locker.

While my parents started to shop around again, looking for another private school, I spent all my days identically. I'd get up in the morning and go to Loebman's candy store, which was right near my house, steal the money off the newspaper counter they kept outside (I had a real nice move for that—I'd put my nickel down for a newspaper in case I was being watched, and then in the same motion slip all the change on top of the paper into my other hand) and then go in to have English muffins with jelly, a discovery which for six months was the most exciting thing in my life. For exercise, I'd take an occasional jaunt down to the "Y" in the afternoon to beat up whoever was available.

Within a few weeks my parents found a private school that didn't have a "wanted dead or alive" poster of me in the principal's office, and I was enrolled, kicking and screaming all the way. This one was called the Franklin School and I gave it a month.

An amazing thing happened at Franklin: I began to enjoy school. I wasn't going to win any scholarship awards, don't get me wrong, but at least I stopped burning down classrooms and blowing up lockers. I don't think I felt any more studious, but the teachers at this school really seemed to care about their students and I could feel the change in attitude. As a result, an occasional B or sometimes even an A would show up on my report card, shocking the hell out of me and causing my parents to think I was blackmailing teachers. Between enjoying Franklin School and boxing, I was beginning to like life for the first time ever, but then I had a setback in family relations and personal happiness—something called a bar mitzvah.

I thought I'd taken care of this bar mitzvah garbage by getting thrown out of Hebrew school—I can still hear Rabbi Ellman telling my mother they didn't want my kind there, which was some nice thing to say, considering I was Jewish. Instead, fighting the good fight, my parents went and hired a private tutor.

When I heard the guy was a seventy-year-old retired cantor, I didn't bitch. I mean I just didn't want to go through with this nonsense and no seventy-year-old Rumanian had a chance to change my mind. If he got rough, I'd sic my dog Scotty on him and make him into chopped meat.

When the day came for my first lesson, I was up in my room holding Scotty hard by the collar, so he'd go extra crazy if I let him loose. Just then there was a knock on my door and in walked this stooped-over, elderly man who spoke in a heavily accented, yet firm voice, "Hello, Alfred, my name is Cantor Buckman," he said, and for no reason, I sat straight up in my chair.

The guy seemed pretty sure of himself, like he had walked up plenty of stairs to tutor plenty of bratty Jewish kids, and his confident manner made me nervous. I could contend with someone telling me to go to bed at ten o'clock if I wanted to grow up and be big and strong. I knew that meant nothing, so I'd nod my head "yes" and leave the radio on until 4 A.M. But this Buckman talked to me like an adult.

I remember once, a few weeks after we'd started meeting, he showed up and asked me to read him a section of Hebrew I was supposed to have studied over the weekend. To be obstinate, I'd done no studying at all, making the cantor's visit a complete waste of his time and my parents' money. Instead of going into a song and dance about becoming a man or making my family proud, he simply got up from his chair and, taking a very deep breath to let me know he was disappointed, said, "Alfred, I'm too old a man to walk this far for nothing. If you won't study, I won't teach." With that, he left, leaving me sitting there with Scotty and fifty-seven back issues of *Ring Magazine*.

From that day on, I tried to have my lessons ready whenever the cantor came to the house, and for a kid that never had anything ready for anyone, that was quite a step. Of course, I still refused to give him my word that I'd go through with the ceremony, but he took care of that three weeks before the big day.

Cantor Buckman simply put his arm around me and, in the warm yet firm tone he used that made me respect him when all I wanted to do was bite everyone else, said, "Alfred, if you go through with this bar mitzvah you will be uncomfortable for forty-five minutes to an hour and you will have to be in the company of your relatives for an afternoon, but for these small inconveniences you will receive thousands of dollars in cash and bonds."

At the time I was getting 75¢ a week in allowance, and if the Yankees kept winning, that was gone Wednesdays, so this was something to think about. If my parents had talked to me this straight, we could have saved a lot of trouble. I didn't want to hear about becoming a man, but money to buy all the English muffins I couldn't steal was a different story.

After a night of mulling the thought over, I decided to give it a go. With cold cash as an incentive, I attacked my lessons like a diehard rabbinical student, and I was so good at the ceremony my parents nearly fainted from joy. Cantor Buckman came and stood in the back of the temple with his eyes closed and his fingers crossed. I think up until the last line of the service they all expected me to do something humiliating, but with all those white envelopes I saw sticking out of pockets there was no chance of that.

I spent two hours accepting congratulations and tucking $50 savings bonds into my suit, and then I snuck out of the reception to watch the Kentucky Derby on television. Native Dancer was a big favorite of mine but he lost that day—the only race he would ever lose—and I felt momentarily depressed. Of course, I recovered quickly when I remembered how much money was in my coat pocket and went back inside.

If I had had any idea of what was in store for me, I would have stayed outside, ransacking the guests' cars.

In the summer of 1953 the bottom fell out of my parents' business. Their firm was solely dependent on the fabric imported from the Orient and because of the Korean War restrictions my father had gradually found himself with a shrinking source of supply, exorbitant costs, and fewer customers, until one day he looked up from his desk and we were broke. Since he had poured all the money he'd ever made back into the business, we had nothing to fall back on except for a semivaluable collection of badly chosen paintings. Worse, my parents were in their late sixties and knew how to do absolutely nothing else. So while other people might 'suffer business reverses and slip from one economic class to another, because of my parents' bad luck, old age, and lack of planning, we went from being very rich to being poor . . . very poor.

While my father tried desperately to reorganize his sinking business, we moved out of our sixteen-room place in the Colorado and into a four-and-a-half room apartment further west on 79th Street near West End Avenue. Having been quietly spoiled, I found this sudden turn of events annoying. I mean, I was ready to begin appreciating nice clothes, and a bigger allowance. Instead, it was hello IRT and goodbye limousine.

In the fall I realized I'd seen the last of private schools and sensed my family would never have big money again. Hymie was plugging away, trying to launch a pajama business, but he was simply too old and too set in his ways to make a go of it.

In September I was enrolled at Commerce High School and, boy, did I miss all those horrible private schools fast. I mean, they might have been boring and petty, but at least they were safe. Going from places like Ethical Culture and Columbia Grammar to Commerce High was a lot like going from the Eden Roc Hotel to Rikers Island, and I didn't like it. I was downright scared. I barely knew about things like black kids and gangs and knives, and here I was being asked to join the "Stomping Hornets." How could I join? I had to be home by 9:30.

Well, Commerce High was no treat, but after a few weeks there it became clear that I had nothing to worry about. This wasn't a rough city school with roving toughs, and wild gangs who'd rumble over who had the best leather jackets. This place was crawling with organized crime. Some kids sold porno; others peddled stolen exams, one group dealt dope, another rented out guns (38s not zips), and they had Commerce divided up like it was the south side of Chicago. So as long as I wandered around minding my own business, smiling, and pretending to be retarded, nobody bothered me.

Quickly, Commerce's fine qualities began to rub off on me and I made my first trip to a whorehouse, which wasn't difficult since there was one across the street from the school's front door. It was in the Marie Antoinette Hotel and it figured to be easy setting things up because most of the girls working there were students at Commerce.

It happened on a hot, humid day early that October when I saw this beautiful Filipino-looking girl leave school and walk into the hotel. Like a magnet, I followed her in, made a fumbling, stuttered agreement on money, and wham, we were in a room together . . . alone. I was glad we didn't have company because this was my first time, and I knew as much about girls as my mother knew about playing second base. Maybe less, and it didn't help that the temperature was 80 degrees outside, and since the fan didn't work, and I couldn't get the window open, at least 110 in the room. Anyway, after she coaxed me into bed I was still glad we were alone but I would have preferred being there by myself. Nervous to begin with and sweating like a pig, I almost drowned the girl for openers. Then I whispered "I love you" into her nose, and came under her arm. After that all I remember is her getting dressed in eight seconds and running down the stairs in four, leaving me in bed, naked, drenched, and embarrassed. And $5 poorer.

Well, my education at Commerce turned out to be more of a farce than my education at the Marie Antoinette. Nobody in the entire school was interested in learning anything but safecracking or headcracking, and the teachers all but kept running charts on how many days were left until their pensions began so they could get the hell out of there.

In a class fifty minutes long it took forty minutes to call the attendance, and I remember having one term of English consisting of a roll call, the first line of *A Tale of Two Cities,* and the bell ringing.

Obviously, it wasn't too hard for a student like me to find distractions in this circus atmosphere, and one popped up in the spring of 1954 when I got myself a job working at a newsstand on the corner of 79th Street and Broadway. I didn't want a job but my allowance was down to 25¢, my parents had nibbled away my bar mitzvah haul, and it was a matter of working or no lunch money. Anyway, the owner of this stand was a guy named Max Kramer and did he love the horses. He went out to Jamaica every day, and it was my job to run the stand while he was at the races, for which he paid me the sum of one dollar an hour. In those days a dollar an hour was plenty and getting it four hours a day, five days a week, could add up. After working there a few weeks I'd accumulated a tidy sum and asked Max if I could go to the track with him on Saturday when his wife ran the stand. I'd never been to the races before, but I'd watched a few on TV and had a feeling I might like them.

Might like them? . . . Come on, was Napoleon short? . . . Before you could say "Gimme the 7 horse," I was there every day I had off. I was only thirteen but I never had any trouble becoming a track regular. I was tall, almost five foot eight, wore thick glasses, seldom smiled, and always had my nose buried in the racing form like every other improver of the breed. Besides, I was the kind of kid who looked fifteen at ten, and twenty-one when I was twelve, so whenever other kids came with me I'd get them past the guard by telling him they were with me.

It was a good thing I looked old because to me the track was heaven. I hated school more than ever, girls still terrified me, and my parents were more miserable poor than rich, so outside of boxing it was all I had going for me. At the track I was outside, around animals, nobody was there to tell me what to do, and on top of all that it wasn't bad catching old "Banana Nose" Arcaro on a 9 to 1 shot.

Soon I talked Max into letting me switch my hours to early evening, and whenever I had more than $10 in my pocket I was long gone. Other kids went to school with their books under their arm and lunch in a bag. I went with the *Morning Telegraph* hidden beneath my sweatshirt and a pair of secondhand binoculars squeezed into a lunch pail.

As my interest in the horses grew, my marks got worse than ever. They'd been bad up to this point in my freshman year but now I was really bombing. Anything under 65 was failing, and I was knocking out forties and fifties left and right. But despite my marks and poor attendance, I never came close to getting anyone upset. You see, when I showed up in school I behaved myself, and at Commerce if you were white, pleasant, and had no felony convictions, the teachers would make sure you were promoted on gratitude alone.

I milked that looking-good-by-comparison trick pretty good. Like in May I started on one stretch when I was at the track every afternoon. I'd stay in school until 11:30 each morning, then duck out during the 90-second monitor change between periods. I had that escape down pat but, unfortunately, I tapped out eight days later and as a punishment for being broke had to return to class on a full-time basis.

My homeroom teacher that term was a very strict lady named Miss Schmidt, a German terror who wouldn't take back talk from anyone. Well, when I walked into her homeroom my first day back, Miss Schmidt had an absentee list in front of her that looked like the Manhattan phone book.

She began with Luis Rodriguez. Luis would come to school about five or six times a month, but I think the only reason he ever dropped in was to pick up a cut of his gang's hunting knife sales. "Rodriguez," Miss Schmidt said in a clipped German accent, "you've been out weeks. What's your excuse?" "I don't feel so good, teach, I stay home," Rodriguez snapped. "What was wrong, Mr. Rodriguez? Why were you home?" Two questions was Luis' limit. "I don't feel good," he screamed, "I stay home." Then he turned his back to show he'd had it with this crap.

"Mr. Simpson, I hope you can give me a better answer than Mr. Rodriguez. Where have you been the last six days?" Miss Schmidt said. Leroy Simpson came to class much less than Rodriguez, and he'd been through this so many times he had his answer memorized. "My head felt bad, teach. You know I don't come in when my head feel bad." Two hoodlums was Miss Schmidt's limit. "Mr. Simpson, stand up when you talk to me," she fumed, "and tell me what was wrong with you." Leroy would just sit there with his legs sticking out into the aisle and he'd answer without even thinking about standing up, "I said my head don't feel good, teach. Sheet, it don't even feel good now, but I come in anyway."

At this, the class went hysterical and Miss Schmidt started banging her ruler against the blackboard, threatening to put people on report. When the roar quieted down she turned to me. "Alfred Talcum, you've been absent over a week. What was wrong with you?" I might have been a dummy in geography but I was always prepared for homeroom, and this time I'd got a small piece of cotton, swabbed it in iodine, and stuck it in my ear. As I stood up, she looked ready to goosestep on someone's face, but in my best king's English I said, "I had an abscess on my eardrum, Miss Schmidt, and since I don't react well to penicillin, I stayed home until the infection receded. Last evening it broke and now I'm here to resume my studies." Then I sat down. Miss Schmidt didn't believe me but it didn't matter. I was like Winston Churchill seated among thirty-five convicts, so she excused my absences without an argument and by Thursday I had enough cash to get me back on the $6 combination line at Jamaica.

I stayed on that line for a good chunk of my next year or so at Commerce, and I only left when I was tapped or had an amateur bout to fight in. I don't think I had one date with a girl in all that time but finally, in the fall of my junior year, I stumbled upon my first "free" sexual experience. It happened as I was walking to a bus stop on my way home from a gym on East 86th Street. I was alone as usual. The young boxers I knew were friendly to me around the gyms and rings, where we shared a common bond, but outside we went our separate ways.

Anyway, when I got to the bus stop, I heard a car horn beeping. I ignored it but, as the beeps continued, I turned and saw that they were coming from a white convertible parked across the street. The car was occupied by a gorgeous red-headed girl who looked to be in her mid-twenties. She seemed to be staring in my direction but, since I couldn't believe that, I glanced behind me, thinking someone else must have been standing there. When all I saw was a litter basket, I walked over to the car, hoping she wasn't an attractive truant officer, and within a minute I realized I was being picked up, and it wasn't for truancy. I mean this was just like being in the movies and everything.

I acted pretty cool for a while, which was amazing because I was scared the moment she suggested we go to her apartment. Even as I jumped in Carol's car I was thinking of the Marie Antoinette fiasco and on the way over to her 3rd Avenue place she began to sense my nervousness. Near 54th Street Carol asked if this was my first time. Wanting to maintain my suave image, I tried to get my mouth to say, "Hell no," but instead, I leaned forward, looked at her softly, and in my deepest voice said, "Are you kidding? Yes." Was I glad Carol laughed.

There was one last obstacle to overcome before we got to her apartment. Candid and loose as the girl seemed, I would have stopped boxing before telling her I wasn't as old as I looked, and I would have quit breathing before I'd admit having to call home. So I made up a story about needing to talk with my boxing coach and asked her to pull over to a phone booth. Carol said okay, parked the car, and waited.

"Listen, Mother," I whispered, "I won't be home for dinner, please start without me." Now that's not a terrible thing for a fifteen-and-a-half-year-old kid to say, but she acted like I was leaving the country. "Alfred, why aren't you coming home for dinner? Why? Where are you going?" I could see I wasn't going to win this decision so I pulled out my ace in the hole, good old Lenny Roth. Lenny Roth was the type of kid every parent dreamed of raising and for years a day didn't go by without me hearing about it. "Give me strength," my mother would chant. "If only you behaved like your friend Lenny" was one of her staples, and another biggie was, "God should hold a hand over me, Alfred, but if I could trade Muriel Roth for her son, I'd take him."

Well, I didn't like the kid, but he was good for something. I could tell my mother I was joining a band of gypsies and if Lenny Roth was coming, I'd leave with her blessings. Anything I'd do with him was okay, so to get out of this smelly phone booth before Carol discovered I was a phony, I said, "Mother, I'm going out with Lenny tonight. Don't worry." That did the trick. "Such good news you should keep secret," she said. "Enjoy, enjoy and say hello to Lenny for me. He's such a fine boy."

Ten minutes later I was up in Carol's place, and I still didn't know what the hell to do. Fortunately, Carol was less subtle than good natured and she began unbuttoning her blouse while I was still mumbling about the weather. When she finished undressing, I took my clothes off and lay down in the bed next to her. I might be there yet, commenting on what clean sheets she had, but this girl wasn't there to talk.

Despite my inexperience, it proved to be some night. We must have stayed on those Springmaids for five hours and there was never a minute my body wasn't finding out new and wonderful things. Carol did tricks with my feet I thought only caterpillars·were capable of, and she was so good in the sack I felt like a young Errol Flynn. By the time I got home it was close to midnight and after a light interrogation from Inga ("How's Lenny? What did you do? Where did you eat? Why can't you be like him?), I went right to sleep. It was the first night in weeks I didn't dream about fillies and mares.

I figured the whole thing was a one-night stand for Carol, but surprisingly she began picking me up outside the gym regularly and we were making it two and three times a week. By December I was running out of Lenny Roth stories, but I didn't think I'd need many more. There was just so far a woman would go with a kid who kept leaving for home before twelve o'clock.

Sure enough it ended a few weeks later as suddenly as it began. I came out of the gym on a Tuesday afternoon and there was no Carol. My first thought was my mother had somehow found out about us and scared Carol off, but that was impossible. I never called her from our apartment, I didn't have her name in my address book, and I didn't talk in my sleep. And not even Lina would have me followed by a private detective, so I knew it must be something else. I stopped at the first phone booth I saw and called Carol's place, hoping this was just a mistake but an operator got on the line and said the phone had been disconnected. There was no new number, nobody in her apartment, and no forwarding address. It was over.

Years later, I saw Carol's name mentioned in a gossip column blurb about some screen test she'd done for Universal, but I never checked it out, and I never saw or heard her name again. I was just glad we'd met. I had liked her. That was good enough.

I went right back into my boxing and track shell and made it through the rest of the school year. Then, in the summer, I got a job at Grossinger's, a large resort in the Catskill Mountains ninety miles from New York. I got the job the way every kid gets one in the Borscht Belt: My uncle knew someone's cousin who knew the night manager's sister and boom, I was an assistant lifeguard. I could swim about as well as Buster Crabbe could pick horses, but it wasn't important. Not many people ever drowned from an "8 point knock," and that was all the guests did around my pool—stayed out of the water and played gin. Even the guys who got "underknocked" were lucky not to be swimmers because I was never awake on duty. I started to play poker up there, and in the mornings I needed my sleep.

I'd played poker before, only the games had been on and off nickel-and-dime stuff in the bathrooms at Commerce. But now that I had a chance to play a little more seriously and a lot more regularly, I took advantage of the opportunity. There'd be games that would go all night, every night, and I'd wind up sitting at a table with four guests, three kitchen helpers, and between yawns, my share of winning hands.

My pattern was to play until I had to show up at the pool. I'd arrive, put some chaise longues around me, get in the middle, and go to sleep. Then I'd awake in midafternoon, and if there were no bodies in the water, I'd punch out, take a shower, eat, and go back to the card room.

I missed plenty of petting and necking and carrying on with girls vacationing with their families, but there were benefits to spending the summer of my sixteenth year drawing for flushes and choking on cigarette smoke. I was slowly learning to play poker and making money as I went. It wasn't a hell of a lot of money, but it was better than diving into the pool to find Mrs. Goldfarb's earrings for a 75-cent tip—much better.

I learned to play poker the same way I learned things as a child, not by watching and copying, but by watching and doing the opposite of what I saw. It was clear to me there was only one way to be a consistently good poker player, or any kind of gambler, and that was through discipline. Not many people had it, but I found playing for long hours with a maximum of control was like having an extra card.

By the end of August I understood the game and what it took to win well enough to be making more money from it than from lifeguarding, and even though I went back to school in September, I knew I'd discovered something. About myself, about people, and about gambling. I was going to come back to whatever it was—not right away, but I was definitely coming back.

My senior year at Commerce started out just like the first three. I was failing my subjects, winning my bouts, and disappearing at 11:30 most mornings to make the "first." But through it all I stayed in school, still using the totally barbaric conduct around me as a shield.

To spice things up, I organized a new poker game in the third-floor boys' room. This one consisted of myself, four members of the Commerce varsity basketball team, and Franklin Paxton. You should understand that if you played basketball for Commerce High School, you were something special. In a school whose biggest claim to fame was its crime rate, the basketball team was worshiped. The entire squad was black, they could all hit twenty-foot jumpers, everyone dunked, and in a city with plenty of good high school basketball teams, Commerce had one of the best. Team members took advantage of their position and never went to class. I mean, there was no way Marcus Washington, who could stuff a basketball with either hand, was going to get thrown out of school, and between him, George Ramsey, Calvin Curtis, and Leon (The Devastator) Williams, Commerce had its best team ever. The more games the team won, the fewer classes they'd attend, and by the time they were 14 and 0, our little poker game was really cooking.

I didn't play basketball, but I didn't go to class much either, so every morning at 9:15 I was in the bathroom waiting with my phony pass, just in case a teacher came in and asked why I wasn't in Spanish with everyone else. By 9:30 the boys would arrive and they didn't need passes because one, they were 14 and 0, two, they were big and strong, and three, no teacher really cared if Leon (The Devastator) Williams was in biology lab; I mean, Leon was twenty and he could barely spell frog.

We didn't play for very much money because none of us had very much, but even at the 50¢ limit we set, by 11 A.M. every morning I was up $15. The big loser, all the time, was this guy George Ramsey. We'd play on a newspaper spread out over the floor in front of a row of toilets, but while everyone else would sit around the paper, George, who was six foot five, would sit on one of the toilet seats, towering over the rest of us. Occasionally when he'd lose a big hand he'd smash the door to the stall closed and start moaning, "Sheet, I ain't gonna open this door 'cause every time I do that Talcum gots aces up." Eventually George would open the door and ante, but this went on at least two or three times a game and never failed to get a laugh.

The game went on for close to four months—ending when the team tapped out—and I don't think I lost more than twice. This could have been fatal, because any one of those guys was capable of throwing me out the window, but I was saved because of Franklin Paxton. Franklin would lose slightly more often than I did, but never for very much, and when he won nobody knew I was living. Instead of slinking out the door, apologizing for his good luck like me, Franklin would strut around the bathroom counting his winnings, and telling George he was the only dude alive who could lose to himself in solitaire.

Franklin (Don't Call Me Frank) Paxton was the one person in my four years at Commerce High School whom I got remotely close to. He was a seventeen-year-old black who talked in an accent that was a cross between Cary Grant and Sidney Poitier and who dressed like a maître d' at a Hollywood cocktail lounge. We never did anything socially because Franklin wouldn't have considered hanging out at a track or going near a gym, but in the confines of Commerce High we were some good buddies. Franklin came from the same poor background that most of the kids at Commerce did, but he was a hustler and had those "street smarts" you could only get in New York. He spent his time at Commerce selling dope in the hallways and porno in the back of the lunchroom and I'm sure he made more money in a year than half the teachers.

Outside of playing poker, we had nothing in common. I liked Franklin because he wouldn't take any crap from anybody, plus he was smart and sassy enough to pull it off. He was a black militant years before anyone thought of coining the phrase, and that was one reason we related. I didn't treat him like a white man usually would, with that forced courtesy and pleasantness people trot out when they feel vaguely uncomfortable with someone. I didn't fake emotions. There were so few people I liked, even a little, that if I found someone real, I didn't care if he was gray or blue, short or tall, rich or poor, and, believe me, Franklin Paxton might have been crazy, but he was for real.

Whenever we had a class together, he and I sat side by side, and I looked more like his hamper than his friend. I'd show up wearing the same things everyday—a dark sweatshirt, dungarees, and sneakers—but Franklin never dressed the same way twice. Sometimes he'd come in a suit with black patent leather shoes, and now and then he'd wear a shirt with a six-inch-long collar and the initials F.P. etched on the cuffs. On Fridays he'd really go wild and wear a pink ascot tucked into his shirt, which always caused a stir in the lunchroom. Once in a while my lack of neatness would get him annoyed.

We had this chemistry class that was really boring, and whenever I was there, I'd doze off fifteen minutes into the lecture and fall fast asleep. One time it happened when Franklin was sitting next to me, dressed in a white suit. As I was snoozing, my head occasionally drooped down and landed on his shoulder, and every time it happened, Franklin shoved it away. "Goddammit, Talcum," he'd say, looking at the Wildroot cream oil stain I'd left on his lapel, "can't you put that honky head of yours somewhere else, boy? Shape up, now," he'd conclude in a tone Henry Aaron might use on a rookie third baseman.

Our whole relationship was conducted in the same manner. We'd never admit we actually liked each other, we never stopped trying to get under each other's skin, but beneath it all we really cared. I mean, we didn't have to sit together and eat together and walk together but we did, and that counts for something.

Of course, Franklin would often try to get a rise out of me. Talking about girls was his favorite way because he knew I knew almost nothing about them. Franklin bragged that he'd go to the Palladium Friday nights, which was the "boss" spot in Harlem then, and carouse until late Sunday, when he was finally too exhausted to unzip his fly. Monday mornings he'd tell me the details (how many girls he made, how much they loved him, how big their breasts were) and I'd ignore him completely. That didn't stop Franklin. As a matter of fact, that's why he told me.

Every Monday we'd go through the same act. After he'd tell me these incredible stories of teenage lust in Harlem, he'd look at me like I was a worm and say, "What'd you do this weekend, Talcum? You get laid?" I'd look him square in the eye and answer, "Franklin, I've told you, I almost never get laid so stop asking me." Then he'd say to me, like he was shocked, like this didn't go on every Monday, "Talcum, you really didn't get a woman this weekend? Damn, you sure missing out, boy!"

With that, Franklin would get up from his desk and walk around the class, stopping at everyone's seat to tell them I was afraid of girls. I'd sit there feeling like an idiot until he'd made his rounds and after a few minutes he'd sit back down, lean over, and say in a voice the whole class could hear, "Well, if you didn't get laid this weekend, what did you do?" "I did the same thing I do every weekend, Franklin," I'd reply with a straight face, hoping he'd quit. "I went to the gym Friday and boxed, I played poker all Friday night, Saturday I went to the track, and Sunday I slept. Is that okay with you?"

By then Franklin was usually bored with that routine, so he tried his racial approach on me. "Listen, Talcum, I'm only telling you this because I feel sorry for you. There's gonna be a race riot Wednesday so knowing how weak you are I thought I better warn you." I'd lean over, stick out my nose about an inch from Paxton's face and say, "Tell me something, Franklin, what side are you going to be on?" He'd stare back at me for a few seconds but by the count of ten he'd get up from his seat and walk away to another desk in disgust. "Jesus, Talcum, you is some kind of freak. You don't ever get laid and you don't even know enough to miss it." Then he'd sit down at an empty desk, turn his seat sideways so his back was to me, and as the teacher would watch, he'd smash his hand down on the desk and let out one last, "Talcum, you ain't never gonna be a ladies man acting like that."

To this day we might still be friends, but in April, two months before graduation, Franklin finally went too far. It happened in a public-speaking class we had with Mrs. Rosinger. Mrs. Rosinger was a nice Jewish lady from Queens who'd been teaching at Commerce for twenty-five years but would not accept the fact that no one in her class had a shot at making the commencement speech. Anyway, this one morning some girl named Melissa was giving an oral report on how she spent the Easter holiday. I was reading the racing form so hard I didn't even hear her, but Franklin was giving me his version of what she was saying. "She wasn't on no picnic," he kept repeating. "She was with me at the Palladium. Damn, I got her drawers home to prove it." I wanted Melissa to finish so I could stop listening to Franklin's fables but as soon as she did, Franklin said, "Talcum, watch this," and followed her to her desk. Franklin never got up unless the bell rang, so "this" figured to be trouble.

Sure enough, he walked right over to where Melissa was sitting, whipped out a picture and held it up in front of her face. You could hear the squealing if you were dead, and in a flash Mrs. Rosinger raced to the back of the room, grabbed the picture, and turned green. It was a moment before she could speak. Franklin was looking right at her. Finally, Mrs. Rosinger said, in a small voice cracking with emotion, "Franklin, how could you think of doing something like this?" Without blinking, Franklin Paxton put his hands on his hips and replied indignantly, "Shit, what's a guy with a ten-inch dick supposed to carry a picture of?"

It was ironic. With all of Franklin's dope pushing and porno selling, he never got caught. But for a stupid thing like flashing a dirty picture he got thrown out of school. I guess Mr. Wasserman, the principal, must have known about the other stuff. Franklin came to say goodbye the day after he was bounced, but he showed no emotion and didn't mention keeping in touch. His last words to me, as he walked down the hall dressed in a blue sports jacket with plaid pants and blue suede shoes, were, "Talcum, you keep wearing those sweatshirts and you never gonna see any pussy at all."

I spent the last couple of months of my senior year behaving, almost never missing a class. My marks really weren't good enough to graduate, but I knew if I showed up and went through the final motions I'd get my diploma, make my mother happy, and get out of this place. With the bathroom poker game finished and Franklin gone, I was ready to move on.

Then about two weeks before graduation day, the entire class was notified by mail to go downtown to have our pictures taken for the yearbook. Unfortunately, when I reported to the building on West 23rd Street, I forgot what floor the Commerce photographer was on. I began walking through the hallways looking for a familiar face, but that day there must have been forty other schools taking class pictures there and the place was a madhouse.

After twenty minutes of searching aimlessly, I gave up and got into the elevator ready to go home. It made three or four stops on the way down, and one of them was on the third floor. As the doors opened, all I could see were New York City cops running everywhere with their nightsticks drawn and their faces beet red from anger. Quickly I moved out of the elevator and strolled down the hall. At last I had found the right floor.

After graduation I made a beeline back to Grossinger's to reclaim my assistant lifeguard post and resume my poker education. Usually the same kids worked there every season, but this summer there was a new face around, and it was on a young guy who stood out like a piece of white bread in a loaf of rye. He had a blond crew cut and a deep tan; was about six and a half feet tall, every inch of it muscle.

I found out his name was Dean Neely, he was twenty-four, from the South, and fresh out of the Marine Corps. He'd made friends in the service with a kid who knew someone at the hotel, and his job that summer was to water the fairways on the golf course.

He wasn't a poker player, but I was drawn to him because he made a habit out of breaking the hotel's rules and regulations. "Borrowing" guests' cars from the parking lot for 3:00 A.M. joy rides and trying to make it with every woman except Jenny Grossinger were two of his specialties. Dean began to notice me when he saw I was the only kid up there who didn't make a fuss over him. I guess I was supposed to, with his being twenty-four and having big muscles and ways with women, but I didn't care about big strong men unless I could beat them at poker. Besides, it was fun ignoring Dean. He'd occasionally drop in on a poker game to brag about the Cadillac he "borrowed," or the manicurist he made it with, and while the whole room hung on his every word, I'd sit there blank-faced, pretending not to hear the "boys," "wows," and "reallys," patiently waiting with a full house and knowing he was dying to just hear me clear my throat.

I was right. Dean began coming around nightly, so I'd have no choice but to acknowledge his hulking presence. Soon we were talking and teasing each other and, to my surprise, he was fairly sharp, although with his deep Southern accent you'd never know it. He'd sit behind me and say things like, "Talcum, y'all never gonna pull a'nuther jack. Why don't you drop out now and save yo'self the grief?" Whenever I'd draw the winning card, Dean's eyes would open wide but he'd never let on he was impressed. In fact, Dean showed almost no emotion or feeling toward anyone, and I needed a guy like that. I was getting pretty good at poker and very good at Ping Pong (a game I took up after discovering the hotel had tables, players, and action), and I wanted to start "baby" hustling some guests. A partner couldn't hurt. Dean even helped a little. I mean he still hung out in the hotel bar looking for women, but he always kept one ear out of his shot glass, listening for "baby" food.

In early July he found some, "Anxious Arnie" and his wife Dotty. Arnie was a tie salesman from Brooklyn who came up to Grossinger's every weekend looking for action. It was like he had a sign hanging around his neck saying "take me." He'd check in, go right to the bar as fast as his white loafers could carry him, put down a double Cutty Sark and water, and head for the card room. You could hear Arnie coming before you could see him because after that first drink he'd start spouting off lines like, "I feel hot tonight. Let me at those cards," or, "I hope you fellas got plenty of money because you're going to need it." By ten o'clock most Friday nights he was writing checks like they were postcards.

Dotty was worse. She owned a dress shop on Eastern Parkway in Brooklyn that must have done a ton of business, because on those rare occasions when Arnie dropped out of a pot, Dotty would make sure to stay in. You know, so someone in the family was always involved. Neither of them ever missed a weekend through Labor Day and three or four times, as a bonus, they'd come up with a friend of theirs who was dubbed "Stay-up Stan, The All-Night Crap Man." While Arnie and Dotty played poker, Stan would wander through the staff's living quarters jumping from one dice game to another. Stan was so compulsive he never bothered to check in, but with his luck, he should have. I mean you could sleep in a gorgeous suite for $60 a night, and Stan dropped five times that much to squeeze in a cramped bungalow with hot bus boys, cold sandwiches and freezing dice.

Dean found a few more poker turkeys in the bar, but by the end of August I was concentrating on the Ping Pong room. It was the perfect game for me to hustle. I looked like a clod, played clumsily, and never slammed, but quietly I could put the ball wherever I wanted to, and while my opponent made mistakes, I'd return a hundred shots in a row without breaking a sweat. As a result, guys would lose twenty games in a row to me and think they could take nine out of the next ten. I won $80 from a man who didn't have a chance if I played with a ukulele, but every game I'd let him get ahead 20 to 17 before finishing him off, and I'm sure he would have staked his shorts that he was twice as good a player.

Unfortunately, the season ended before I could win the guy's Munsingwear, so I returned to New York and Dean came along. He'd saved a little money, he knew a few girls, and besides, he kind of liked running around finding ways to make extra money. I settled back into my parents' place, while Dean rented a studio apartment on 81st Street.

I didn't consider going to college. I didn't want to, my parents couldn't afford it if I did, and with the atrocious marks I got at Commerce, even a Ping Pong scholarship was impossible. So I hid my Grossinger's winnings, and to keep myself busy, worked at Max Kramer's newsstand.

Dean didn't give working a thought but, as I found out, he was a very good pool and golf player and made money that fall by doing both. Still, by mid-December he was restless, and on a freezing cold day we sat down to talk. I told him about snow and reminded him that in addition to his skills, I knew how to play poker, Ping Pong and the horses. Before the first flake hit, we began making plans.

Within two weeks I quit my job with Max, broke the news to my parents, grabbed my binoculars, and got my $1,000 stake out from under the mattress. Dean broke his lease and packed his golf clubs, and in late December we gassed up his 1955 Chevy and left for the South, where men were men, women were women, and the sun was always shining.

We headed for Miami but decided to make a quick stop at Dean's father's house in Ft. Lauderdale. Dean didn't care for the old man very much, but we agreed the place might come in handy in case we went tapioca. It wasn't that we weren't confident—in fact, I thought we were pretty cool—but taking this little act on the road, where you had to make thirty bucks a day to cover expenses, wasn't easy. I mean, I was eighteen and still learning, and Dean couldn't shoot pool very well if he was in the hay somewhere making a Southern belle blush all over.

We arrived in Florida on schedule, stopped in Lauderdale, and speeded down to Miami so I could try my hand at busting Hialeah. Wow, Hialeah. It was everything I'd heard and some of what I'd imagined. It had flamingos in the infield, palm trees in the parking lot, and white linen suits everywhere. There was class here. Style. Even the black men's room attendants mopped their tile floors with a bit of pride, but occasionally they had to miss a spot. I was standing on it, hiding from Dean.

I'd gone through all but $140 of our money. l mean, I couldn't pick up my binoculars the right way, much less pick the winner of a race, and I gave up on a horrible, rainy Friday afternoon after losing my sixty-first consecutive bet. We hadn't missed a Saturday at the track since coming South, but by now it wasn't hard convincing Dean we should go to his father's house for the weekend. He didn't really want to punch me out, and besides another loss would have cost him his golf clubs.

Before leaving, we went out for breakfast, and as much as I hated to admit defeat, it was a relief to eat a 99¢ Whelan's special without having to rush through my muffin to make the daily double. From habit, I bought a form to read at the counter—just the articles—but in a few minutes my eyes wandered to the "Hialeah Today" page. That was unfortunate.

"Dean, we have to go to the track. There's a horse running in the first who can't lose." "No way, Al." "Dean, listen to me. I know I've been cold but this one's a lock. Let's go for just his race, and I swear we'll leave when it's over." Dean glared at me hard. "Okay, we'll go, but this horse best do some running or I'm gonna put your ass in a sling."

The pressure was intense, but when we got to the track I didn't have to worry if Dean was serious or not because the horse was scratched. We had two choices—go or stay—but once I was on the grounds of a racetrack, a mortar attack couldn't budge me. We stayed. We also lost $80, $40 of it on a horse in the last race named Irish Love. He had an eight-length lead deep in the stretch, but in the last hundred feet his legs got like rubber and he finished ninth. Sure.

I didn't get "punched out" or "ass slung," but let me tell you, there was some bitching and screaming in Dean's car leaving the lot. There we were, two assholes, stuck in Saturday traffic with $60 between us and a losing streak that wouldn't quit. Still, we weren't going back to our room at the Gaston Lodge, $1.99 a day at the height of the season and that was too much, so we miserably crawled out onto the highway, headed toward Ft. Lauderdale.

Even after Dean and I quit threatening each other, we were in a spot. We both wanted to spend a couple of days lounging around his dad's place, but we couldn't go up there empty-handed. Since we'd been in Florida, Dean and I had already visited three or four times, scavenging through the house like two bears, and the old man didn't like it. He lived on a small pension, and whenever he heard our car come up the driveway, he'd hide all his food in the rear of the refrigerator and put ice trays in front so we couldn't see the good stuff.

Occasionally, I'd find some American cheese or a very old loaf of bread he'd forgotten to hide, but that was about it. Worse, he was anti-Semitic, and each time we walked through his door he started up. The old man never talked to me directly, but he'd use Dean to get his point across. "I see you brought the Jew over," he'd greet Dean, or sometimes it would be, "Hiya, bum, you got the 'Heeb' with you again, don't ya?"

I'd always ignore him, but as we stalked through the house looking for scraps, he'd follow us. "I never heard of no starving Yid," I'd hear as we flopped down in his carpeted den. But I never flinched. The house had a yard and a shower that pumped hot water, and an old bigot's insults aside, it was better than the Gaston Lodge.

To avoid being locked out of the house completely, we stopped at a Food Town supermarket to pick up a few token groceries. It was close to 8 P.M. and the store was almost empty. I was reaching for a can of tuna fish when I noticed a gigantic steak sitting all by itself on a shelf in the meat department. I'd been going to the track so much I'd forgotten the word "steak" didn't have to have the line, "$50,000 added," tacked onto it, and my mouth was watering. "Dean, would you look at that steak," I whispered. "Can you grasp how happy your father would be if we brought it with us and cooked it on his barbecue?" We couldn't afford to buy it, but Dean agreed it was worth stealing, so I threw it in the basket, took a few steps, glanced around, and whipped it under my jacket. Then I went to the check-out counter while Dean got the car, paid for the cold cuts and beer we bought, and stepped outside.

The second I set foot out the door, two seedy guys walked up to me. "Okay, buddy," one of them said, "we saw what went on in there." I thought they were bums trying to hustle me out of the score so I kept my mouth shut, stalling until Dean got back with the car. "Listen, kid," the other one said angrily, "we saw what went on in there. Let's have the goods."

Dean was nowhere in sight, so to kill more time I tried a little double talk. "Okay, okay, I can see there's no way to tell how big this is," I babbled. "You saw it right through me." Then I looked away like it was a closed issue while the seeds stood there in total confusion. Meanwhile, Dean must have found a honey in the parking lot because he wasn't back yet and I was stranded there with the steak melting under my arm, trying to ignore my new-found friends.

Just as I was ready to make a run for it, Dean came driving up. When the two guys saw him and realized he was with me, they whipped out their badges and announced themselves as Food Town security men. "Why didn't you tell me, fellas?" I said. "My favorite uncle's a bank guard." Nobody laughed. "Walk back in the store, kid, and tell the manager what you did. If he's in a good mood he might let you go." Not having much choice, I slinked inside, followed by the two security men, and found the manager busy locking up for the night. I took the steak out from under my coat and told him I stole it. The guy looked too tired to care, and after all that crap, he made me sign a form stating I could never work for the Food Town Corporation. Then he took the steak and let me go.

Dean giggled like an idiot all the way to the house, and

by the time we got there I was totally disgusted. So disgusted that when his father came running out to meet us yelling, "If you and the kyke think you're gonna stay here and eat my food, you can go fuck yourselves," I didn't even look at him. Sleeping most of the time, we managed to last the weekend, and by Monday we'd hocked Dean's golf clubs and were back in action again.

For the next month we made ends meet, but it was tough. I remember one day things were so bad—we had $65 and were cold—that I went to the Sans Souci Hotel, applied for a job, and was told by the manager to "forget it," he'd just laid off his own brother-in-law.

Sometimes, we'd get our meals by sneaking into hotel buffets, intended solely for guests. What we'd do was lie on the beach in front of one hotel or another, usually the Shelbourne, and at about five o'clock in the afternoon we'd hear a voice come over the loudspeaker. "Good afternoon, ladies and gentlemen. Welcome to another beautiful day here in Miami. Isn't it nice to be in Miami? Tonight, per our custom, we're having a 'howdy buffet' for all the new guests of the Shelbourne, 6:00 to 8:30 in the Surf and Sea Room. Don't forget, 6:00 to 8:30. See you then." We'd always be starving by that time, so we perfected an act to get into these things.

For me it was fairly easy, but slipping Dean into those buffets was like sneaking Herman Göring into Temple Emmanuel. I mean, I could pass for somebody's son but nobody would believe this man was anything but a raving Gentile. To get in, he'd go back to the Gaston Lodge, put on his best clothes and my eyeglasses, and march right into the lobby. Before the doorman could say word one, he'd say, in his best nondrawl, "Would you get my car, please. It's a white Buick. I'm Mr. Levy." The doorman would be so startled he'd run to get the car and we'd be knee-deep in chopped liver before anyone caught on.

Occasionally, we got into those free buffets after two days of eating nothing but candy bars. Then I'd sit down at a table and start very slowly and steadily to make roast beef sandwiches so big I almost couldn't get my mouth around them. For every one I'd eat, I'd slip another into my pocket for the next day, while Dean would casually be drinking three martinis at a time. When he'd tear himself away from the bar, he'd mosey over to the buffet table and just about scoop it into his mouth. The guests would be standing there picking at tidbits with their little toothpicks while Dean would stand behind them, swallowing jello molds. He looked like a dressed-up gorilla and I'm sure the guests realized he had no business there, but no one had the guts to kick him out.

Late in February, two weeks before our return to New York, we hit the low point. We had $60 and owed hundreds, Dean's father wouldn't let us near the house, and the golf clubs and binoculars were in hock. When we couldn't find a pool or poker game to take our last shot in, I talked Dean into letting me give Hialeah one final go. If I hit it, we'd go back to the city in style; if I missed, we'd have to get jobs to make gas money.

I studied the form for three days without making a bet, but on a Thursday morning I saw our chance. A horse named Hidden Gold was running in the fifth race that afternoon; it was pouring rain, and I remembered seeing the same horse once win a race by twelve lengths in the slop at Jamaica. Today he was 20 to 1 on the morning line, and Eddie Arcaro was riding in the race on a horse named Roman Princess who was going to be the big favorite. I didn't think Roman Princess could beat us in the slop if we pulled a howitzer, and on the way to the track I pleaded with Dean to let me bet the whole $60. He was willing to go along, but being a little gun-shy from my past selections, added one condition.

There was a small blood bank not too far from the front gate at Hialeah, and Dean said that before we got to the track I had to go in there and give up a pint of my blood. Now, I'd done some pretty desperate things in my young life, but this was pushing it. "Listen, Dean, that's not fair or right and, besides, I hate needles." "Al," he said, without taking his eyes off the road, "we've gone through most of my money and all of yours. Y'all want to bet this here horse, you putting up something besides money." The way I saw it, if I gave in I'd be jabbed with a needle, disgusted with myself, and humiliated. On the other hand, I'd get $15, a cup of coffee, and a piece of danish. "Okay, okay," I said as Dean made a U-turn, "but if you ever tell a soul about this, I'll kill you. I swear I will."

When we got to the blood bank there was a goddamned line outside like they were giving away color televisions. Dean still wouldn't let me back out, so I waited for over half an hour, finally got called in, gave away a pint of my precious blood, and left. One nice thing happened. In addition to the coffee, danish, and $15, on the way out a nurse handed me two passes to the grandstand. No wonder this place was busy. It was full of horseplayers.

Well, at least I got the satisfaction of picking the right filly. Hidden Gold ran away and hid from the field, winning by four easy lengths and to make it sweeter he paid $48.40 to win. Dean and I got back over $1,400 for our $60 investment and went into immediate shock. We hadn't made over $100 at any one time all winter and in a little over a minute, on our very last gasp, we hit the jackpot. For once, the ride back to the Gaston Lodge was bitch-free, but with all that money I could barely smile. Instead, I sat the whole way with my head hanging out the window, fighting back the nausea I'd felt coming ever since I left the blood bank. "Dean," I burped out as we pulled into the Lodge's parking lot, "this is one you're going to owe me for a long time."

That week we paid our long-overdue bills, got everything out of hock, and spent three nights on the town before leaving for New York. A few days later we chugged through the Lincoln Tunnel, and Dean dropped me off in front of my parents' apartment house, exactly where he'd picked me up four short months before.

The winter had taught us plenty, and the best lesson was that we both had a lot to learn. Dean left quick-like for some upstate waitress, but that was expected. December was nine months away and we had those two hundred and seventy days to live the best we could.

As soon as daytime TV got boring, I took a job at a Vic Tanney reducing salon on Lexington Avenue at 49th Street. I was hired as a pot measurer, a job which paid two bucks an hour and consisted of measuring men's waistlines and saying, "Congratulations, Mr. Reynolds, your waist is down to a forty-four. Six more inches and you can join the human race." I stuck it out a couple of months, aware it was a waste of time—what could I steal, a rowing machine?—but one day I noticed this beautiful woman who came in for a swim and steam bath every afternoon at 5 P.M. I liked her. I wanted to communicate. Why couldn't she have been a horse?

Slowly, I made progress. Her name was Anna Carrillo, and if she had looked like my hound Scotty instead of a small, dark Ava Gardner, I still would have fallen for her. She was smart and funny and seemed to like me. For a kid with binocular strap marks on his neck and a thank you note from a blood bank, that was nice.

Anna was a call girl, but in the best sense of the word. She didn't particularly like selling her body for money, but she was desirable, enjoyed the finer things in life, and had long ago accepted herself for what she was. No pretense, no games, no telling lies.

What I liked most about her was that she knew truth from jive. The first time I was in her apartment, Anna talked to me about her view of life and the way it really was, what was important to people—sex, money, power—what was up and down, left and right, forward and reverse. I listened with both ears. "Al," she said in a tone a teacher would use on her favorite pupil, "people give you things for two reasons in this world—either they're forced to or they think they'll get something for it." With that, Anna got up from the couch, took me into her bedroom, and threw open the doors of her clothes closet. Inside was a rack of mink coats, designer dresses, and suede suits and a shelf of imported shoes. She ran her hand across the mink, then looked at me. "I have these clothes because I fuck for money, Al. You have to decide whether the price you have to pay to acquire what you want is worth it. I have, and once you've made that decision the rest is easy."

Our relationship made it through to the late spring of 1958 because I never tried to get the one thing from Anna every man wanted, her ass. But even I had a limit. I really did want to sleep with her, and since I didn't know the first thing about making a woman want me, one night I simply told her how I felt.

Anna wasn't very surprised, or enthused, but after giving me a what-took-you-so-long look, she took me into the bedroom and this time it wasn't to see the closet. When we finished I felt great. Not only was I learning about life outside the racetrack but I was involved with a woman other men paid money for. It sure beat hell out of picking losers.

The more Anna and I talked, the more I realized we shared many of the same traits. The difference was that mine were just forming while hers were fully developed. She expected nothing from most people, looked out for herself above all else, and let her good side show only when she was very sure of the situation. "I'm a cynic, Al," she said, "always have been, always will be." When I found out what the word meant I knew I was one, too.

Of course, I was sometimes rudely reminded that I was a seventeen-and-three-quarter-year-old cynic still living at home. One night Anna and I were at her place around 1:30 when the phone rang. She asked me to pick it up and tell whoever was on that she was out. I reached over, lifted the receiver, and said hello. "Alfred, it's past 1:00 A.M. and let me tell you something, Mr. Big Shot, you can run away like a wild animal all you want but as long as you're living under my roof, you'll be home when I say so." When would this woman give up?

I hung the phone up, hoping she wouldn't call back, and told Anna it was a wrong number. Naturally, the phone rang again ten seconds later, but I said we should let it ring until it stopped. Anna was too tired to argue. I got home after 3:00 and caught plenty of flack the next morning, but it was my own fault. With a Jewish Sergeant Preston of the Yukon for a mother, you don't leave a girl's name and number sitting on your desk.

Anna and I never got into much of a sexual thing; I was more like a younger brother to her than a lover. And in May that price to pay she always talked about broke us up. We were friends but business was business, and she left for Chicago to keep some guy company at a sales convention. It must have turned into a good arrangement, because she began spending a lot of time out of town and soon we lost contact.

Anna never called me, I never called her, and neither one of us ever wrote. All the little things that go wrong when you don't really care anymore. After it was over I remember thinking how much she'd reminded me of the old Jewish cantor my parents had hired to help me with bar mitzvah lessons. He was the first person ever to speak plain English to me and then, five years later, when I met Anna, I'd found the second one. Two people in over seventeen years who told me the way it really was—an East Side call girl and an old Jewish man. Quite a parlay.

I quit Vic Tanney's before June 1 and started going to the track regularly. One day, coming home on the degennie bus, I got into a conversation with a guy named Sam Winston. I knew Sam casually from seeing him at the races. He was about twenty-five years old and was nicknamed "The Ninth" because he had an uncanny knack for losing the first eight races and almost always winning the ninth. Sam said he had a problem. He worked for the post office on the night shift, which made him a salary to stay in action but kept him from attending the trotters. What Sam needed was a bookie, and when he mentioned he was looking for one, the wheels in my brain began turning.

I'd gone to the trotters plenty of times when I was at Commerce, but there was something about harness racing that stopped me from taking it seriously. I'd bet $2 a race, sometimes $4, but I'd never plunk down a ten or twenty like I did at the "flats" when I thought I had a good thing. To begin with, the trotters had a shady reputation, which put me off right away. If it was true, I had better ways to waste my money than betting on some driver who only let his horse out a notch on days beginning with the letter T. But even if they were honest, it was still a risky proposition. The tracks in New York were sharp-turned half-milers, so racing luck was often more important than ability. I also thought standardbreds (the formal term for all horses who paced or trotted) were less consistent than thoroughbreds, and to make matters worse, they had a nasty little habit of losing races by breaking stride.

In other words, I figured trotters were a lousy bet, but Sam was more interested in action than opinions.

Well, I had close to $1,000 put away, not doing much of anything, so as the bus passed over the Triborough Bridge, I said, "I know a guy who's a bookie, and if I ask him he'll probably take your bets." It was like I'd told Sam he'd just inherited a million dollars. "Al, that's great. Jesus, I can't tell you how much I'd appreciate it. I got a bunch of friends at the post office itching to find a guy. Jesus, Al," he repeated, this time putting his arm around my shoulder, hugging me as if we were lovers, "call me tonight at the Chelsea post office and let me know, huh?"

Of course, I didn't know a bookie, but maybe Sam didn't have to know that. He might not have minded doing business with an eighteen-year-old kid, but I couldn't be sure. What was the difference anyway? I'd pay if I lost.

So when I spoke to Sam hours later, I made up a cock-and-bull story about the bookie not wanting to deal directly with anyone he didn't know and told him he and his friends were to deal through me. I said I'd wait on the corner of 86th Street and Broadway Monday through Saturday nights from 6:30 to 7 o'clock, that the bookie's policy was trot action only and not for more than $20 a race. Sam must have been carried away with joy at the thought of being in action for eighteen races a day, because he agreed to the whole shmear, thanked me, and hung up. I'd done it. I was proud of myself. If I knew what the hell I was doing, I might have even been happy.

The next night I finished eating dinner in record time and burst out of the apartment at 6:20, leaving my mother's baked apple behind. Running all the way, I got to 86th Street in ten minutes. It was lucky I was fast, because Sam was already there, surrounded by four or five young guys and, boy, did they look pleased to see me.

I could see the corner of 86th and Broadway was a choice spot. It was the center of an incredible amount of seamy goings-on, the least of which was bookmaking. On one side of the block the addicts hung out, dealing bags of heroin to each other, for laughs rolling around on the sidewalk smacked out of their heads. Then there was a bunch of peddlers who'd set up their stands at five o'clock and begin hawking everything from umbrellas to girdles, all of it hot and none of it good.

Prostitutes and derelicts were all over, and last but not least, a pack of pickpockets almost lived next to the New York Bank for Savings, looking for easy marks. So, even when Sam and his friends spotted me and stuck money into my face yelling things like, "Put down ten for Harry on Adios Bird in the fourth," I never gave a thought to getting in trouble. If a cop ever showed up, he'd be so busy nabbing hookers, perverts, and addicts I'd hardly be noticed. Hell, compared to my neighbors, I was performing a public service.

It turned out Sam and his friends were small bettors, five- and ten-dollar-a-race types mostly, and after a couple of weeks I wasn't making much money but I was meeting some strange characters. There was one guy in particular, called "Recytum," who was totally gone. To begin with, he had the nickname Recytum because he was famous for doing everything ass backwards. Sam told me that before Recytum made his bets he'd lock himself in his room, turn off all the lights, and get in a closet. Then he'd pretend the closet was a time machine which could project him into the future so he could get tomorrow's scores and results today. He said Recytum swore he heard voices and would tell this story to anyone who asked him. I never asked, but whoever Recytum thought he heard couldn't have been too accurate. On some nights, he'd bet two or three horses in each race and none of them ever won.

Recytum quickly became my favorite trot degennie, not just because he always lost, but because he was my first freak customer. He'd split his time between driving a cab, playing in schoolyard basketball games, and sitting in that closet. I can still see him dribbling a basketball down Broadway, feinting left, faking right, imagining Bob Cousy and Bill Sharman alongside, always dreaming (which helped if you thought you could make money betting on the trotters). He wore the same outfit daily—black, low-cut Boston Celtic-type sneakers, a sweatshirt with cut-off sleeves for easy lay-ups, and a rolled-up trotters program in his back pocket, which looked like it had been chewed by a dog.

It was a sad day when he tapped out a month later, but I gave him my home phone number and told him to stay in touch. I didn't want to lose contact with a guy who made his bets after talking to a coat hanger.

By late June I was making as much as $100 a week off Sam and his boys, but the whole business was getting to be more trouble than it was worth. They were bugging me to take sports bets, for one thing, and I didn't know what to do. "Ask your boss, ask your boss," they'd say until I couldn't stall any longer. Finally, I decided to get out. I knew nothing about booking sports professionally, didn't want to learn, and wouldn't have known how to find out, even if I did.

Figuring that if I could create a boss I could just as easily make him disappear, I made up a story about his quitting suddenly and said goodbye. It had been an interesting couple of months but it was again time to move on.

I think if I had grown up on the Lower East Side my boxing career might have ended when I was nine. I would probably have joined an athletic program in a rundown Delancey Street boys club, fought a tough, hungry kid, got a concussion, and headed back to the zoo to talk to the animals.

But, because I'd kept boxing through high school—winning twenty-one consecutive amateur bouts—and was so excited about having found something I was good at, I never stopped uppercutting long enough to remember who I was beating up. Unfortunately, that summer I found out.

Having nothing to do, I began visiting the 86th Street gym every day, and after a month of working out, occasionally winning a bout over a college kid home until September, I was in the best shape of my life. Such good shape that I got the incredible idea of taking a crack at boxing professionally. I asked Tommy Wilton, a punchy old fighter who hung out at the gym, what he thought. "Go ahead, Al," he said, "you're young and strong. All you can lose is a few teeth."

It wasn't much encouragement, but since he didn't laugh in my face, I went downtown to the state boxing commission and with Tommy's help, a physical exam, a few weeks of red tape, and a forged consent note from my mother, I was licensed to box as a professional in the state of New York. That left only one problem—talent.

For my first pro fight, Tommy talked my way into a preliminary bout at the old St. Nick's Arena on 65th Street off Columbus Avenue. As I slipped through the ropes, I thought about how far I'd come from punching out pansies like Irving Conklin and Dickie Bradley. It was my last clear-headed thought of the night. What I remember about the fight was the other kid was Irish. He hit me with a short left hook that I blocked with my mouth, and inside of a minute I was down. Also, I received $23. I was supposed to get $50, but by the time Tommy got back from the Arena office, $27 had disappeared. From then on, the only way I ever got to fight was as a favor. Not a favor to me or Tommy, but to the other boxers. If a promoter wanted to keep a young fighter around and ready for an upcoming match that would draw a nice house, he'd schedule a bout for him with clods like myself. The favor was in making the guy's record look good—TKO, eighteen seconds of the first round—and letting him pick up a small purse with no risk.

I got my second bout like that a month later. I was pitted against a good up-and-coming lightweight, a black kid from Trinidad whom I had no business being in the ring with. I mean the guy's cut man looked like he could beat me. Naturally, I went out—like all good favors should—in the second round, and on my way down to the canvas I had my first flash about this boxing business being a big mistake. I got $75 and a split lip I couldn't hide from my mother when I got home. I told her it happened fooling around and hoped she'd buy it. It was better than telling her the truth and have her faint. I didn't have the strength to pick her up.

Stubbornly, I fought four more times in August and September and lost them all. The final two fights were interesting, the next to last one being so because it was the first time I was actually scared. It was at St. Nick's again, and somehow, I was matched against a black fighter named Elvin James. The program called him a contender for the light-weight crown. Contender, C-O-N-T-E-N-D-E-R, Contender.

My past fights had been pushing it but this was absurd. I'd gotten the notion of boxing for a living beaten out of my head, but come on, I didn't want to get k-i-l-l-e-d for being a dreamer! By the time I saw James in the ring, it was too late to back out, and I can still see the look on the referee's face when we took off our robes. James couldn't have weighed more than 130 pounds, but it was all muscle. He had a shaved head and a savage-looking face. I had a good build, but I was pale as a rabbit and had a tiny clump of hair on my chest that looked like someone had pasted it on. Also, the shorts I wore were too big for my twenty-eight-inch waist and I had them hitched up so high any punch below my neck would have been a low blow.

I guess James had a heart under all his muscle, because in the first round he cornered me, zapped out a couple of stiff jabs, and backed off when my knees buckled. In the second round he did what he had to and hit me with a shot that nearly took my head off. As I struggled to get to my feet and pull my trunks up from off my shoe tops, I recall James leaned over me and said, "Hey, Whitey, raise up yo' aching head so I can get me some more." For no good reason, I got up and Elvin hit me again, just like he promised, and the fight was over.

I wanted to quit in the dressing room, but Tommy talked me into another bout. So for a hundred dollars and a last shot at winning one fight, I boxed again two weeks later. My opponent was a Puerto Rican kid, and we fought at a club in Queens with a hundred people in the stands, all of them Spanish. The kid didn't look too tough and when the bell rang for the first round, I thought I might have a chance. The kid was tougher than he looked. After a minute, I was taking lefts and rights like a sponge when something happened that gave me a niche in boxing history. Out of nowhere, with no visible sign of collapse, or blood, or giving up, the referee stopped the fight. Then he raised the Puerto Rican kid's arm in victory and told me to go to my corner and stay there. It went into the record books as "Fight

Declared No Contest" and if it wasn't the only bout ever declared "no contest," it was one of very few.

I never wanted to see the inside of a fight ring again, but in case I changed my mind, the state boxing commission made sure it wouldn't happen in New York. On September 15th they revoked my license, and I wasn't about to ask for a hearing. I simply put away my heavy-duty athletic supporter, knee pads and high-top sneakers. I didn't even ask those dummies why they gave me the goddamned license to begin with.

I was playing a little poker before the swelling on my face was gone, but I kept getting smacked around. The only difference was the surface. It was felt instead of canvas. Four nights a week of three, five, eight, jack, king, and all the discipline in the world couldn't help. My bankroll started to disappear, and my confidence was going with it. Worse, if my luck stayed bad, wintering in the South with Dean would have gone out the window. I had to get some steady money coming in. Where from, was the question, and slowly and reluctantly I began to think about Sam and his eager-beaver friends. It was worth a call. And when I called Sam to let him know "my boss" was back in action, he was ripe. He said he and his friends had been dying because they couldn't find a bookie who'd handle their tiny action. Since it was the perfect size for me, we agreed to resume our old arrangements, and I reclaimed my spot on West 86th Street. The first night back made me think I never left. At six-thirty, I arrived at the corner, and Sam, Recytum, and Harry were already waiting. I wrote down their bets on the night's races, told everyone we'd settle the next day, and went home to pray nobody would hit a horse.

Well, not only didn't anyone hit a horse, but in my first three weeks of making book I made $600. That was with nobody betting over $20 a race. It was beautiful. There were six guys, and through the third week in October not one of them had a winning day. Recytum personally lost eighteen bets in a row and he was driving his cab twelve hours at a clip just to pay me off. One night he drove up to the corner in his cab, rolled down the window and threw out an envelope with $80 in it. "Here, Talcum," he screamed, pulling away. "Give it to your boss and tell him to choke on it. I can't turn my fucking meter off I'm losing so much money." Unfortunately, even trotter degennies had a limit, and soon the boys wanted me to take football bets as well. I'd seen this coming and didn't want any part of it, but I was trapped. The "boss" quitting story wouldn't cut it again and if I didn't give them a chance to win back some money, Recytum might have run me over with that cab of his.

Telling Sam my "boss" had given his okay for me to take their football action was easy. The rest called for fast footwork. First, I said the limit was $25 a bet, which was okay only because none of them could afford to bet more, but even that could have been serious. Football teams never paid off at 20 to 1, but they didn't run sixth either.

Next, I had to get a phone put in my room and give everyone the number. I knew I'd have to put up with my mother's listening at the door, but if I was going to have to make book nights, plus weekends, I wanted to get off 86th Street. There were five weeks left in the season, and New York street corners could get awfully cold in late November. As awkward as working out of my parents' apartment was, it still beat freezing to death.

So, on the last week in November, I had the phone installed, my fingers crossed, and my mother constantly wondering—but never finding out—what I was doing. I made it my business to be home 6:30 to 7:00 Monday through Saturday nights for the trotters, and an hour Saturday and Sunday mornings for football. In two weeks, I was being taken for granted. It was unbelievable. These ninnies were actually depending upon me to take their action regularly.

On weekends I'd get up early in the morning and go out to get the *New York Daily News*. In the sports section there'd be printed a betting line for the day's pro and college football games, so when Sam and his friends called, I'd read from it like it was a menu. If the paper said Ohio State was a 14-point favorite over Northwestern, I figured that meant Ohio State had to win by more than 14 for a bet on them to win and I assumed a bet on Northwestern would win only if they lost by less than 14 or won the game outright.

I almost blew everything when I asked Sam to pay me on a game he laid 7 points on and won 28-21. He got mad and said I should ask my boss because he was sure games like that were called pushes and were regarded as no bet. The next day I told him he was right; he was, but at the time I was merely guessing. Sam apologized, and we continued on.

I mean Sam knew about a push, but neither he nor I nor his friends knew what vigorish was. After three weeks I was behind $100, and if I'd been dealing with smart bettors, I would have been losing $25,000.

By the fourth week, I was dying to quit. Not my "boss"—me. Besides losing money, I was tired of having to play the radio full blast to keep what I was doing a secret, and I hadn't had a free weekend in what seemed like forever. Worse, I had to stay in my room every weekend so Harry Platt could bet $10 on Auburn. Who needed it?

Because, and only because, there were two weeks left to the end, I stuck it out, and on New Year's Day, in the last gasp of the season, I had my first big game. Syracuse was playing Texas in the Cotton Bowl. They were 14-point favorites, and every one of my six ninnies bet $20 on them. The money mattered, but now there was pride involved. If I won the game, it would be like winning a who-was-the-least-stupid contest!

I glued myself to the television, but before the bands were off the field, Ernie Davis scored an 87-yard TD and through the first half Syracuse pushed Texas around, taking a 15-point lead. In the second half, Texas played better, more confidently, tougher. Syracuse began getting into third-down-and-three situations, expecting Ernie Davis to gain nineteen yards on the play, but Davis was tired, Texas was fired up, and instead of gaining nineteen yards, he was losing six or seven. By the fourth quarter, it was anybody's ball game. Texas never did get the lead, but they held Syracuse down, scored two touchdowns of their own and wound up losing by only nine points, 23-14. The Southwest Conference lost prestige, the Longhorns lost the game, and I won the contest. In the next four days I collected $120. Better yet, I didn't have to make up an excuse for my "boss" not booking anymore. Everyone was tapped.

A week later, Dean came back from his upstate romance, and by January 10th, we were on our way South. We headed for the Washington-Baltimore area, where Dean had heard about a poker game and I quickly found that all the degennies in the world didn't live on the West Side of New York.

We stayed in D.C. for over a month and this game never stopped. It was run by two guys named Charley and Dave, out of a house in the Georgetown section of the city. It was straight five- and seven-card draw, $4 limit, and it was madness! There was one regular there, called Charlestown Joe, who never spoke to anyone about anything. He was called Charlestown Joe because every day he'd drive from Baltimore to West Virginia to attend the races at Charlestown Race Track. When the races were over, he'd get back in his car and drive right to the poker game until the next day, when he'd leave for the races again. When I was told he'd never missed a day at either place for months, I had to find out what made him tick. He wasn't an easy guy to talk to, but I tried to start a conversation by asking if he had a family. Joe picked up the deck of cards lying in front of him, took out a ten, jack, queen, king, and ace of spades and held them up in front of my face. "Boy, this is all the family I ever had or ever want."

Without Joe it would have been a rough game to beat, but there was another guy playing in it who made my breaking even worthwhile. His name was Hank Taylor, a Princeton-educated hustler, and I learned more about playing poker by watching him than I knew existed. I had discipline, but Taylor was a vise. He'd sit at the table for hours, folding his cards time and time again, playing only when he knew he was a big favorite to win. I'm sure he threw in an occasional bluff, but he'd have everyone so intimidated by his style no one would call, and he'd take $100 pots with a pair of nines. Watching Taylor didn't make me any money, but it confirmed what I had first learned at Grossinger's: Play it tight to the vest long enough, and you could make money just on other people's mistakes.

When we left Washington, we traveled through the Virginias and Maryland, even down through mid-Florida. We didn't hit any big action spots, but the trip served a purpose. You see, Dean was so big and powerful-looking that he often had trouble getting pool games up anywhere but in the sticks. There, even if a redneck was terrified, he'd never show it, and since Dean could act like a big, ol' country boy himself, most of them thought he was just a bigger variety of themselves. They'd stop thinking that after he'd run forty balls and walked out with $60, but by then it was too late.

Dean taught me one gimmick that was a little shady, but I didn't mind because it never failed. Down South every bar had a pool table and every small town had its local hustlers. So Dean and I would walk into these places holding a brown paper bag and start playing pool. Dean would pretend he was hard-pressed not to rip the felt, and we'd start cursing and yelling, pretending to be drunk when all we had inside the bottle was iced tea. I couldn't hit a pool ball in a pocket unless it was set up right in front, but Dean was so good that when he'd play he'd leave shots for me even I could make. We'd go through six or seven games like that, making sure I'd lose the last one, so I could curse him out and walk over to the bar acting like I was angry. Then somebody would challenge Dean to a game or two, thinking if he was pressed to beat me he couldn't be too good. I don't think we ever made less than $75 a night on that act. Of course, we'd get plenty of rednecks hot under the collar, but none of them ever got pissed off enough to make an issue out of it. Dean was just too damn big.

We kept hustling all spring and summer, but despite the gimmicks it began to feel like a treadmill. We'd make enough money to pay expenses, but the road was tough and we never seemed to find that big hit: the poker game with four turkeys or the rich kid with his own pool table and customized cue.

By September we decided to split up again. Dean went down to Florida to hang out in Miami hustling golf and mooching off his old man, and I grabbed a bus back to New York still looking for that pot of gold.

On my arrival, I found a letter waiting from the United States Army. It informed me that prior to induction, I was to report to Whitehall Street on September 11th for my physical exam. I spoke to that letter. I told it I didn't want anything to do with marching and rifles and Russians acting up in Berlin. When it didn't say, "Okay Al, forget I asked," I threw it in the wastebasket and got busy. Luckily my neighborhood was full of professional draft dodgers and all of them told me the pilonidal cyst I had at the base of my spine was a great way to stay a civilian. My doctor said they were right and gave me a note to prove it, and brimming with confidence, I went downtown on the eleventh, eager to flash it around.

I had to wait four hours just to get undressed, but finally I was called into a room along with a huge bunch of recruits. The officer in charge asked for anyone with a medical reason disqualifying him from service to step forward. Only three of us budged, me included, and in the second it took for me to see who I was standing between, I wanted to inflate my cyst with helium. The kid on my left couldn't have been over five foot six, but it would have taken a truck scale to weigh him. The only one there was for humans. Dismissed. The kid on my right was fat too, but that was the least of his problems. In addition to having his head connected to his body without a neck, like on a snowman, he had bowed legs and pink, shapeless feet that looked like chuck steak with toes attached. An army doctor came over to him and said, "Okay, son, jump up and down." And after a couple of spastic little ascents, this kid started going, "Aha, aha, aha!" like he was about to die, so the doctor stopped him before he did, and told him he could join Fatty. I was next and you better believe I looked like Rocky Marciano compared with those two. The doctor said, "What's your story?" and I showed him my note. He read it, jotted down something on a pad, and walked away. I went through with the rest of the exam and went home afterwards a lot less confident than when I'd walked in.

Two weeks later, I received my second letter from the army. It said, "Dah-da-dah . . . 1-A. . . . Dah-da-dah . . . Ft. Dix. . . . Dah-da-dah . . . report 10/14. . . . Dah-da-dah. . . . Sincerely yours." Sure. I was afraid my cyst didn't have a prayer after seeing those geeks at Whitehall Street but, fortunately, I had a cousin who was an army officer. He told me that if I appealed, I could get a ninety-day extension. So I put in for one immediately, got it, and waited. The days passed slowly.

To kill some time, I called Sam to see if any of the crew was flush enough to try the trotters again. This time I was out of luck. Sam was broke and Harry was unemployed, and the best he could do was promise to pass the word around that I was back in town. It turned out only Recytum was interested, and his bets were so small and infrequent my schedule was: "If I'm in I'll take it, if I'm out, too bad." But I was grateful for his loyalty. Tum, as I called him after we became friends, might have been a stone loser but he was an okay little kid. I even told him I didn't have a boss.

In late October, I got my third letter from the army. My

case had been reviewed, my doctor's note checked, and I'd been reclassified 1-Y. I didn't know if that was very good or very bad, so I called my draft board and was filled in. The way the clerk on the phone put it was, "Talcum, if the Russians overrun Jersey City, we'll give you a buzz, otherwise relax."

With the bazooka scare out of the way, I settled down, going to the track and booking 100 to 200 bucks a week in trotter action from Tum and a couple of buddies he'd introduced me to. Really, I was biding time until winter when I knew I'd get my annual itch to hit the road, but in November, I got my first lesson in getting wiped out. Incredibly, it was done at the hands of one of Tum's buddies, my very newest ninny, El Groovo.

El Groovo's real name was Dennis Turner, but no one ever called him that. No one ever explained why his nickname was El Groovo either, but after I'd dealt with him for six weeks, I didn't care if his name was Baron Hanover. He never bet more than thirty dollars a night yet in those six weeks he lost $400. I'd figured Tum had losers for friends but this kid was like a deposit slip. (This same El Groovo is a customer of mine to this day and his luck is still the world's worst. On Sunday mornings he gets calls from his friends wanting to know who he's betting in the afternoon. Sometimes, after he tells them, they call me and bet the opposite way.)

Anyway, one night El Groovo called and asked if I'd take a $100 bet on a trotter. Normally, I wouldn't let anybody bet $100, but considering it was El Groovo, I said okay and wrote it down: $100 to win on Mr. K. Braden in the seventh at Yonkers. Later, I went to bed, put on radio station WADO, and waited for Jocko, a popular black disc jockey of the time, to announce the race results. Jocko was pretty cool. (His opening went: "E tidilly Op, it's back with the Jock, and I'm on the scene with my record machine.") But he liked to steam folks on race results or sports scores, knowing people staying up to listen for them late at night were probably BMs or degennies or, in my case, both. The later the hour, the worse he'd get, and his biggest steam jobs were reserved for West Coast baseball games, especially when a very bad team like the Phillies were playing out there. Then he wouldn't give any score at all until midnight when he'd say: "I got a second-inning flash on the LA-Philadelphia game for all you sportin' men interested in such things. The Phillies, 1. . . ." Big pause. "The Dodgers, 3, 3, 3, 3. . . . !!!!!!" He had this way of making the 3 echo over and over again, and no matter how many times he did it BM's would get furious, because they always needed the Phillies. By giving their run total first, Jocko made them think Philly was winning and then they had to listen to "Dodgers 3" echo over the mike for ten seconds while Jocko chuckled in the background.

Well, Jocko wasn't above messing around with the race results either, and about 11:45 he said, "I got the seventh race in from Yonkers for all you boys. Afton Wick"—he paused for effect—"ran second and paid 7.20 to place, 4.40 to show. The winner was"—he'd pause again and by now I had my ear in the radio—"Mr. K. Braden paying 17.60 to win, 9.80 to place, 6.20 to show. I just know boxcar prices like that made somebody out there happy."

Not me, you fat creep, I felt like screaming. I swear if somebody had given me a white sheet with a hood, I would have burned a cross in his studio that night! I knew how to win money pretty good, but I was a long way from being a good loser. And a trotter yet! All I thought about was how many ways they had to lose. The driver could have stiffed him. The horse could have broke, been interfered with, got parked outside by Hugh Bell, fallen over his hopples. Hell, I'd once seen some horror named Widower Creed lose when his sulky got a flat tire, but tonight none of those things happened to Mr. K. Braden and it cost me $780.

Bitching and whining aside, I assured El Groovo I'd meet him Friday morning to settle, per our regular arrangement, and he was waiting in front of the Embassy Movie Theatre on West 72nd Street when I got there. "El Groovo," I said, as his eyes bulged out of their sockets counting my ex-money, "how did you ever pick that horse?" "I didn't pick him, Al," he mumbled, still counting. "Tum gave it to me, you know, from that closet he sits in." "But $100, El Groovo? Why such a big bet? You know his closet's a joke." El Groovo looked up at me for the first time since I'd handed him the envelope. "Hey, Al," he said, "all I know is Tum swore he'd been hearing Mr. K. Braden's voice for a week. He hears one horse that long, I got to give it a big shot."

I walked away speechless. It was two days before I cracked a smile, but by then I'd thought the whole thing over and came out of it with my first Talcum Law of Bookmaking. Booking bets was a good way to make a buck, but you could still get bopped. The important thing was not to let it happen often. Hopefully, my second would tell how.

By mid-December, when the trotters stopped running for a while—"Yonkers wishes you a Merry Christmas"—my business was gone but it was okay because my traveling itch had arrived on schedule. Quickly, I gave Dean a call at a small apartment he'd taken in North Miami. "Al, sure glad you called. Listen, I got myself an assistant golf pro job down here at a country club and I'm gonna stay put. I'll hit the road with ya'll again but this here set-up is too good to pass up. I'm making bucks hustling golf. There's plenty a fine, rich women around. . . . Well, you understan' how it is, Al, don't ya? . . . Man gotta take care a number one."

I was annoyed Dean hadn't told me this earlier, but I let it go, said I'd do the same in his place, and hung up with a promise to stay in touch. Now, not itchy enough to travel South without a partner, I was faced with spending the winter in New York and, like a squirrel, I got busy making sure I had the necessary provisions. I wanted to find something I could do inside, make money at, and enjoy. Playing poker sounded good.

The reason I was so confident about poker was that I thought my experiences on the road had taught me plenty since I'd last played in the city, but nothing could have prepared me for the game I landed in a week later. It was played in a loft not four blocks from where I lived and it was referred to as "Proppo's Sodom and Gomorrah Game." Proppo was the guy who ran it and I figured he was called Proppo in honor of his being the proprietor of the place where we played. It took me five sessions to figure out the second part of the title. Then, that came to me too. It was called "The Sodom and Gomorrah Game" because every vice imaginable—and I mean every vice—must have been practiced by someone in the game sometime during their lives.

Proppo looked like a young Fred Astaire, but he ran his card game like Ziegfeld staged the Follies. Nobody floated down a white staircase, but the production was an extravaganza without one. We'd start playing Friday nights and between then and late Sunday, when we quit, there were never less than ten, fifteen people in the room, maybe six playing poker.

For instance, there'd always be girls around, but they weren't there to kibitz. I remember one dubbed "Cuntola" who used to weave through the apartment for hours trying to pick up men like men would try to pick up women. I mean if you didn't have typhoid fever you were okay with her. One time, Proppo had a friend from Yugoslavia staying with him and the guy could barely speak English. So, whenever he'd see a girl, he'd point to her and say, "You fuckee?" With that approach I'm sure he never picked up anything except dirty looks, but the first time he said, "You fuckee?" to Cuntola, she had him in the bedroom so fast I thought a rubber duck was going to come down and give him $100 for saying the magic words.

During the course of a weekend everyone would take a break to ball Cuntola at least once, except for a super degennie named George Abrams who wouldn't have gotten up from the table if it were on fire. In fact, the minute one of us as much as pinched Cuntola, he'd start grumbling, "Come on, huh? Let's play poker." Mind you, that was after thirty-six hours of doing nothing else but.

George got even angrier when the game was interrupted by a Canadian marijuana salesman who used Proppo's apartment as a hotel room when he was in town. It seemed Proppo was one of the first big grass heads in New York and he'd have his guy up there to talk business while we were playing. A lot of times he'd pass joints around the table, wanting to get our opinions on whether he should buy or not, but after a couple of go-rounds, we'd get too stoned to help him out. Cards would start getting dealt face up. Guys were bumping bets when they were "beat on board" and almost everybody'd be smoking away as if playing the hands were an inconvenience. Soon four players would be zonked out, Proppo would be mumbling, "Okay, maybe I'll buy a pound of this stuff for $300," and George would be screaming, "I just raised the pot eight dollars! If no one calls me in fifteen seconds, I'm taking the whole thing!"

Eventually, George quit the game in a rage—after winning a $260 pot only to have his three kings voided when a stoned-out Proppo realized we'd played the hand with forty-seven cards—but shortly thereafter there was no game to play in. You see, Proppo had another insane habit of playing phonograph records as loud as possible and, finally, on a hot, humid, Saturday night in May, with the sound of Xavier Cugat blaring in the background and Cuntola running around the table in her panties, the landlord showed up. He had two cops, a city marshal, and an eviction notice with him. Nobody put up a fight. Proppo was too busy hiding his stash in the bedroom. Cuntola was behind the drapes and the rest of us left quietly, lucky not to be arrested. I was the only player really upset. After all, I'd just faked smoking Proppo's grass, and walking away from a game that brought me $1,100 in six months wasn't easy.

Thinking a good move was to keep playing poker, I again applied for a summer job at Grossinger's and got one as a bar waiter in the hotel lounge. I was twenty-one years old and sick of telling guests I was working my way through Cornell so I'd get bigger tips, but the lure of Catskill pickings was too much to resist.

Unfortunately, there were none because, as the old song went, "there'd been some changes made." Jenny Grossinger and the golf course were still there, but most of the employees I'd known were gone. They'd been replaced by lots of guys who looked like they spent winters playing baseball in the Caribbean League. Fine for holding labor costs down, terrible for a young Jewish stud player who'd failed Spanish three years running. After a couple of months of saying "Que pasa?" fifty times a day, only to be totally ignored, I was upset, and worse the guests weren't coming through either. A couple of years before you had to stand in line to get into the card room but something had happened—maybe junkets to Las Vegas, maybe a bad spring season on Seventh Avenue— and the hotel wasn't getting its share of gamblers. There were days the pool was actually filled with swimmers and by the end of July, desperate for action, I'd become a regular at Monticello Raceway.

If anyone I knew saw me there, I would have died. I'd sit in the grandstand for seven races a night, telling myself not to give in and bet these ridiculous, broken-down trotters, but my will power always blew by the eighth. Then I'd bet a day's tips on some 6-to-5 shot who looked unbeatable, watch him never come off the rail—finishing fifth behind some shipped in hotiola from Roosevelt—and go back to my room to jerk off into the next night's Monticello entries.

Since I wasn't a total masochist, I got fed up with waiting in the hotel parking lot for Cadillacs full of poker players that never showed and trotters that never placed or won. So, I decided to get myself fired. The problem was I wanted to do it in a way that wouldn't get anybody too upset. I wanted severance pay, but having spent some nice moments there, and having a few fond memories left, there was a limit to what I'd do to get it. I spent a week groping for an acceptable out, but by the last few days in July I hadn't thought of a thing. Then, by pure luck, I got my chance and it happened so unexpectedly I never realized it was taking place. It began on a Wednesday, a little past 9A.M., by the hotel pool. I'd had a restless night of groping and was in an irritable mood to begin with. I pulled up a chaise longue to stretch out on, but before I could get comfortable, I heard approaching footsteps. It was a middle-aged woman staying at the hotel, and although there were at least 150 empty chaise longues around she pulled one up right next to me. I closed my eyes and tried to ignore her but it was no use. She'd just checked in and wanted to know where the bar was? Could she get a free drink? What was for dinner? What time was lunch? For a while I held my tongue and rolled over on my stomach hoping she'd leave me alone. No good! This woman's mouth was a nonstopper. I mean I hadn't answered her in five minutes and she hadn't paused to catch her breath. Finally, I couldn't take any more. I turned over on my back and faced her. "Listen, lady," I said, "you won't be able to sit out here much longer. A convention of Mau-Maus from Nairobi checked into the hotel last night and they've reserved the pool area for a breakfast seminar at 11:00A.M." For the first time since this woman had arrived, no words were coming out of her mouth. It was still open, just no words were coming out. After her moment of shocked silence passed, she said, "Mau-Maus are here? Here at Grossinger's— Mau-Maus?" Suddenly, it dawned on me that she really believed this story. There was no way I was stopping now. "Lady, a lot of hotels across the country have agreed to have large groups of Mau-Maus as guests to better our relations with Africa. Don't worry, they'll be kept under guard and, anyway, they haven't caused any trouble since they speared that bellhop at the Fontainebleau.

Well, that did it! There had been stories in the newspapers recently about Mau-Mau uprisings in Africa, and this woman was terrified. She sat up in her chaise longue and stared at me with a face of a fifty-year-old Jewish woman paying forty-five dollars a day for a room that she wouldn't have stayed in if Paul Newman were there for a singles weekend. Without saying another word to me, she walked off in a daze, and as she made it to the lobby door I could hear her mumbling, "Mau-Maus are here? Mau-Maus are here at Grossinger's?"

Later, the hotel manager saw me in the hall and told me that much to his regret I was being dismissed. It seemed some woman had gone to the front desk that morning to check out because, she said, the Mau-Maus were coming. Naturally, the clerk called the manager and after he calmed her down enough to put her at ease, he found out just where she got this little piece of information. By the description she gave him, he knew it was me and without even realizing it I had got my $147.00 wish.

It was rough saying goodbye to prime ribs for dinner three times a week but good food didn't fill a wallet. So, I stopped back in New York to raid my dwindling savings account, and on the same day boarded a bus for Oceanport, New Jersey. I didn't care for the seashore but Monmouth race track was open. I was in the mood to play the horses—real ones, not trotters—and with the racing in New York having moved to Saratoga for the month of August, the "Big M" would have to do. Besides, renting a room in Asbury Park beat spending the month apologizing to my mother for getting fired from her favorite hotel.

My move to Jersey proved to beat a lot more than apologizing. The Monmouth course was baked hard as a rock by the summer heat. Its turns were sharp, and I was even sharper. Since a hard racing surface and sharp turns favor speed horses—horses which are very fast leaving the gate and like to run on the lead or close to it—I began betting accordingly and soon was hitting some nice winners. What I'd do was look for a race with one outstanding speedball in it and then bet twenty-five, thirty dollars on it. When I was right, the horse would get the lead in a hurry and never get caught. The track didn't seem to tire out the front runners as much as soft yielding ones did. The tight turns made it harder for the others to come from behind, because as each turn approached, they had to slow down as their riders looked for racing room; and once the field hit the stretch, the jockeys who still had a live horse under them wound up humping and whipping for second money as my choice won, as the form would put it, "easily."

I wasn't the only handicapper in the stands to figure that pattern out, but in Oceanport the insight paid off especially well. For every serious handicapper around, there were ten tourists and twenty retirees out to get a little sun, bet two bucks, and have some fun. Consequently, some of my Talcum specials went off at 7 to 1 when they should have been 9 to 5, and the $900 I made before Labor Day was a nice way to cap off what had started out as a lousy summer.

When I got back to the city I was floating. Hell, I only came home because the horses were back from Saratoga and I had plans. Now, I wanted to bet the New York horses plus the Jersey ones, and I was hot enough so that the idea of betting with a real bookie instead of pretending to be one didn't look so bad.

I began asking around and in a week, a guy named Julian Berg, a high-low poker player I knew through Proppo, found one for me. He said the bookie was a friend of his named Jo-Jo and that he ran a small cash-and-carry operation (cash-and-carry meaning you bet in person, put the money in the bookie's hand after you bet, and if you won, collected the next day). Julian also said Jo-Jo was honest, had made enough money from bookmaking not to have to do it any more, but stayed in business because he still liked the action.

Then he told me Jo-Jo worked out of a luncheonette in East Harlem, gave me the address, and promised to call him at home so he'd expect me. I thanked him for his trouble and the very next morning took the subway uptown, got off near 116th Street, walked toward Second Avenue, stopped at a flapping Coca-Cola sign and walked inside.

It wasn't the first luncheonette I'd ever seen with tables, napkin dispensers, a grill, shelves, and a counter with a cash register on the end, but it was the first one I'd ever seen with no food anywhere. Since I knew the pack of guys milling around weren't waiting for luncheon reservations, I approached the middle-aged guy standing behind the register. He figured to be Jo-Jo, and I said, "Hi! My name's Al Talcum. Did Julian Berg call you last night and mention that I'd be dropping by?" He just stared at me. For a second, I thought I had the wrong guy or that I was supposed to act like I didn't know you could starve here a lot easier than you could bet, so I said, "All I want is an English muffin to go." That broke the ice.

It was Jo-Jo all right, and a minute later he took out a little pad of paper, asked me who I liked, and wrote down the names of three horses I gave him. Then I handed him the $45 to cover my bets and left to get something to eat. The next day I came back to collect the money I was owed after two of the three won. I still couldn't get an English muffin, but I didn't have any trouble getting my $120. I stayed hot for another week or two, but then I started to cool off. Not wanting to blow all my Monmouth money, I quickly cut down my betting to one day a week, usually Saturday, when I'd drop in to put twenty bucks on an irresistible stakes race. But, the less I bet, the more I was going up there, and for a while I didn't know why. At first, I thought it was the laughs and kicks I got from soaking up this whole new atmosphere.

Like some mornings I'd get to the place real early just to

take in the scene, and if Jo-Jo was late, maybe twenty, twenty-five guys would be outside, waiting for him to arrive. They'd nonchalantly loiter around, leaning on cars, or sitting on fire hydrants, and the general impression everyone tried to give was that they lived right out there on 116th Street. Nobody would budge until Jo-Jo showed up, unlocked the door, and nodded his head for them to come in. Then, in the instant he switched the luncheonette's lights on, the same guys, who, five minutes before looked like statues, came barreling through the door so anxious for action Jo-Jo had to jump behind the counter to avoid being trampled.

As the newness of the atmosphere wore off, I got to know some of the guys who hung out there, and then I figured it was them bringing me back. They were interesting. Like Theo. Almost every day he came into the place with the same opening line. "Señor Jo-Jo," he'd say in Spanish-English, "had to wire dinero to sick mother in Ponce, mucho dinero Señor Jo-Jo, mucho." Then Theo would ask for some tiny dinero in credit and Jo-Jo would extend it to him until Theo ran out of "muchos gracious's," pesos, and sick relatives. Or Hugo. I loved Hugo. He used to roam around betting on everything from cock fights to coin flips, and once he asked me if I wanted to race him to 110th Street for $20. When I said only if I could start on 112th he walked away, but if I hadn't been wearing my Keds he might have taken me on just for the action.

There was another guy from Haiti who ran a poker game with cash right out on the table. I don't remember his name because he was banished from the luncheonette the very day I met him. It happened after he called a pot with a pair of aces and was beaten by another player who had a full house—a two 9's and three aces full house.

After I met all the local talent, I was still going up there regularly. So I figured maybe the big attraction was being involved in something slightly illegal. But that wasn't it either. I mean it was hard to remember anyone was breaking the law because nobody seemed to care. Least of all Jo-Jo. Instead of complaining about the carrying on he ignored it: All he did was go back and forth to the phone in the rear of the store to take action, or do it in person, at his register. Not having a neon sign in the window flashing, "Bookmaker inside no waiting," was about the only concession he made to the law.

In fact, I was still wondering why I was spending eight hours at a clip there when a cop walked in the luncheonette exactly five weeks from the day I first had. He was a black patrolman and he sat right down at the counter. Everybody got pretty quiet when they saw him but all Jo-Jo did was casually put away his betting slips and send someone out to bring back coffee and a Drake's cake. The two of them killed five minutes laughing and joking and when the guy got back with the eats, the cop wolfed his snack down and Jo-Jo said it was on the house. Then the cop headed into the garbage-littered street with a big smile on his face, acting like he hadn't just spent ten minutes in a luncheonette where the owner had to send out for a 40¢ order. (Months later I'd find out it cost Jo-Jo $75 a month to keep that cop jolly.)

The moment the door closed behind him, Jo-Jo strolled back to his stool behind the counter, nodded his head, and after those ten minutes of peace, it was instant chaos again. The betting and hustling started, the money and pesos began changing hands, the shrieking and arguing grew louder, and as I sat at one of the chipped formica tables I finally realized why I felt so at home in this crazy place.

It happened as I watched Jo-Jo sitting on his stool, too busy stuffing money into his overworked cash register to notice I was staring at him. I wasn't ready to stop being a degennie, but I wanted to start learning how to be a bookmaker. Boy, did I want to start learning. The question now was how to get from one side of the counter to the other.

The question soon became how to get out of a pile of 116th Street chicken and rice, because when I began trying to get over the counter that's where Jo-Jo told me to stand. I think his exact words were, "Al, I'm not here to teach freshman bookmaking. If you're not betting, go outside so they'll be room for the people who are." It was nice to have Hugo join me after Jo-Jo bounced him for paying a gambling debt with a forged welfare check, but it wasn't enough to make me stay there and get eaten by flies.

The first thing I did was to give Dean a call around October 10th to see if he wanted to run around that coming winter. Unfortunately, he said his job was solid, that he was in love with a golfer's wife, and that all he wanted to do was get her to take lessons so he could screw her in a sand trap. Since I still didn't want to hit the road without having a buddy along to share the excitement of making a score—or the *letdown* of not making one—I decided to stay in New York. Unhappily.

Then my parents put their two cents in. They'd been on my back about how bad business was, and how I should have been working to help them out for a while, but I thought I'd taken care of their complaints. For weeks I'd just said, "Here's forty dollars for my share of the grocery bill," and it had stopped. With good reason. Their favorite foods were farmers cheese, herring, and overcooked chicken-in-the-pot, none of which I could be in the same room with, much less eat. Suddenly they got rough. Now I still had to chip in, only they were serious about my chipping with money I got from a job, and worse, a job that was "meaningful."

I didn't have to ask Inga or Hymie what they meant by "meaningful" to know I'd find it meaningless, and when I got hit with a midmonth barrage about Lenny Roth being in his last year of pre-med at Columbia—the same Lenny Roth whom I hadn't seen since 1956 and might never stop hearing about unless he became the AMA's malpractice king—I was doubly unhappy. In fact, I was triple unhappy because near the end of October I was spending more time at Jo-Jo's and he was appreciating me less each day. I'd say I didn't enjoy being a pest, try to tell him my problems, and kept asking questions about bookmaking. Jo-Jo would say he was too busy to listen to my troubles, never answered my questions, and kept asking me to join Hugo unless I wanted to bet.

I was ready to pitch a tent halfway between my apartment and his luncheonette and never come out, when, at the end of the month, everything began to change. What seemed to do the trick was my mentioning to Jo-Jo that I had booked football one season. Ten minutes later I was listening to him gripe about having more action than he could handle because football, he said, was in the midst of a betting explosion that had started with the good Giant teams of the late fifties. Jo-Jo went on talking about how it was the most heavily bet sport in New York (in the years to come would account for 80 percent of all bookmaker action throughout the country), even before the AFL was formed, and how people bet more on it than anything else, and while I was still wondering how he could complain when all I'd ever seen him do was win, I got myself a job.

Answering the phone in his place on weekends for $125 might not have been "meaningful" to my parents, but it was to me, and that's where I was heading at 11:00 A.M. on the first Saturday in November.

I was a little nervous walking down 116th Street thinking Jo-Jo might have wanted a more experienced "helper"—as he called me—than I'd led him to believe I was, but I figured I could fake it. Hell, he said all he needed me for was football bets so how big a schmuck could I have made out of myself? Try this: when I got in, around eleven forty-five, Jo-Jo said, "Al, here's the line I want you to use today," and I said, "That's okay. I'll just use the one in the newspaper I bought on the way over." Besides some out-of-character cursing, and a look like I was a 140-pound infielder who'd just hit his first home run since leaving the Dominican Republic—in the ninth with two men on and Jo-Jo needing the team in the field—he was pretty nice. After I admitted never booking anything except tiny horse bets and straight football action, Jo-Jo just said he was glad we hadn't met when he was making big book, told me to write down the lines on about thirty college football games, and said I should inform everyone who called that he'd explain everything Monday. He said the word "everything" like his throat hurt.

I lasted until one-thirty that afternoon. A lot of guys I spoke to didn't sound happy. Jo-Jo was in the booth with me at least twice each fifteen minutes. When he could speak at all, he sounded very bad, and when he said I didn't have to work the hour he'd originally wanted me to that night, I had a big feeling it wasn't a reward for having answered his twelve o'clock question of, "What's doing?" with a bewildered, "I wish I knew."

I got a second chance. On Sunday, I came in at 11:30. Jo-Jo gave me the lines on the day's pro football games and said it would get hectic fast. He was right. By one o'clock I'd had a customer of his hang up in a rage when I asked him what he meant by an "if bet," had another click off after I said I didn't know what the hell "give me the chalk in that Patriot game thirty times" meant, and had Jo-Jo tell me to be back "real early" Monday morning so we could have a talk. Oh, did I know it wasn't going to be about a raise!

Well, I was there by 9:00 A.M., but at least twenty-five people were already inside when I arrived and I could recognize some of the louder voices. They sounded remarkably like several people I'd had very brief conversations with over the weekend, many of which had ended in groans. I remember sitting there, sure I was about to get fired, and miserable at the thought, even though I'd made an ass of myself. I mean, with all the raised voices, Jo-Jo was still putting plenty more money in his cash register than he was taking out, and I wasn't embarrassed enough to forget I still wanted to find out how.

Around 11:00 the place emptied, and Jo-Jo was annoyed. He said he had hired me because he thought I was going to make things easier for him, that he'd given some of his old customers the number so they could get some action on the weekends without coming up to Harlem, and that after dealing with me, three-quarters of them were ready to take up needlepoint. I said I was sorry and started to slink off the stool. I wasn't even going to ask for my $125 but Jo-Jo handed it to me and said to come back at 3:00 P.M. When I asked him why, he said, "If I don't teach you a few things about bookmaking you'll never make it through another weekend."

I walked around Harlem those four hours not believing I was getting a third chance. I also was wondering why. Was it because Jo-Jo was just a nice guy, or liked me, or desperately needed help, or what? By Friday, I didn't care.

I mean, Jo-Jo didn't tell me the secrets of the pyramids, but the bare essentials he slipped me that week were good enough. His first lesson was on bets. He told me about parleys (betting on two teams where both had to win for the bettor to collect) and "if bets" (a wager where a guy would put a certain amount of money on one team and specify that *if* the team won, he then wanted x amount of money to go on a second team. Then he tried to tell me about a few other exotic wagers, but when he noticed I was looking at him like I was in Latin class, he said he'd explain things like "if and reverse bets" as they came up.

Next he ran down a few gambling terms he thought I should know. He made a special effort to explain that when a bettor used the expression "a time," it meant $5, as in, "give me Green Bay thirty times," which even I understood meant $150. He also said it was a good shortcut to use in writing down action because a time was written as an X, and re-marked that I might get less ink on my neck if I wrote down a $400 bet on Denver as "80X."

For my final lesson, Jo-Jo told me about vigorish. He was still pretty secretive about telling me anything I didn't have to know to work for him, but he said, "vig," as he called it, was special. He said it was the most important thing in bookmaking, the reason it was illegal, and the key to the whole business. (Simply put, vig is the built-in edge a BM has on every bet he takes. In football and basketball it's the 10 percent a bookie gets on each losing bet he books. For example, when a customer bets $100 on the Baltimore Colts and loses, he has to pay $110. If he bet $200 and lost, he'd have to pay $220, and that 10 percent vig remains constant no matter how big or small the wager. Theoretically then, if a bookmaker takes a 100 or a 1,000, or any number of bets for exactly the same amount of money and wins half and loses half, he'll still come out ahead because of the vig he collects on each of the losing ones. The vig varies in other sports, like in baseball and hockey—but it's always there, and as Jo-Jo first said and which I gradually found out was my first important lesson ever, "Without the vig, you're not a book-maker. You're just another gambler taking a shot.")

There were a zillion other things I wanted to know, not the least of which was whether I could call Sam and the boys and collect their back vig, but, like I said, Jo-Jo was tight-lipped, and after my vig class he clammed up again and let me loose on the phone. When I didn't create any riots for a few weeks, he didn't tell me much else for months. He'd always find an excuse to slough me off. If I asked him to tell me how baseball was bet, he'd say it was too complicated. If I bugged him about hockey, he'd say he had no customers and that it wasn't bet heavily enough to matter, and it wasn't until January that my routine changed. By then, I was calling customers by their first names instead of "sir" and writing down their bets without too much trouble, and Jo-Jo opened up a little.

At first, I was excited about getting a $25 raise and being shown how to do the work, and dealing a little basket-ball, but soon it seemed like he'd gone about as far as he wanted. By March, I had, too. Even after Jo-Jo asked me to work extra hours and for more money, I about had my fill of being a "helper." In fact, when Dean called me around the middle of the month and said he'd quit his job and wanted me to meet him in Orlando for some "easy pickin's," I jumped at the chance. Better yet, Jo-Jo said he understood, told me to come see him as soon as I got back and I was on a bus South five days later. The last thing I did before boarding was to leave a note for my parents. It said, "Gone to Florida to meet with 'meaningful' goyim. Love, Alfred." Of course, I left a fifty-dollar bill underneath so they wouldn't get too mad.

Dean picked me up when I arrived in Orlando and immediately took me to his pool hall hangout. I was just glad to be out of New York, but when we walked into the place and I looked around as Dean boomed, "Hey, I want you boys to meet a buddy!" I suddenly got this real nice feeling about being in Orlando.

It looked as if Dean had found every dummy in a twenty-mile radius and had them assembled in there like they were bowling pins. First he introduced me to a guy who was playing pool. "Al, meet Jimmy Nelson, a helluva 8-ball player from right here in Orlando. Jimmy, say hello to Al Talcum." Since Jimmy had a pool cue in one hand and a bottle of beer in the other, he just nodded, which was okay with me because I could have lived without shaking hands with a guy with nothing in his mouth but gums, and nothing on his feet but skin.

Then Dean took me around and introduced me to the headliners, most of whom were sitting down picking alfalfa off their clothes. My favorite was this guy who said his name was Phil Culver, and then spelled it out for me like they do in a spelling bee. When he followed that by saying he hoped we could sit down and play a little draw poker, it was all I could do not to whip out a deck of cards right there.

After Dean and I got back to his apartment, I got the lowdown. He said if I thought that pool hall was turkey heaven I was going to die when I saw the poker game he had for me. He said it was run in a house on the outskirts of town by a guy called Dan Tepper, that it was eight-dollar limit, five-card draw, and stud only, and added, "Hell, I'm ahead a couple of hunerd and y'all know I stink!" I had to admit it sounded promising. At 8:00 that night I met the host.

Dan Tepper tried real hard to look like an idiot, but by 8:10 I could see he was a lot sharper than he wanted anyone to know. He was dressed in jeans and a work shirt like everyone else I met that day, but his hands were smooth and uncalloused. His house wasn't much to look at from the outside, but when I got in I noticed he had a 21-inch color television, a brand new hi-fi, and a very well-stocked bar. He also had a nice modern kitchen, and smack in the middle of it was a poker table. In the same minute I saw the players sitting at it, I looked out the kitchen window and saw a new car parked out back. No one had to tell me whose it was.

I sat down to watch for a while, looking to see who was good and bad, and, sure enough, in twenty minutes, it was obvious that Dan was my only real competition. He played tight, bluffing when the time was right, going out when he knew he was beat. Around 9:00 P.M. I started playing, and I didn't stop until close to 4:00 A.M. when the game broke up. I won $160, Dean won $180, and Dan must have made $500. At the door, he said they played every night, invited me back, and as I left, said, "Y'all a pretty good card-player, Talcum. I just might have to keep an eye on you."

Well, over the next three months I never missed a night, and after Dean quit to hustle more pool, Dan and I never took our eyes off each other. I was doing fine, Dan was doing finer, and there were a few country boys who could play a little, but the turkeys in the game were so bad they all but gobbled. One of them was called Ga. He owned a dairy in Georgia (hence the nickname), but he didn't get home more than once a week. He went back to his motel room a lot, though, and Ga. was so bad that we ran a $5-a-man pool on him, guessing the exact time he'd tap out and leave for it. Another one was a ranch hand named Carl. I didn't know where he got the money to play but he'd show up night after night smelling from horse shit and let me tell you about 3:00 A.M. on a hot, humid one, you needed nose clips just to survive. We put up with it because he never, ever won, but finally Dan couldn't take it any more. One night he just said, "Carl, next time you come here, I want y'all to stop before-hand and take a bath. Most o' my tropical fish have died since you been visitin'." All Carl did was say his wife thought he smelled fine, and all I did was imagine what this place would have smelled like if she sat in too.

On the 15th of June, I stopped worrying about it. For weeks I'd been taking a few hundred out of the game while Dan was in a deep slump, and that night he came up to me as I was leaving. "I'm sorry, Talcum, but I'd appreciate it if you took your business elsewhere. This game's been feeling a little cramped with you in it." Since it was his house I didn't argue, but I noticed he seemed to have lost his Southern accent and on the way down to Miami I told Dean I thought Tepper was definitely from the Bronx.

There wasn't much to do in Miami in the summertime, but Dean and I managed to stir things up a bit. We even made a score with a young guy named Rick Newman whom I spotted in a bar about three weeks after we arrived. He was wearing the two things that turned me on most—white loafers and gold jewelry, a combination which usually meant one of two things: either the guy wearing them had money and wanted you to know it, or didn't have any but sure would have liked some. I found out Rick had money when he took me for a ride in his private plane and, better yet, we got $800 of it when Dean found out he liked to play golf.

There were laughs, too. Between the time Rick left for Tulsa and Dean and I sold a pound of oregano to some poor schmuck who thought it was grass, there were plenty of them. I was proudest of the chuckles we got from beating checks in restaurants. Mainly because I got so good at it. I could walk out of a coffee shop without paying if I was naked, and that includes toughies like the ones where the cashier sits right by the door. What I'd do was send Dean to get the car after we ate, then I'd wait for a group of people to pass my table, follow them closely, and, like Jimmy Brown picking up blocks on an end sweep, use them as interference until I was out the door and in the parking lot. For variety sometimes I'd make Dean dress up and drag him to one of the hotel nightclubs. We'd take in a show, eat dinner, have plenty of drinks, even buy a round for the people at the next table, and when the bill came, I'd sign it, "Max Cohen, Room 407." Then I'd smile and give the waiter five bucks, and by the time anyone realized I wasn't one of the 197 Max Cohens the hotel had registered, we'd be careening down Collins Avenue, busy trying to keep Dean's car off the sidewalk and hysterical thinking about the frazzled maitre d'.

Somehow, though, with all the laughs, and with all the white-loafered turkeys hanging around the bars and lobbies of Miami, by late August the thrill was gone. I didn't know where it went. Hell, I'd always thought plucking turkeys, and living out of a suitcase making $400 one day and spending

$300 of it the next was what I wanted and enjoyed. But now, suddenly, I was just as sure it wasn't. Dean looked shocked when I told him I was leaving, yet I think he sensed that this time it was for good. All I said was I hoped we might run into each other again, we shook hands, and I was gone. Ex-hustlers don't go in for long goodbyes. Especially one who wanted to be a BM's helper.

I left Florida in a 1959 Chevy I bought with the money I'd won in Orlando, and on a Monday four days later I was back in New York. I stopped home for an hour and then drove up to Harlem to see a man about a steady job. I made it to 116th Street in less than fifteen minutes. The Coca-Cola sign was flapping just the way it was the first time I ever saw it. The luncheonette was there, too, and so was the garbage outside, but when I walked in, all it took was one look to see the only job I could get there was as a short-order cook. The guy behind the counter was making french fries, the people sitting on the stools were munching on them, and unless shrimp salad was the name of a horse, I had just made a big mistake.

Ten seconds later I was dialing Jo-Jo's home phone number. It rang seven, eight, nine times. No answer. Finally, Jo-Jo picked up the phone, and, as relieved as I was to hear his voice, I barely let him speak. "Jo-Jo," I said, "do you know people are eating in your luncheonette?" He knew.

Forty minutes later, I was sitting in his house in the College Point section of Queens, and before I could finish my coffee, I found out what happened. He quit. One Sunday Jo-Jo got home from booking baseball and found his old lady waiting for him with her bags packed. She told him that she'd had it with his seven-day work week and long hours and trying to raise two kids by herself, and she was going to walk out on him unless he stopped making book. Jo-Jo said at first he didn't know what to do, but when he sat down and thought about how much money he had saved, and the kids he never saw, he realized his wife was doing him more of a favor than anything else. So he got himself lined up in a nice

job with an insurance company, was playing golf, tak...
easy, and never felt better.

When Jo-Jo was done telling me all this, he asked how
much money I had. I told him a few thousand dollars, maybe
a little more, and knowing I had a phone in my room, he
said, "Al, if you're still interested in making book, I know
four, five guys whose action you could handle. They just bet
football and none of them ever go for over 100 a game. If
you want, I can give them your number and help set things
up." I said I'd like to give it a try, and Jo-Jo told me to be at
his house at one o'clock the next day.

As soon as I arrived, the pyramids started to open nice
and wide. "Okay, Al," Jo-Jo said. "The guys' names are
Felix, Benny, Fred L., and Bobby. I told them you'll be
working on Saturdays from noon to two and six to seven and
Sundays from twelve to two. All four of them happen to be
gentlemen but let me give you a few tips on how to keep
them that way. Listen to me good, Al. I made book for
twenty years and the things I'm going to tell you hold water
if you have four customers or 400. First, run your operation
like it's a machine. Win or lose, settle up fast as possible, and
when you pay, do it with a smile even when it hurts. Deliver
your money on a pillow Al, like it's a goddamned pleasure,
because if you act like that, one day it'll all come back.

"And don't make mistakes. Do your figures right. Be
polite, show up on time, and know what you're talking
about. It's a business, Al, and if you want to be treated like a
mench, don't act like a slob. . . . Another thing: Be honest.
You don't have to cheat. No good bookmaker does. It's only
the petty liars and the never-made-it gangsters, and the "take-
a-shot" gamblers who call themselves bookies, who have to
do that.

"Hell, I'm getting carried away with this," Jo-Jo said.
"Here's a number of a bookmaker I know. I'll speak to him
tomorrow and on Saturday morning you call him around
eleven thirty and just say you're Al for Jo-Jo so he'll know
who you are. Say that every time you call and he'll give you a

line to deal." Then Jo-Jo asked, "What do you know about hedging?" I said,"Nothing." By the way Jo-Jo sat up in his chair and lit a cigarette before continuing, I was sure he was again saving the best lesson for last. "Look, Al, all I can really tell you about hedging (also called "laying off" or "hedging off") is that it's what a bookmaker does when he gives part of his action to another BM, but since everyone has his own method, I'm just going to explain mine.

"To me the ideal situation is to have the same amount of money bet on every team, in every game I book. Like when I have ten games bet for a total of $1,000, 500 a side. If I lose seven or eight I'll get killed; if I win seven or eight, I'll make a killing. But the bottom line is that most of the time a bookie figures to win as many games as he loses and if you're holding equal amounts on each of them, you wind up making money because of the vig.

"Listen Al, some bookies hold whatever they get; a grand, ten grand, a million—they don't care as long as it's action. They don't look at the vig the way I do, that having it means you win $50 when you book a split down the middle thousand. How do you think they built Vegas, Al? They got vig, that's how. They got double zero, they got gamblers shooting for a hard eight. To me, it's simple. You got the edge. Use it.

"Nobody makes a bookie play it any way but his own. If he wants to sit with one game where he has five grand bet on one side and five hundred on the other, and another bet $3,000 to zero, it's his choice. Me telling him that he can win seven out of ten games and lose money because the three he lost were bet the heaviest isn't going to change his head around. Anyway, the reason I'm telling you all this is because the guy you're going to get the line from takes hedges, too, and if you want to lay off money, just ask him. Here's how you do it: Say that on Sunday your customers bet three games and on two of them they bet a total of $400, $200 a side, but on the third they bet a total of $400, only they put the whole package on one team. Like, for argument's sake, on Green Bay favored by 10 points over the Bears. If what I've told you makes sense, you just call him and say you're Al for Jo-Jo and tell him you want Green Bay -10 for $200. I don't think he'll ever say no, because your action is too small for him to worry about, and after he takes it you're sitting pretty. If Green Bay wins by more than 10, you get $200 back from him so you only have to lay out a deuce of your own money. If they blow the game or win it by less than 10, you'll make the $400 from your customers and only have to give the guy $200, and in the other two games the worst that can happen is making the vig. You won't get rich quick, but you won't take as many baths either.

"That's it for now, Al. There's a ton of things I haven't told you, but if you ever decide to become a serious book-maker, you'll find the rest out. At least, you got some free advice." With that, Jo-Jo saw me to the door and said to call him if I hit any snags. Then I got into my car and drove back into the city. It had been a very good afternoon.

Well, as far as my customers were concerned, things stayed good for months. They were always courteous, and between their betting small and my following Jo-Jo's advice to the tee, I never won more than $600 in a week, or lost over $400. In fact, I only had two real problems. One was Jo-Jo's bookie friend. He had this set-up where he used an answering service to screen his calls. (I later found out bookies used answering services in an attempt to fool cops. What they'd do was have their customers phone in, leave their names, and ask to have the "doctor" call back. Then the BM would call the service, pick up his messages, and return the calls. Of course, when the police got serious, they'd just bust the service without too much trouble. I mean, if they tapped one they thought was being used as a front and heard, "Dr. Gross" get 175 calls between six and seven o'clock on a Friday night, it didn't take Frank Hogan to know what was going on.)

Anyway, for a while it was pretty exciting. You know, just calling the service and asking for the doctor to call back

"Al for Jo-Jo." I can still remember what a wonderful feeling it was sitting in my room, waiting for the phone to ring, knowing it was a real dyed-in-the-wool BM on the other end. What eventually made my excitement go away, and my wonderful feeling vanish, was having the guy always sound like he hated to hear my voice and constantly remind me he was taking my calls only as a favor to Jo-Jo.

"Hi! This is Al for Jo-Jo," I'd say. "Can you give me the line on the St. Louis-Washington game again?" I'd ask. "I forgot what you told me last time. Is St. Louis favored by nine or nine and a half?" "Jesus Christ, Al!" he'd say. "The spread's nine and a half. Don't bother me with this shit, will ya. I'd like to bite you sometimes." "Okay," I'd say, ignoring his remark. "Can I have St. Louis minus the nine and a half ten times?" "Ten times, Al? Is that what you want? St. Louis ten times?" and he'd repeat it back to me in a disgusted tone of voice just to let me know he could have been on the phone with ten other guys betting twenty times as much.

My other problem was my parents, but that one disappeared fast. When I started, I made up a story about selling magazine subscriptions over the phone, and, through October, it held up, thanks to my radio blaring out The Coasters singing, "Get a job" every fifteen minutes.

Then, one Sunday, I opened my locked door and Inga was there. I'd heard her heavy breathing for weeks but this time she must have put a stethescope to the wood, because the minute I stepped out I got hit with, "So, Mr. Alfred Talcum. How many subscriptions did you sell this morning?" In a minute, my father joined her, and they both started shaking their heads wildly and then, in that tone that I knew so well, my mother added, "Ah, Hymie, a wise guy wasn't enough. Now we have a gambler to boot." I just shrugged my shoulders at their sarcasm, said I was what I was, and really never worried about it again.

In fact, by the last Sunday in November just about everything was fine. My parents hadn't bugged me in weeks, my customers had lost $250 Saturday, and when the

"Doctor" called me at 11:45 that morning to give me the line, I got it right the first time around. Boy, I was feeling frisky.

Too frisky. Come 1:55 I could have roughly evened out my action by hedging off a total of $500. (I'd already found out a BM almost never wound up holding the exactly equal amounts Jo-Jo spoke of, but the object was to try.) Instead, I said the hell with being a monk this weekend, hedged off almost nothing and lost all but one game. And I only won that one because of a last-second field goal that bounced off someone's helmet and caromed over the crossbar.

Well, I blew about $800 thanks to my daring move, and Monday I settled with a forced smile on my face. The last guy I saw was Felix and I gave him the $300 I owed him outside the building he worked in on Madison Avenue. I spent around five minutes with him talking about the field goal and whatnot, and right after he left some guy came up to me. He said his name was David Dale, that he'd overheard me talking to my friend, and wanted to know if I'd consider taking his bets. I was just standing there thinking about whether I should or not when Dale said, "Come on up to my office. It's just across the street and at least we could chat."

I didn't have anything else to do so I said okay. In the elevator he told me he was in the advertising business and when we got inside his office I figured he owned the agency. It had paintings on the walls, and thick carpeting, and a desk the size of a piano. Dale started talking about himself and showed me this picture of his wife and kids posed in front of this huge house somewhere in Westchester. After I was there around fifteen minutes, I said I'd be glad to take his bets but added that I only worked weekends and just took football for a $100 limit. Dale said that was big enough for him, I gave him my number, we shook hands, and I left.

I finally had a customer who wore a suit.

To most bookmakers, the world's population is divided up into three groups: good customers, bad customers, and people who don't bet. The first two are the only ones that matter. Good customers for several reasons: They pay on time, don't ask you to meet them on top of the Pan Am Building to settle, are generally pleasant to deal with, etc., but the most important, they usually refer you to other good customers. Bad customers also count for several reasons: They pay late, sometimes ask you to meet them on the antenna on top of the Empire State Building to settle, are generally ball-busters to deal with, etc., but the most important, they usually refer you to other bad customers.

Now, referrals are important because they're the main way a BM's business can grow. (After all, we can't advertise in the Yellow Pages.) But equally valuable is their predictability. Besides the good-customer, bad-customer pattern referrals follow, BMs also find that ninnies refer them to other ninnies, $100 bettors to other $100 bettors, college hoop freaks to other college hoop freaks and so on right down to twenty-dollar spot players who cheat at pinochle to their friends who do the same. So while knowing that nine times out of ten an honest ninny will not slip a BM's number to a dishonest hoop freak isn't everything, at least it comes close.

Of course, there are times when a BM can get a referral and still not know what to do—like if they meet a prospect for lunch who says, "You'll buy, I'll leave the tip." In those cases, they check the guy's pedigree—a pedigree being an unofficial word of mouth opinion that floats around among gamblers. Customers have good and bad reputations just like bookmakers, and if you ask enough questions and a guy's been involved in gambling before, you can find out plenty. Sometimes you'll hear a person is rich but cheap, loses heavily or wins big, pays by cash or check or offers you his watch in lieu of either, but the main thing a BM looks for is whether he's honest.

Obviously, then, if a BM knows who a guy is referred by, and gets his pedigree to double-check, he can make a pretty solid decision about whether to take him on as a customer. Unfortunately—very, very unfortunately—when I met David Dale, I knew none of this.

My first dealings with Dale began that following weekend. He called Saturday morning and bet $75 on four Big Ten teams. Three lost. On Sunday, he called again and bet $50 on five pro teams, $75 on two, and $100 on another. This time he did a little better, though not much, and when I went to his Madison Avenue office Monday morning, he owed me over $300. I got an envelope with the full amount in cash, a smile, and a courteous walk back to the elevator. That house in Westchester must have been even bigger than it looked in the picture.

I didn't hear from Dale again until the next Saturday, the last one of the regular season college schedule. He bet thirteen games at $100 a shot, but he did it so matter-of-factly and he'd paid me so fast the past week I didn't give it a second thought. Until that night I didn't give it a second thought, I should say, because when I got the scores old "matter-of-fact Dale" had lost ten out of the thirteen and owed me $800.

I didn't know whether to be excited about winning the money or nervous thinking I'd have trouble collecting it. I mean big house or not, $800 bucks was a package, and come Sunday morning I was confused. Part of me wanted to get the $800 and run, and part wanted to stay and have him lose more.

Regardless of how many parts I had, Dale called at twelve forty-five and went very wide. He bet ten pro games, all for the $100 limit, and without a crack in his voice. In fact, when he gave me the action, his voice was smooth as silk, but when I read it back to him, mine was squeaking like it was me taking a $1,100 shot. Just to see if Dale was as cool a customer as he seemed, I said, "Wow, you're really getting involved today!" He didn't say anything except "Goodbye," and I swear, when he hung up, the biggest part of me wanted this guy to break even, pay me the $800 and become a soccer fan.

Well, the first scores I heard were bad for Dale, and by six o'clock, he'd lost all seven of the completed games and I wasn't confused any more. I was nervous. What if he didn't want to pay? Moved overnight? Died? Took his own life? Then again, what if he paid in full? Without a bitch? Without a peep, without a fight? That was possible, too, and by 11 P.M. when all the finals were in, I was praying for it. David Dale went 0 for 10 and owed me $1,900!

By ten o'clock Monday morning I'd paid my other customers—four had won—and at 11:00 I called Dale's office. Before noon, I'd called three more times, left three more messages, and was getting jumpier with each: "I'm sorry, but Mr. Dale's in a meeting." Twenty-four hours ago this guy would have left his wife on the *Titanic* to take my call, and when he hadn't phoned back by 3:00, I knew I had a problem. What I didn't know was what to do about it.

I called Dale a few more times Tuesday. By five o'clock, I hadn't reached him, but I gave it one last try. "Hello, this is Al Talcum again. You know? The same Al Talcum who called seven times since yesterday? Is Mr. Dale in?" I was ready to smash the phone if Dale's secretary told me he was in another meeting, but surprisingly, Dale got on the line and sounded like his old melted-butter self. "I'm sorry about not returning your calls, Al," he cooed. "I've been tied up the last couple of days. Tell you what: Meet me in front of the Track 38 entrance in Grand Central at six sharp and I'll give you a check. I owe you $1,900, right?" "Right, right, Dave," I mumbled, "$1,900 is right. Right as rain, Dave. You sure are accurate," I kept mumbling, and if Dale didn't say he had to run, I might never have stopped babbling.

Sure enough, when I got there, Dale was waiting. He handed me the check, commented on his lousy luck and left for White Plains. On his way down the steps I followed him, thanking him over and over like the money was for cerebral palsy and I was there to pick up his donation! I wasn't that polite a kid, but I'd gotten carried away with the season ending like this. Hell, nobody ever told me bookmaking was this easy. And even after I paid the Doctor the $600 I'd hedged off to him, I still felt pretty good.

"What can I do for you, Al?" were the first words out of Jo-Jo's mouth when I called him six days later. I told him the story. He said he didn't want to know about it. I pleaded until he gave me the number of a guy who might be able to help. I called it immediately, and whoever the guy was promised to meet me the next day on the corner of Lexington Avenue and 63rd Street. I wasn't sure what I was doing. All I knew was I had a $1,900 check in my pocket marked "Insufficient Funds."

When I met Jo-Jo's friend at four o'clock the next afternoon he said his name was Frank Hirsch and to tell him the whole story from the beginning. When I finished, Frank asked for my phone number, told me to relax, and promised he'd call in a day or two. I agreed, but in the meantime phoned Dale a couple of times hoping against hope the bad check had been a mistake. By late Thursday, Dale hadn't returned my calls, and I stopped trying to reach him. It was obvious the only mistake had been in my taking this guy on, and when Frank called me that night I found out how big a mistake it was.

"You might as well send Dave's check to Goodyear, Al," he said. "They can use the rubber." "That bad, huh?" I asked, and Frank told me the whole lousy story. David Dale was a genuine, sick, degenerate gambler, and the only reason he'd bothered to get involved with me was because no other bookie in New York would touch his action. It seemed that two years ago Dale had won thousands of dollars from a big-time BM in Queens, then lost all of it back plus a few grand and refused to pay. The bookie, who, like most BMs, was completely nonviolent and willing to compromise on any point to avoid unpleasantness, got so mad at Dale that he lost his temper and roughed him up pretty good. After that, Frank went on, Dale not only still refused to pay but told the BM he enjoyed getting beat up. The BM thought Dale was sick enough to be telling the truth, and since the only other alternative was to drop him off a bridge, he wound up writing the whole thing off to experience and forgot about ever seeing the money.

Now I was really upset. For the first time, I was seeing bookmaking wasn't fun and games, and getting clipped for $1,900 was a tough way to learn. "I don't go in for strong arm stuff myself, but for this Dale character, I'd find someone who would," Frank said. I thanked him for the offer, but I didn't want any part of violence. Instead, I asked him to call me in a week and decided to try and reason with Dale. I mean the guy had a house, a job, a family, and blond-haired kids. How sick could he be?

I began calling him on the phone hourly. I must have called him fifty times in five days, and by Friday his secretary would hear my voice and hang up. Finally, that afternoon, I went to Dale's office, marched right by his secretary, opened his door, and sat down next to his desk as he stared at me in disbelief.

My knees were knocking loud enough to tap out "Begin the Beguine," but my mouth was working. "Look, Dale, we both know why I'm here. You can't come up with $1,900. Fine. But you could at least agree to pay it off a little at a time." Stop making your threats rhyme, schmuck, I said to myself, but I don't think it mattered how tough I came off because Dale was ignoring me. "Well?" I said. There was a moment of silence, and then Dale suddenly bolted up from his desk, ran to the open door, and pointed for me to leave. "Listen, Sonny Boy, I don't have $1,900, and when I get it I'm certainly not going to give it to you." I went quietly, as he smashed the door closed behind me. I was fuming.

The next day I called Frank. I told him what had gone on, that I wanted my money, and asked for his help. "Please, no real rough stuff," I begged. "If you can't help me scare him into paying, I'll just have to forget it." Frank said to call him back in an hour, and when I did, he gave me a phone number. "Call there tomorrow morning, Al. They'll fix you up."

For all I knew he'd slipped me Murder, Incorporated's number, but it was too late to back out. At 9:00 A.M. I was dialing. Forget about a "Hello." The first sound I heard was a very rough "Yeah?" "How are you?" I said. "My name's Al Talc——." "Yeah, we know all about it," the voice interrupted. "Tell me where and when, huh?" "Would noon in the lobby at 412 Madison Avenue be okay?" I asked. "Goodbye, Talcum." Before the voice hung up, I said, "Hey, how will I know who I'm meeting?" "Don't worry, kid," the voice answered. "You'll know."

Let me tell you when I got off the phone after that conversation I felt like paying myself the $1,900. Then I remembered I didn't have it, so I took a bus over to Madison Avenue and was in the lobby of 412 ten minutes early. When no one who looked even a little tough showed up by five after twelve, I'd just about talked myself into leaving. Then I saw it. Emerging from the revolving door was a six-and-a-half foot, 350-pound thug with the face of a giant, dark olive, and the body of a sequoia tree!

This hulk stood by the door for a second, wearing an

overcoat that would easily have wrapped around two or three people. Since there wasn't much chance he was the account executive for Jergen's Hand Lotion, I walked over to him. "You Talcum?" "Yes, I am." "Where's de guy who owes de cabbage?"

I was scared Dale was in danger of being killed. So scared I asked this thing to wait a moment thinking that maybe one last call to Dale would get him to budge. Then, I looked up and saw Dale coming out of the elevator. By now the lobby was packed with people on their lunch hour, but I zigzagged my way across quickly and grabbed him by the arm. "Dale, listen to me. There's a guy with me here whose business is collecting money. Please, Mr. Dale, this thing is out of my control unless you promise to make some kind of payments. Five dollars a week. Anything! Just say you'll do it." Without even realizing it, I'd been screaming, yet Dale didn't seem to be hearing a word I'd said. In fact, he was looking over my head with this twisted half smile on his face, and when I turned around to see what he was smiling at, I saw the Olive standing right behind me.

"Dis de guy, Talcum?" the Olive said. "If you think this goon can scare me into paying, you're sadly mistaken," Dale said, and I swear he looked like guys do before they have sex, like he couldn't wait to get it. He got his wish. Just as I noticed we'd gathered a crowd of spectators, the Olive stepped around me, took Dale by the shoulders and smashed him up against the wall. Sick as Dale was, I'm sure he never expected anything like that, and as he peeled himself off the marble, his whole body was shaking and I could see he was about to come apart.

Sure enough, Dale began begging for mercy and at the same time he was emptying his pockets at our feet. Out came a football betting card, an old fifty-dollar pari-mutuel ticket, a late payment reminder from HFC, at least three pawn stubs, and to top everything off, a notice from a collection agency threatening to put a lien on his salary. I mean this man was an educated, polished executive who must have made thirty, forty thousand dollars a year and here he was on his knees, shaking helplessly at the feet of a mindless thug and a twenty-two-year-old kid.

It was so pathetic, even the Olive seemed affected. Almost gently he put his arms around Dale and said, "I ain't gonna touch you no more but you'd better come up with a hund'erd a week till you even." Dale nodded frantically in agreement, but just as I thought the whole thing had ended the Olive, as if to punctuate his last remark, took Dale by the collar of his jacket and literally threw him down the lobby like a bowling ball. Dale came to a stop in a heap by the lobby newsstand, and the crowd we'd attracted ooh-ed and ah-ed like this was an act on the Ed Sullivan show.

With that, Dale got up and ran into an elevator and the Olive turned to me and said, "Some sicky, huh, kid?" Then he lumbered out of the building, leaving me standing there in a daze, with sweat falling off of me like it was rain. Looking straight ahead, totally ignoring the stares I could feel from the people all around, I strode out the door, walked half a block away, stopped outside a shoe repair shop, and threw up all over the sidewalk.

I was through with bookmaking.

On a Wednesday, two weeks into 1963, I received a $1,900 money order from Mr. David Dale. Seeing his name again, even as a signature, made my stomach churn like it had that day on the sidewalk. Was it stolen? Forged? I wouldn't have been surprised if it was ransom money from kidnapping his own kids, but then I noticed a note tucked inside the envelope. It was from Dale's father. He said his son had borrowed $10,000 from him, turned over a new leaf, and wanted to start a fresh life with a clear conscience. I cashed it a few days later, put the money in my pocket, and didn't feel a bounce.

Poppa Dale's generosity was nice, but it didn't solve my newest problem. With bookmaking and hustling gone, I was bored—inside-bored—the kind an ace high flush or a 14-to-1 shot couldn't cure. I didn't think a straight job could cure it either, but I was twenty-two years old and ready to give it a try.

Unfortunately, there were a few stumbling blocks between me and the key to the executives' men's room. No college was one; a résumé listing experience as a pot-measurer and a Mau-Mau storyteller was another, and an attitude of automatically looking down on what most people did for a living was the third.

The want ads didn't help change my mind. There were jobs open for cab drivers, window washers, cashiers, assistant-this, assistant-that, management trainees, Wall Street trainees, tool-and-die trainees, trainee trainees. One ad promised great opportunity; one hinted at unlimited advancement; another mentioned a boundless future, yet as I scanned the pages I noticed beneath all the big print, all the various come-ons, every ad had one thing in common. Each started you on your way to fame, fortune, and success at eighty-five dollars a week.

Nevertheless, I tried, and after a month of "I'm sorry, but we're looking for a young man with a, shall we say, more acceptable background." Or, "I'm afraid we can't use you, Alfred, but before you go would you tell me some more stories about Commerce High?" I got a job as an estimator-salesman with the household-moving division of Greyhound Van Lines. The job consisted of following up on phone calls from people interested in hiring movers, and the starting salary was the minimum wage plus a percentage of sales made. Before my first day, I figured out that with Greyhound's percentage arrangement I'd have to talk forty families a week into moving to Albuquerque to make a good living, but it was the best offer I had, so I bought a suit, fixed a smile on my face, and joined society.

For over a month I made zilch over my base salary. I don't mean ten or twenty dollars either. I mean zero like in less than one. Day after day, I'd go to people's homes or apartments and, using a method taught by the company, leave them estimates on how much a move would cost. Most of the time I'd get a cup of coffee, questions on how much less it would be if the piano was left behind, a comment on what a nice tie I had, and a promise to call back at the end of the week.

I couldn't figure it out. Not one sale for a kid who sat in a stifling hot apartment in the Bronx for two hours listening to a man bitch about moving to Staten Island to get away from "niggers," and with a smile on my face, while all I wanted to do was smash him. Something had to be wrong! A week later I found out what.

I thought the straight world meant acting straight, being open, pleasant, reasonably honest. You sold a frying pan for $9.98—it fried. A television set cost $200—you got to see "I Love Lucy." You bought a fur coat for three grand—you got mink, not crap. I thought only hustlers—guys who could find out what someone wanted, make them think they had it, and then sold them something else for more money—carried on, but if the moving industry was any standard, legitimate business was hardly Winnie-the-Pooh time.

The trick to this one was that there was no such thing as competitive moving prices. They were set by law, like airline fares, or postage rates, and there was no difference in cost between Allied and Bekins and Mayflower, or any licensed mover. What there was a difference in was estimates, and while I'd been going around New York telling people what moves would actually cost, other estimators were out there saying, "Well, Mr. Jones, I'd estimate the whole thing shouldn't cost you more than $1,300, give or take a hundred either way." Jones would sign a contract. The salesman would get his commission, and a month later the guy would get a bill for $2,900, while I'd be home playing with my pud because I'd told him $2,875 six weeks ago.

Seeing the house rules weren't what I thought was a mild surprise but not one I couldn't handle. In fact, I used this white-collar dishonesty to my own advantage. From then on, I'd go to someone's house and the first thing I'd do was ask if they'd already been estimated. If the answer was yes, and if it was for a figure not even close to what I knew it would cost, I'd explain the estimate was low and tell them about each company's rates being set by law. Next, I'd add the only things that should really count were the firm's honesty and reliability, concluding with a smooth ". . . and you know Greyhound." By May, I was making $200 a week.

Also, I was getting very close to flipping my cookie. I had sales meetings to attend two mornings a week, a sign-in sheet, a sign-out sheet, three assistant sales managers to report to, and a dress code to abide by. Plus a company vice-president in charge of pep talks who took me to lunch one day and said, "Al, I was a young, ambitious estimator once myself. I struggled, and pulled and kissed the right asses and now I have a house in Jericho, a pension to fall back on, and one of the best-looking little Ford station wagons you'd ever want to see."

Well, if Greyhound, or any other boob-filled, nine-to-five, sign-in-and-out company paid me five times what I was making, I would still never be able to stomach that kind of life. I wanted money, sure, but I needed some fun and excitement too. It didn't take the Mardi Gras to turn me on, but dealing with the same thirty or forty white-shirted dullards every day, filling out forms, and talking to people about moving pianos made doing nothing great by comparison.

It got so bad, I spent my last month there signing out for made-up appointments, going to the movies, and coming back grumbling about what a tough day it had been. Finally, somebody got wise, and a couple of weeks before I was going to quit, an assistant boob came into my cramped cubicle and said, "I'm sorry, Al, but somebody upstairs thinks you're not giving us your best. We're going to have to let you go." I think the guy might have thought he was ruining my life, so I got up slowly, shook his hand, and, as I left, turned and said, "Don't feel bad. After all, now I know Greyhound."

At least, getting fired instead of quitting made me eligible to collect $30 a week in unemployment insurance, and for months, the leads the unemployment office sent me out on were the only things I had to look forward to. Not because any of them filled my growing need to find a niche for myself somewhere, but, in fact, because they did the opposite. They allowed me to see the incredible variety of people and places I wanted nothing to do with.

Like the time in August when I was sent out to see a guy who needed a shipping clerk for his brassiere factory in Brooklyn. It was a very hot Monday morning when I arrived, but when I walked inside nobody offered me a lemonade. The factory consisted of about thirty-five pathetic human beings locked in a room with no air conditioning, sewing brassiere cups together. I didn't think anyone there ever heard of minimum wage laws or unions, but I was sure that the guy who ran this place was going to hire me no matter how disinterested or stupid I tried to appear. Sure enough, it took some foreman about a minute to interview me, say I was okay, and could start the next day. I told him I wanted to think over his $67.50 a week offer, and would be there in the morning if I decided to take it.

I stayed up half the night racking my brains, but it wasn't over whether I should take the job or not. My problem was that if I turned it down, the unemployment office would cut off my benefits, and worse, stop sending me out on these leads I was reverse learning so much from. Finally, around 3:00 A.M., I got an idea that was so good, I was amazed I'd thought of it. Five hours later I was at the factory, and after I told the foreman I wanted the job, he showed me into the boss's air-conditioned office.

The guy looked startled when his foreman said I was the new shipping clerk, but he got over the shock of having a white employee fast enough to whip out a few forms for me to sign before I could change my mind. I said I'd sign whatever he wanted if he'd just let me put my paper down so I could use the pen. He told me to go right ahead, but the moment I placed my copy of the *Daily Worker* on the edge of his desk, I could see him tense up.

I had figured he might. I mean if I employed thirty-five people inside a sweatbox, and paid them $9 a week while my wife spent $15 on her hair and a thousand for the three kids in summer camp, I would have been tense. After all, the *Daily Worker* was the house propaganda sheet of the American Communist Party and anyone who read it figured to be at least a Socialist, and maybe even a Commie rat.

I have to admit the guy was pretty cool about not tipping his hand. When I gave him back the signed forms and asked if I could start immediately, he pretended to read them over, then looked up and said, "I'm sorry Al, but I've reconsidered. Business is pretty bad, so I think I'll just have to wait on hiring a new employee. Thanks for your trouble, and when things pick up I'll give you a call." I gave him a quick disappointed look and scooped up my *Daily Worker,* and by 10:00 A.M. I was in the unemployment office to report my latest rejection and pick up my weekly check.

Over the next month or so I was sent on at least ten more leads. Some were laughable, some were miserable, most were somewhere in the middle, but with every interview and each uninteresting job offer, it became clearer and clearer that I just couldn't feel comfortable living and working in the straight world. I didn't want to rob banks or kidnap babies or mug old women, but there had to be something in between that and $67.50 a week.

By October, I wasn't any closer to finding it, but a call from an old acquaintance named Case Cohen led me into a situation that seemed to have possibilities. I'd known Case on and off since meeting him at a basketball game in the Garden five years ago. He was about my age, very crazy, and known far and wide as the "Garden-mooner" because he had a habit of dropping his pants at crucial moments during basketball games. He'd drop them to start rallies, to celebrate charging fouls called on the team he bet against, and occasionally, just to make his friends fall off their chairs in hysterics. If either of us ever stayed in one place long enough to make friends, we probably would have been close ones.

Anyway, the day after Case called, I went over to his big, messy studio apartment on 93rd Street, anxious to see what he'd said was "some stuff I want to talk to you about." When I got there I was stunned! Spread out over the bare floor were sports jackets, gloves, clock radios, typewriters, ivory chess boards, attaché cases, jewelry boxes, and an incredible array of cuff links and tie clasps. Considering Case owned a Dumont television that hadn't worked since he had, I knew something was up. "What's going on here?" I said, pawing a carton marked: Fragile—Toaster Oven. Case grinned like an idiot. "I don't know, Al. I think I got carried away. I was helping out this friend of my father's in this warehouse he owns in Brooklyn and I guess, well, you know, I guess . . . I had the key and . . . I got carried away, that's all."

"Case," I said, shocked. "Al," he said, not shocked, "the guy's a millionaire; he won't miss it. Just help me get rid of this crap. Al," he whined, as he opened a closet and pointed to a box marked: Leather Belts. Size 38. 12 Dozen, "please say you'll help me unload this shit or I swear I'm going to mail you the 140 pairs of moccasins I got under the bed."

I said, "Okay." I didn't really want to get involved with stolen merchandise, but dealing with Case and his story about some schnook's father made this seem more of a game than a real crime. Besides, I knew of a guy in Harlem who could take the first two floors of Davega off anybody's hands.

His name was José Strello and he owned a transmission shop on 111th Street that fixed transmissions like Jo-Jo used to fix ham and swiss sandwiches. I'd known José ever since I won an electronic guitar in a poker game and sold it to him for forty-five dollars, songbook included. I hadn't been there since, but I'd heard the back room of his shop had become to hot merchandise what Yankee Stadium was to baseball, and when I arrived there the next afternoon, the action was hot and heavy. José was in one corner buying raincoats; his brother, Ramon, was in another unloading portable televisions; and right in the middle of the floor was a marble statue that must have been hotter than charcoal briquets.

José remembered me, said hello, and I gave him a list of the stuff Case wanted to sell. He paced around a minute, consulted with Ramon, and said he'd take the lot for $750. I knew I could have jacked up the price, but I was a little nervous with that statue staring at me so I said okay, and in the morning Case and I loaded up the trunk of my car and drove back to deliver the goods.

Five minutes after we got there, José had the stuff

stashed away and we had our $750. Then, just as we were walking out, José motioned for me to come over to him, without Case, and for a guy who never lost his cool, he seemed a little shaky.

"Al, I want to show you something," he said, leading me through a door into another room. I couldn't believe it. We were in the back room's back room. There were closed cartons everywhere, and just thinking about what was in them got me nervous. As José cut one open, I was prepared to see anything from pounds of pure heroin to piles of counterfeit money, and it was a relief when he took out a couple of beautiful, thick, white, cableknit sweaters. "Gorgeous stuff, huh, Al? Imported from Finland. You buy one in any of those Fifth Avenue places, cost you fifty bucks. You want to make some money selling them to friends? I'll give you six dozen for $200." "Goodbye, José," I said, no longer relieved. Hot? At that price, those sweaters might have come from the ski shop at the Police Academy.

Strello wouldn't take no for an answer. "Al, I swear they're not that hot. I just don't deal with people who can afford them, kid." "No." "Al, you can make twenty, thirty bucks a shot. That's over a grand with no sweat." I was wavering. There was something about a comma followed by three zeros that made me forget myself. After all, it was only a sweater. I could tell the police I knitted it myself. José helped me put them in the car.

The next morning, I put one of them on and began walking down 79th Street. I figured if I paraded around for a couple of hours, people who knew me from the neighborhood would stop to chat. If they noticed I had on a beautiful sweater instead of my customary sweatshirt, and commented on it, I'd say I knew where to get more wholesale. Since the word "wholesale" spread on West 79th Street like the name "Gucci" did on East 55th, I had an outside shot to unload them all by lunch time.

The only thing I was right about was that I'd be done by lunch time. In fact, I was done five minutes after I hit the street and bumped into Willie Thomas. Thomas was a local black hustler who made his living doing everything from loansharking to running numbers to fencing hot jewelry, and the only reason I knew him even slightly was because he used the newsstand I bought my racing forms from as an office. He wasn't the type who'd comment on what a lovely sweater I was wearing, but I wanted to impress him, like one hustler to another, so I told him about José's back room and the sealed cartons of imported sweaters I'd bought for a song. The instant I said "José" and "imported" he grabbed my arm and nearly dragged me into the nearest doorway. "Don't ask me no questions, but if you're smart, you'll take whatever sweaters Strello sold you and burn 'em. You been fucked over, man!"

Thomas wouldn't give me the details, but he looked dead serious, and whatever he knew worried me enough to go home, take off the sweater I was wearing, and put it with the other seventy-one I had there. The next day I went up to see José, but some guy in his phony garage said he wasn't there and that he'd be gone for awhile. It sounded like a brush-off to me, and a week later those sweaters were still collecting dust when I accidentally ran into Ramon on 79th Street. I told him about Willie Thomas and said, "Level with me, Ramon. I'm not mad. I don't want my money back and I won't tell your brother you squealed. I just want to know what the story is with this stuff."

After swearing on my family's life that I'd never tell José anything, Ramon opened up. I got a rash just listening. He said the sweaters had come in from Finland and, like all imports, had to be checked through customs. While they were in transit, two guys hijacked the federal customs truck, not just the sweaters but the whole truck, taking the driver and guard with them. Then the hijackers drove the truck up to Harlem, sold the sweaters to José, and vanished. A few days later, José found out about the hijacking and, in a panic, unloaded the sweaters on the four biggest turkeys he could find.

"Ramon," I wailed, as he hurried down the block, "how could your brother do that to me? That's kidnapping; that's felonies; that's 20 years!" He never looked back.

When I got home I threw every one of those woolen beauties down the incinerator shaft, and if my arms were asbestos I would have reached in for the burnt threads and scattered them over Jamaica Bay. For days afterward I had flashes of the two guys from the customs truck lying bound and gagged in a Harlem alley next to a radio playing "Mama Loves Mambo." The flashes stopped in a week. I didn't wear a sweater for a month.

Obviously dealing in hijacked goods wasn't my forte, so I continued my search for that space between major crime and minor money. There was progress. In late November, it even dawned on me that what I was searching for was a purpose, and I might have found one if it wasn't for the enormous amount of low-lifes I knew. Like Proppo.

It was my fault, too. I could have hung up when he called to tell me about the lucrative position he'd taken in retailing, but, of course, I didn't. "Al, I never thought department stores were such gold mines, but there's five weeks till Christmas and I already feel like Santa's favorite elf." I let him continue. I knew it was a mistake. Purpose could wait.

In a week, I applied for a pre-Christmas sales job with the department store Proppo worked at. I was accepted and assigned to a training class. The three days of training were tolerable only because Proppo had warned me of them and promised the rewards would make it worthwhile. The classes met at 8:00 A.M., and the two instructors must have owned stock in this place. They tried to instill a gung-ho attitude in all of us similar to that of guerrilla terrorists. They expected our dedication, our loyalty, and our spirit all for sixty dollars a week! We were supposed to think about THE STORE, as it was called, constantly, and they wanted us to dress a certain way—high class, but understated—to further THE STORE's image. That was particularly hysterical because if we had to dress on the money THE STORE paid us, it would have been tough getting a job for Goodwill Industries.

After sitting through those three mornings of morale-builders, I was given an employee badge and assigned to a counter in the men's furnishings department. I was so happy to be out of THE STORE's training program, I didn't mind having to stand on my feet for eight hours a day being abused by consumers. Of course, I was following Proppo's own personal training and it spurred me on to bursts of unknown stamina. Even the bedlam created by the hordes of Christmas shoppers couldn't unnerve me enough to forget my most important lessons. Like the one where I switched price labels from expensive items to cheap ones, pitched the overpriced goodies to the customers who looked like the biggest dummies and kept the difference. Or the one about double-digited figures where if a sale came to $22.00, I'd ring up the $2 and pocket the $20. Not only was it too confusing for a harried customer to notice, but the register would never be short, and if I didn't do it while the short, bald guy in the brown windbreaker was looking, I didn't figure to get caught. I mean Proppo knew an undercover security guard when he saw one.

For two weeks I listened to Proppo's tips, and even with giving him 20 percent, I brought home up to eighty dollars a day. Proppo wouldn't say what he made, but from where I worked, I could see him at his register in the store Smoke Shop. Sometimes, he'd notice I was watching him. When he wasn't scoring, he'd shrug his shoulders and look away. When he was scoring a little, he'd smile and give me a thumbs-up sign. When he was scoring heavily, he'd raise his arms over his head like a fighter who'd just won a championship bout. There were a LOT more thumbs and arms than there were shrugs.

Too many. On the Monday before Christmas, a guy from Security—this one had a uniform—told me to close my register and come with him. "Oh, am I needed in housewares again?" I said, but I knew where we were going. When I got to the store manager's office, Proppo was already there. He was arguing with the manager over nothing. All the guy wanted was for us to turn in our badges and leave. There were no threats, no cops, no attempts at getting us to confess. It was obvious someone had seen us carrying on, but the store couldn't prove it and if we left quietly the matter would be dropped. "Proppo," I said, tugging at his coat. But he pulled away. "You can't fire us for nothing. I know my rights," he screamed. "Unless you can prove something, I'm gonna sue you." "Okay, son," the manager snarled. "I wasn't going to press the issue, but now you asked for it." Then he got on the intercom and asked his secretary to have the head of Security report to his office immediately. "Fine," Proppo said, " 'cause now I'm gonna sue you again for harassment of my person."

Meanwhile, I was collapsing. "Proppo, please," I begged, pointing wildly to my pocket, but he was out of control. The manager was furious. The Security Chief was on his way. Proppo was still going berserk, acting like we were innocent. I snapped. I lunged at him, ripped off his employee badge, threw it onto the manager's desk, and half dragged him out to the hall.

I could hear Proppo cursing and bitching behind me as we ran and bumped our way down three crowded escalators and into the street. "Al, you're a schmuck, you know that? They couldn't have proved shit if we stayed there. I could have squeezed out another week in a different store, but now that we ran out like that, I can forget about ever working in one of these places again." I didn't say a word until we got down the block and stopped. Then, I reached into my jacket pocket and took out a gold watch with its $195 price-tag still attached. "Here, Proppo," I said, "take this and set the little alarm on it for six o'clock tomorrow morning. When the buzzer wakes you up, do me a favor and kill yourself."

If anyone ever asked me for another résumé, I'd fill it out in invisible ink.

Chapter 10

I made my next move only three weeks from the day my retailing career disappeared. I made it so fast because it was so good. The first person to hear about it was Tum, and he found out on a Tuesday night in the Nathan's on Surf Avenue in Brooklyn. I was standing next to him eating a shrimp roll and between bites talking about a poem I'd heard at Commerce. I didn't remember the title but it was the one with all the forks in the roads people face in life and how everyone had to choose the path best for themselves. Tum wasn't big on poetry. "Al," he said, "I know two roads: the Major Deegan 'cause it takes me to Yonkers and the Meadowbrook Parkway 'cause it takes me to Roosevelt. Pass the salt." I said I was leading up to something serious. He said, "You always act serious when you get into these 'what-should-I-do-with-my-life' numbers. I wish you'd find something already so I could stop hearing about them." "That's just it. I think I finally know what I'd like to do." "What, Al? Tell me before I die from the suspense." "I want to own a horse." "A what?" "A horse, a thoroughbred race horse. You know, the kind that run around with jockeys on top and pay money for finishing better than fourth."

"Al, I wish you told me before." "Why," I said, "what difference would it have made?" "Forget it, it would only annoy you." "Tum, come on, what difference would it have made? Tell me." "All right. It's just that if you told me five minutes ago I wouldn't have eaten my hamburger." "So?" "Well, I think there was a horseshoe in there, and if I'd poked around a little I might have found some legs, and a neck, and a head, and with a little glue we could have pasted one together." I didn't get mad at Tum for mocking me. He'd seen too many of my brainstorms turn into horror shows to react any other way, and, besides, on the ride back to Manhattan, he was courteous enough to hear me out.

He listened to me go into how I had loved horses ever since Max Kramer first took me to Jamaica, how I'd never let myself think about getting involved in racing as a business because I was always too busy running around finding things to hate, and how I'd just realized the nitty-gritty in life was making money by doing what made you happy. When I got all finished, he said it sounded great, dropped me at my apartment, and drove away. Then I went upstairs feeling tremendous. I had my purpose, my niche, something with a future. Now, all I had to do was learn more about horses, then learn how to pick a winner, and then make enough money to afford one who could.

I figured I'd be able to do the learning. It would take a racetrack with horses who needed to be fed, brushed, walked, and all around taken care of and stables that would pay the bills. The money part figured to come harder. I had a few grand saved but I had dues to pay, and a job on the backstretch wouldn't cover the cost. So, as usual, making some more of the green stuff came first.

Well, I spent that night the same way I'd spent the twenty before it—trying hard not to think about bookmaking. The result was the same. I kept coming out even. I'd think of Dale and get sick and then think of his $1,900 and get better. I'd think about having no customers left and then remember all the degennies I knew. I'd try and justify doing it as a means toward an end and a minute later I'd unjustify it by worrying that the end could be another rubber check and a thug.

Finally, I'd go to sleep thinking of Jo-Jo and all the things he'd told me after Dale soured me on bookmaking. How the whole mess was my fault, how careless I had been, how stupid, but most of all I remembered him saying, "Look at it this way, Al. Gamblers and bookies have no lawyers or contracts or accountants. We got nothing except each other's words and phone numbers. There'll always be a guy or two who won't pay up unless you give him a good scare, but it's still not as sick a business as you think."

On morning number 21 I called Jo-Jo. I said I was considering making book again. He said if I made up my mind, he'd arrange for me to deal with a bookie he knew. Then I told him I was only hesitating because I was sick of doing illegal things. He didn't like that. I got a speech about how gamblers had been betting since the Romans made the Lions eight to one and out over the Christians, how they weren't going to stop now, and how he didn't see anything illegal about bookmaking. "Let me tell you something," he said. "The cops say it's against the law because bookies use vig but I had a customer who was a dentist and he charged his patients $300 for root canal work when all they needed was a filling. To me that's a lot more illegal than taking bets from people who want to give 'em to you." I had a feeling he'd break the tie.

"Jo-Jo," I said. "you got me so excited, I can't wait, but I still want to tell you one last thing. I'm only doing it to make enough money to buy a horse." "Sure, Al," he said, taking me much less seriously than Tum, "just don't let him answer the phones. It's hell on their hoofs."

Since the sound of basketballs thumping on hardwood floors had been going on for a few months, I called Case next, hoping he could get my ball rolling. He was a basketball degennie, owed me a big favor, and figured to know plenty of hoop freaks. Sure enough, a week after I told him that I was going to make book from my room again he called back with six prospects. That was an incredible haul even for a hustler like him, but after meeting all of them, I wound up with only three as customers. The trio I never got to deal with were a wealthy friend of Case's father's who wanted to bet a lot more than the $200 a game I'd take, and two friends of Case's who swore they had money but didn't have jobs. My new customers' names were Tony, Larry, and Stewy, and they all worked at the same talent agency Case had recently joined. I took them on because they were music agents who made pretty good money. As a reward for Case's finding them, I said I'd let him bet with me, too, even though he was working in the mail room. I mean, he couldn't have been making more than $65 a week, before taxes, but he swore he was pulling down plenty extra by selling "Promotion Only" record albums he stole from the head of the rock department's incoming mail load. Case, I believed.

A day later Jo-Jo phoned with the name of a small, but good BM called Johnny G. and two more customers—Sal something ending in an "O," an attorney, hitter and vouched-for bettor; and a free-lance illustrator named Catch, who split his life between drawing pictures and being a ninny. I added a few old standbys and with my roster set, the rules laid out and Johnny G. ready, I began taking action the third week in January.

Basketball proved to be an easy sport to handle. There were lines on the pros and on forty or so major college teams. The games were almost always at night, only piled up weekends, and since the sport wasn't all that popular, the line never came out earlier than the day each game was played.

At first, I didn't mind hoops not being too popular, but by mid-February, I was winning regularly and beginning to wish someone would give it a boost up the ladder. Still, I couldn't bitch. Not many BMs had four guys—Case, Stewy,

Larry, and Tony—who bet on the New York Knicks like they were the team's fan club, and in 1964 just rooting for them took a lot of guts.

The Knicks weren't bad. They were horrendous! Johnny G. told me most people who bet basketball in the city either ignored the team completely or bet against them. That made sense. What didn't was hearing my four fanatics bet cash money on the Knicks when they played the Boston Celtics, and it didn't matter how many points they got. Bill Russell was so good that if he showed up with four leaping midgets instead of Sam Jones and Tommy Heinsohn, they would have covered whatever the spread was. I remember attending one New York-Boston mismatch that must have been the cigar game of all time.

It was on a Saturday night in late February at the Garden. Boston was favored by 9 points and the fan club bet $200 on New York, 50 a member. For a half, the Knicks played as well as they could and left the court drenched in sweat trailing 70 to 49. Then they came back for the last twenty-four minutes with blood in their eyes, turned the ball over the first five times they got it, and when I left, with a couple of minutes to go, they were losing, 131 to 99. I stopped on the exit ramp to watch one more play, a Russell dunk after a Knick travel. After all, I wanted to make sure New York didn't rally.

There were some changes in the next six weeks. Case went tapioca; Stewy, Tony, and Larry began betting less money less often; Catch and I were becoming friends; and Sal took his wife on a cruise to Europe. In fact, the only thing that didn't change was the Knicks. Tom Hoover kept missing from four feet. Billy McGill's hook shot kept falling short, and if it wasn't for Art Heyman, I wouldn't have ever gone to a game. Art would have been my favorite player even if he weren't on New York, because I loved just watching him. What he'd do was stand in a spot, about twenty feet from the Knick basket, for five, ten minutes a game, and no matter which team had possession, Art would stay there, waving his hand for the ball. Whenever he'd go into one of those seances and the Knicks managed to get to their half of the court and pass it to him, Art wouldn't go toward the basket. He'd simply quit waving long enough to throw up a jumper that never missed and wind up scoring 27 points while the rest of the team scored 54, and the Knicks would get blown out night after night.

Obviously, I had some kind of season! By May, I was ahead over $2,400, and since nobody bet baseball, I called it a wrap without a complaint. The money was great. My not forgetting what I wanted it for was better, and now that I had it, I was chomping at the bit.

I chomped for six months. Oh, I got a backstretch job all right, only I got it in New York, and, slowly, I began to see that for someone who wanted to get into racing with two grand of patience and three grand of bankroll, it was the worst possible place to be.

For starters, the job I got was with one of the most famous stables in America. Its owner was rich enough to use it as a hobby. The trainer wore three-piece suits, with the vest buttoned, and in the A.M. yet, and if their horses were humans, they would have been kings and queens! That was the crux of the problem. You see, their horses were so valuable that if one as much as coughed, there'd be a mob scene in the barn. The trainer would show up—if he was in town—with his assistant, a vet and an exercise boy, and the horse's groom and a couple of people I didn't even know. Now, I didn't expect anyone to ask me whether a coughing horse, worth a hundred thou should have a chest x-ray or take two aspirin and see how he felt in the morning, but with all the employees in the way, I could hardly see into the stall. In fact, my main duty turned out to be moving manure from one spot to another and after five months, the only thing I'd learned was that their best stakes' horse took the biggest craps in the barn!

Anyway, I quit as soon as I was sure my perfecting a manure scoop wasn't getting Brooks Brothers favorite trainer's attention, and in October, at Aqueduct, I started looking for a job with a different stable. All I wanted was to find one where I could learn more about horses than what they had for lunch, get to take care of a few before the season ended, and buy one before I ran out of money.

It took me less than three weeks to realize I wasn't going to make my deadline, the reason why, and where I had to go to turn things around. As I'd been slowly finding out, just being in New York was the reason I was going to blow the deadline. I mean, it was a great place to watch the best horses, jockeys, and races in the world, but because of that, I knew now, I had to get away. The least ambitious trainers and owners on the grounds were more concerned with making a profit than giving a rush course in horsemanship to Al Talcum, and, besides, the only horses they'd sell were either too expensive or ones I didn't want. (For example, expensive in New York meant $15,000 and up. I had $3,500. Secondly, the ones I didn't want but could afford were low-priced claiming horses. For a horse to be claimed, he has to run in what's called "a claiming race," which is a race where each horse entered can be claimed—bought—by a trainer. The only requisites are to have the money to pay and, at least, one horse quartered at whatever track he makes the claim. At New York's major tracks, a claiming horse can cost anywhere from $3,500 to $30,000 or $40,000, and, whatever the price, they're the backbone of the racing industry everywhere. They consist of all the horses whose ability lies between that of riding academy nags and the tiny percentage of really good and great ones, and they make up the fields in six or seven out of every nine races run daily. One more thing: The reason I didn't want a claimer was that the same day I'd decided owning a horse would make me happy, I'd also decided that the first one I'd buy wouldn't be used, or given up on, or have a pretty-well-thought-out price on its head. In other words, I wanted to buy a horse with a little mystery to it—a young untried one with potential and looks and a shiny coat. One that I could dream about becoming a star: Unfortunately, in New York just taking a pot shot on an unknown quantity cost too much.) As for where to go to get a mystery horse I could afford, the answer was a smaller track, a much smaller track, and, after a few weeks of thinking about all the dumps I'd been to during my days down South with Dean, one stood out.

Its name was Sunshine Park. It was in Tampa, and the reason it stood out was something I'd overheard there over four years before. It was a conversation between a woman trainer named Lola Steeple and a young jockey who was telling her that he was giving up race riding and going back to playing pool for a living. When the jock finished, Lola said, "Son, my daddy once told me every hustler he ever knew rode a gold mare and that gold mare was always in front comin' into the stretch. Only thing was, a hustler's stretch goes on forever, and by the finish his mare was always a beatin', crawlin' last."

Well, any woman who knew that much about hustling— especially a redneck who probably hadn't been in a city with more than two traffic lights for twenty years—figured to know even more about horses. I gave her a call.

Since the track wasn't open yet, I reached Lola at her ranch in Umitilla, a nothing town eighty miles from Tampa. The first words I heard were, "Operator, I don't know a soul in New York City. Y'all sure your party got the right numbah?" I could see finding her alive was going to be the easiest part of this maneuver.

"Hello, Miss Steeple," I said after the operator assured her the call was for real. "My name's Alfred Talcum and I'm coming South to learn about horses. I was at Sunshine Park a while back and you impressed me quite a lot. . . . Miss Steeple! Miss Steeple! Are you there?" I could hear her breathing. "Miss Steeple, all I want to do is work for you, and I was just wondering if you might give me a job." Finally, she spoke, "Talcum! Alfred Talcum? I don't know any Talcum boy ever worked around here." Silence. I was paying for the call. Even her breathing was getting faint. "Miss Steeple, I'm coming down there and you don't have to promise me anything. Just remember my name." I didn't think she would.

I arrived in Tampa with the Sunshine Park meeting still a month and a half off so I checked into a motel and drove out to Umitilla to see Lola. As soon as I turned in the open, broken gate and spotted her little, sunbleached, grizzled form tying a saddle on a horse like a man would leash a small dog, I was prepared for the worst. I got it. After I said I was the Al Talcum who'd talked to her on the phone two weeks ago, she not only didn't remember the call or my name, but she looked at me funny, like I was a human being, but just barely. Then she shook her head and said, "Sorry, boy. I don't need help. I got my son, Orville, to help, and when he gets to drinkin', I just tend chores myself."

I didn't drive 2,500 miles to hear about Orville or to take no for an answer. Even though she was ignoring me, I stayed there telling her how sincere I was and kept saying over and over, "Look, Miss Steeple, all I want to do is learn about race horses and all I'm asking for is a job." She didn't as much as blink until I finally and desperately said, "I don't expect to get paid!" Well, all of a sudden, Lola Steeple looked up from the horse she was brushing and I could tell she was hearing me for the first time. I mean, even down here people knew something for nothing was very cheap, even a barely human something. "I guess if y'all don't get in the way, I kin find somethin' for y'all to do, bein' it's for free. That's right, boy, ain't it? Y'all did say 'no pay'?" I assured Lola that was right, said I wouldn't ask for a cent until she offered, and thanked her for the opportunity.

Before I left, she gave me the name of a trailer park on the outskirts of Tampa, and said starting Saturday she'd be staying there, because from then on she'd be going to the track every day. "Y'all can rent a trailer there right cheap and if you be by mine at four-fifteen, I'll give y'all a lift in." Just to let me know she wasn't being soft, Lola added, "Only reason I offer is so y'all be on time."

I met her Saturday okay and let me tell you it was some strange feeling being up and out at four-fifteen in the morning, sitting in a pick-up truck, driving through the black humid air of a predawn Florida morning. I mean, this was really backwoods country, and Jews from New York and long-distance telephone calls weren't part of it. Suddenly, I could feel every foot of those 2,500 miles between me and Max Kramer's newsstand.

Although racetrack workers are all early risers, we were the first people to arrive, and the second I climbed out of her truck, Lola began explaining my chores. She told me every morning I was to go around to her twelve horses, dump the old water from their pails, and give them fresh. Then I was to give each of them a meal of one scoop of oats. "Not an oat more, boy," she liked to remind me, and by the time dawn was breaking, I was to start my big job, exercising her horses by walking each of them around the barn for half an hour.

It sounded like hard work, but considering I could watch the dawn break from outside instead of through Proppo's window between poker hands, I didn't feel too bad. After I began, what made me feel even better was that as hard as I worked, my lady boss, who must have been sixty years old and couldn't have weighed 100 pounds, worked twice as hard, and she made the thought of complaining or bitching downright embarrassing.

Hell, within a couple of weeks, I must have walked Lola's horses around her barn hundreds of times and I was enjoying it. I talked to them like I talked to the lions, as a kid, in Central Park, only now I went one step further. I had whole conversations. Some I talked to about the weather. Some, I'd gossip with, and I spoke loud enough so other stable hands could hear me. I didn't care. I was busy singing, whistling, and talking and having a good feeling inside like never before.

In late December, just before the meet started, I was joined at six every morning by a stable hand named Bob. We chatted every once in a while and one time he mentioned his last name was Kelso. That struck me pretty funny because of the great horse, Kelso, who was running in those days, so I said, "That's a helluva name for a guy who works at a race track." With that, Kelso jumped up and, sounding insulted, said, "Talcum ain't much of a name, either." Then he walked away in a huff and I realized he hadn't known what I was talking about. He had never heard of Kelso.

Incidents like that always reminded me of just how far removed this track and these people were from the big-time racing I grew up with in New York and Jersey. Bob Kelso and Lola Steeple might be involved in this business for years, but they'd never heard of a lot of things in "the bigs." That was another world of rich stakes and wealthy owners and thousand-acre farms in Kentucky, while 90 percent of all racing consisted of tiny tracks like Sunshine Park and folks like Lola who worked long hours for short purses yet knew more about horses and worked harder with them than people making a hundred times more money.

On rare occasions when I would get a chance to relax and Lola would sit down to talk, she'd tell me about how she went to horse sales and bought crippled but well-bred ones for a nickel on the dollar. Lola said she never spent more than a few hundred dollars on a horse, but she'd take the time no one else would nursing them back to health and eventually getting them sound enough to run at the minor league tracks she trained at. It wasn't much, but she made a living and it was all she knew. Better yet, for me anyway, her horses were so crippled and needed so much attention I couldn't help learning more and more every day.

Aside from getting no wages, my biggest problem was

communicating. Sure, I'd spent time in the South, but this place was no Miami. Hell, it wasn't even Orlando, and because the racing people here were even more clannish and limited than most yokels, I found the best way for me to act was to keep my mouth shut and do my work. It seemed like every time I tried to make a joke or glib remark my sarcastic, cynical big-city sense of humor fell completely flat and, as a result, I kept myself going by talking to the horses and listening to Lola tell me the difference between them and zebras. Once in a while, I'd get real horny and drive into downtown Tampa to look for a semiliterate red-neck woman. They were hard to come by, but when I got lucky enough to find one who could spell "c-o-w," I'd take her back to my trailer and screw her with my eyes closed, hoping she'd disappear into the poinsettia the instant we finished.

In fact, after a couple of months at the track, my best friend was a black stable foreman named Mushy, and hanging out with him didn't help my image. Most of the rednecks around were just average bigots, but there were a few who could have qualified for the Ku Klux Klan's tar-and-feather brigade. Still, I'd ignore their dirty looks, and share coffee with Mushy almost every morning. He wasn't any brighter than the Klansmen, but he was friendly and open and didn't make me feel like I was a Northern troublemaker. Sometimes I'd see him and say, "Hi, Mushy, how they coming?" and with a "Howdy Mr. Al," he'd come up to me, look at my cigarette, and answer by saying "How 'bout borrowing me one of dem smokes?" Then we'd sit around and he'd tell me stories about growing up in Florence, South Carolina, in a shack with no plumbing, and I'd tell him about apartments in New York with stained glass windows and private elevators. I remember once Mush and I were kneeling down outside a stall in a cool morning mist. I was smoking a cigarette and it being my last, I passed it to him so he could take a drag and then pass it back. We kept dragging like that until I looked up and saw Lola standing maybe thirty yards away staring at me in total disbelief. I mean, white folks just didn't share cigarettes with blacks, and if I wasn't such a good slave, I'm sure she would have fired me on the spot. Lola never did say anything to me about it, but later in the week, I overheard her talking to Orville. "Son," she drawled, "if everybody from the big city is like Talcum, this here country's in a hunk o' trouble."

One Sunday Lola came over to my trailer dressed in her Sunday finest and asked if I'd like to go to church with her. I said I was sorry but I wasn't very religious, and besides, I wasn't Christian. "Might I ask," she said, "just what religious persuasion y'all follow?" I told her I was Jewish. Then she smiled, walked away, and I swear, I don't think she knew what the hell I was talking about.

I didn't do much betting down there, mainly because the horses were so cheap the best of them were hard-pressed to make it around the track without a pacemaker, but now and then I'd think I had a "goodie" and always tried to slip it to Lola. It was hopeless. Like this one day in February, a horse named Sergeant O'Hara was running in the fourth race and I thought he couldn't lose. So in the morning I saw Lola near the barn and walked over to her. "Miss Steeple," I said, confidentially, "I think there's a horse in the fourth who's a little special. I know you don't like to bet, but this is a positive certainty, a cinch. I swear, Miss Steeple, he's a sure thing." "Alfred," she said, walking away. "Y'all know I don't gamble and I don't want y'all to, neither. Now git, and tend to chores." I ran after her, stuck one finger in front of her face, danced around her as she kept walking down Shed Row, and said, "Miss Steeple. He's a lock. The jockey won't need a whip. I'll guarantee he'll finish first." Lola never stopped to listen, but later in the day, after Sergeant O'Hara had won easy and paid $14.80, she saw me in the grandstand counting my winnings. "My, my," she said. "Look at all that foldin' money. I guess I don't have to worry no more about paying y'all that salary I been thinkin' on." Sure.

It really didn't matter that much because by then I'd had enough chicken-fried steak and wilderness to last me a lifetime and, besides, I thought I knew as much about horses as anyone. Lola didn't think I knew as much as Orville, who knew nothing, but when I told her I wanted to buy one, she tried to help. She said she knew a wealthy breeder who had a spread near her ranch and she took me out there one day to show me a horse he had for sale. His name was Knight Charger and he was a three-year-old colt who, a few months before, had run second in his very first race. Lola said the horse had bad knee problems but that his breeding was about as good as a horse's could be and the owner was selling him only because he had too many good, healthy horses to keep this one around. I told her it was just the kind of horse I wanted, and she haggled with the guy until he agreed to sell him to me for $1,460. I was so excited, I never thought about why I was getting a horse for $28,540 less than his owner had paid for him just over a year ago.

Next, Lola introduced me to a young trainer-owner named Joe James. She said Joe had been in the business a few years and just had two or three cheap horses but that he was a hard worker and would take the time to help get Knight Charger ready to race. Originally, I agreed to work with Joe only because I didn't have a trainer's license and you needed one to enter a horse in a race, but quickly, he became more than handy. It started when I realized I didn't know how to get a horse ready to do anything except eat and walk around barns. That made me want him as a trainer. Soon he was a friend too. We both loved racing and horses, we were both young and struggling, and best of all, in three weeks my new friend and trainer had Knight Charger looking like he was worth a lot more than $1,460.

So, in late February he entered Knight Charger in a maiden race—maidens being horses who have never won a race. I had my silks registered with the Florida State Racing Commission, I got my name listed in the form and program as owner, and the night before we ran, I couldn't sleep. To give you some idea of how bad the horses were at Sunshine Park, on the morning of the race, the form had us listed as the even money favorite, and the ace handicapper's comment was, "In clever hands—ready for score." And despite the fact Knight Charger hadn't run in a race for months, that our jockey was an eighteen-year-old kid with gonorrhea, who kept scratching his crotch furiously right up until post time, and that one of the "clever hands" the form referred to might have been the one I got tangled in the reins as Joe tightened the horse's saddle, I had to admit we deserved to be the favorite.

The nine horses we were running against had raced a total of eighty-one times and the best one among them had once finished third in a six-horse field. Well, Knight Charger was bet down to 4 to 5, and sitting in the grandstand a minute before the race with Joe and the jockey's girl friend who gave him the clap, I was sure we'd win. Two minutes later I knew we'd lost. There wasn't much doubt because even if Knight Charger liked to save his big run for the stretch, he still would have had a helluva tough time. I mean, not many horses went on to win after coming to a dead stop.

When we got him back to the barn, the track vet looked him over and said, "I got better knees than this horse. He's not hurt real bad, but if you want, I'll shoot him for you 'cause all he's good for now is walkin' fast."

Even spending $1,500 for 1,200 pounds of Gravy Train couldn't make me let him do that. Instead, I gave Knight Charger to a farmer who said he wanted him for his kids to ride.

I toyed with the idea of throwing myself onto the grill in the horseman's kitchen, but fought off the urge to check out of life wrapped in a western omelet and trudged on. I had a little help. In late March, Joe asked me if I wanted to go with him up to Finger Lakes, a small track in upstate New York. He said I could work with his horses and that if I studied I could pass the trainer's test, get my license, and maybe train a few horses. I told Joe the only horses I wanted to train were mine and thanked him anyway, but before he left I asked for all his travel plans so I'd know where to reach him if I changed my mind.

Lola helped too, in her own backwoods way. She saw me one morning moping around the backstretch like a lost soul and said: "Stop pining, son. Y'all take the good with the bad in this business and leave the rest to the Lord." Her dose of old-time religion wasn't going to get the Baptist Church to drop a stable of allowance horses in my collection plate, but it gave me the push I needed to stop dragging my ass.

"Case, how are you?" I said when I heard his New York "Hello" come over the line. "Al?" "Nobody but." "What's doing in the boonies, big fella? You trade in your car for a covered wagon yet?" "Case, a little break," I whined. "The horse is gone and my sense of humor went with him. Just tell me something. Are Stewy and the rest of your friends still living?" "What happened with the horse?" "Case, it must be 105 degrees in this phone booth. I'll tell you about the horse when I see you. What about your friends?" "You won't believe this, Al, but they're flush. They sat out the basketball season because Stewy read a book that said baseball was the best sport to bet on. They might not touch the NBA playoffs they're so worked up. Al, they took a season's box at Shea Stadium and Tony's got the Yankee and Met schedules pinned on the wall over his bed."

The Alfred Talcum stable wasn't dead yet. "Case, tell the boys I'm on my way home so they don't get desperate and look for another bookmaker. I'll call you the minute I arrive." "Okay, but what am I going to get out of this?" "My man," I said, hurrying to get off the phone, clean the oats out of my car, and take off, "you get 1 percent of Stewy's losses for the season and a kiss on the lips. Goodbye."

I got into the city ten days before the Mets home opener. I called Case. "No sweat, Al. The boys are glad you're back." So was Tum. And Catch, and Sal. On a whim I even called Felix and a few other guys from my pre-Dale days, and everyone of them said they'd be glad to do business with me. It was a nice feeling to be greeted with, "Welcome back," or, "Sure, just give me your number and I'll call whenever the mood hits," but I knew why I was so well received.

Having been a polite and accurate little BM helped to avoid boos and nasty cracks about my being out of town so much, but moreover, it was because I always made my bettors feel they could trust me—that if I lost four grand making book I might fleece a department store to steal it, hock myself to raise it, or hustle Ping Pong to earn it, but whatever it took, I'd get it.

I still don't want to be a bookmaker, but I'd come a long way from taking lunch money as a tyke and bad checks as an idiot. A long enough way to get a second phone installed in my room that week, and long enough to come up with another Talcum Law of Bookmaking, one that Jo-Jo really told me almost four years before. Bettors would change doctors or dentists, girl friends or wives. What they wouldn't change was a good, honest bookie, and unless every degennie in the world tapped out or joined GA, that was a helluva nice thing to know.

Thinking Jo-Jo could do more than improve my code of ethics, I called him to discuss pressing matters, like tips on booking baseball, maybe picking up a few of his ex-customers, and definitely asking about him getting me a BM to deal with. After an annoying couple of horse jokes—How come I wasn't at the Belmont Ball? Did I meet Seabiscuit?—Jo-Jo said it was good to have me back because when I was gone he had no one to do favors for and told me to talk fast if I wanted to take advantage of his good mood.

After I said I planned to book baseball, there was a slight pause, and then he said, "Baseball?" in a way that made the word sound like an eight-letter obscenity. "You get sunstroke down South or what?" Jo-Jo added. "You can make with it Al, but it's everyday stuff from April to October; it's a killer. What the hell you need that for?" I asked him if he was the same guy who gave me the speech about bookmaking last year. "Come on," I said, "you talked about making book like it was working for the Vatican." "Baseball's different," Jo-Jo explained. "You handled it for twenty years," I argued. "Yeah, and it almost blew my marriage, remember?"

"Jo-Jo," I said, "I'm single and besides I got a motive." "What?" "I want to get some money together fast and buy another horse." As the "e" in horse was still airborne, Jo-Jo started zinging me for the second time. "Again with the horses. You don't learn do you? I got to tell you something, Al. Booking baseball is rough, but doing it to get a horse is unbelievable. You want to be a cowboy why don't you just go up to the park in Pelham, rent a pony for an hour, and take him on the Grand Concourse. I know a bowling alley that's great for gunfights."

It took a "Please," two or three "Come on's," and some bitching about not wanting to be a straight man until opening day, but finally I got Jo-Jo to stop. He told me a little about baseball and said I'd find out soon enough why it was such a pain in the ass. Then he promised to see if he could get a few customers for me plus a BM I could deal with. His last words were, "Finding a bookie who works baseball won't be easy, but I'll ask around." I thanked him, hung up, and without knowing what I was in for, began wishing the Knicks were in the American League.

I didn't think Jo-Jo would let me down, but five days passed without my hearing from him. I didn't care about the extra bettors, but I had to get a guy to hedge with. It was that or take the line out of the paper and make book with my fingers crossed again. I mean, with bad luck I could lose my couple of grand by Memorial Day no matter how much action I laid off, but with nothing going for me except the newspaper and silent prayer I had a shot at being wiped out before the Astros were 0-4.

A day later, as usual, Jo-Jo came through, this time with two of his ex-customers—a furrier named Max, who bet $60 parleys, and a glazier from Queens named Solomon, who liked to bet the Yankees and Mets and not for more than the $200 limit I'd take. Better yet, he also found me a BM to work with. I was to meet him on Saturday, three days before the season opened, under the marquee of a residential hotel on West 76th Street. His name was Pot Cheese.

I'd just rounded the corner of 76th Street and Columbus Avenue at 8:00 A.M. Saturday when I spotted something. At 150 feet there was no question it was a bookmaker. I might have been able to tell the guy was a BM if he was buried upside down on Rockaway Beach. He was standing outside the hotel dressed in a short-sleeved shirt, two sizes too small, exposing an incredibly large stomach jutting out over his pants. On his head sat a Cleveland Indian baseball cap, tilted to the side like the brim was lightly brushed by a foul tip, and he was holding a transistor radio tight to his right ear.

At seventy-five feet, it was clear it was Pot Cheese because his nickname, like most given to gamblers, was right on the money. The belly, which was looming larger and paler with every step I took, was a mass of bumps and ripples of pale fat, and I half expected to see "Large Curd" etched across its expanse.

Five feet away I heard his voice for the first time when he glanced up quickly at a passing wino, "Lakers win last night—103-101." Then he relit his cigar, put the radio back to his ear and resumed his pose. "Pot Cheese," I whispered, "my name's Al Talcum, Jo-Jo's friend." "Talcum, hummm," he murmured, like he wasn't sure where he heard the name before. "Talcum. Oh yeah, you're the guy Jo-Jo called me about. How you doin', kid?" he said, extending his free hand for me to shake, but before I could, he tore the radio away from his ear. "Goddamn, dem 76-ers!" he moaned. "They losing by fourteen at the half. I go to bed at one A.M. when I hear the game's in overtime. They lose the whole thing by 'tree.' Ah, life's a number, kid. What do you want this business for?"

Without waiting for my answer, Pot Cheese ducked into the hotel lobby, emerging a moment later with a fresh cigar. He said Jo-Jo vouched for me and on his word he'd take up to $500 a game in lay-offs. "$500 a game!" I said, sounding surprised. "My sheet's got a $200 limit, and I don't figure to ever need you for more than a hundred or two." "Okay, kid," Pot Cheese said, switching his radio back on. "Jo-Jo didn't tell me you was just a little BM."

Then I asked him for the numbers I could reach him at. "Forget phone numbers, kid. I haven't sat direct since I found this hotel." "How come?" "They got five booths and the desk clerk's got a tin ear. That's how come, kid. Now stop askin' so many questions. I got a very simple set-up. You give me your numbers and I'll call you with the line starting opening day. Day games I'll call in around eleven forty-five, twelve; night games, five forty-five, six o'clock the latest. I'll come back to you every half hour or so with changes in the line, and when I call you, gimme what you want to lay off and say 'good-night, Gracie.' Any more questions?" "No," I answered, slipping him my two phone numbers, "nothing I can think of." "Good. Jo-Jo told me you were a sharp kid. Have a cigar, call me P.C. from now on, and rest up the next two days. Running bases till October ain't no fun." For a kid who made book with young ninnies to buy old horses I was certainly getting involved with a big bookie.

Well, I spent opening day in front of my television set watching the Mets home opener. The mayor threw out the season's first ball—I thought it would have added some class if there was a bookmaker behind him throwing out the season's first pen. Two hours later I was still watching as Don Drysdale strutted into the dugout with a win and a smile. He was 1 and 0. I was 0 and 1. P.C. called a moment later. "Welcome to the national pastime, kid. Ain't it a bitch?"

I survived the early part of the season, thanks to April showers bringing canceled games along with May flowers, but by early June, when the weather improved, I was getting shaky. Jo-Jo's words about "baseball being everyday stuff" were hitting home, and I was beginning to see why he was selling insurance and P.C. was eating cigar butts. Every week seemed the same.

As soon as Sunday's games were over, I'd get a *Daily News,* check the scores, do the work, and then, nervously, turn to the page with Monday's baseball schedule. Sure. In the old days when there were sixteen teams it might have been an open day, but with expansion teams everywhere except Alaska, there were always a few games. Like two in the afternoon and two at night, which meant I'd have to spend a couple of hours in my room early and late, and run around settling up between shifts. Tuesdays through Thursdays were worse, by Fridays the Dodgers would be in town for a big weekend series, and before I caught my breath Monday's paper was on the stands again. I could have lived without Fire Island, but, come on, never a free afternoon for the races?

Still, I was holding up until a Monday morning in late June. The night before I'd checked the paper to see the schedule, and right under the standings, in big type, it said "No Games Today." Okay, I thought. Finally a freebie. No phones. No Stewy. A day at the track. It was like getting out of prison. I jumped out of bed and began getting dressed. I had one sock on when the phone rang. It was P.C. "Listen, kid, I just called to tell you there's a ball game today. I know the *News* got it listed different, but I got the schedule and the Cubs are at home against the Giants. It's an afternoon job—one fifty-five start. I'll call you later with the startin' pitchers."

It figured. If there was one team I'd grown to hate that summer, it was the goddamned Cubs! The mistake in the paper was making it worse this time, but it was the fourth day the Cubs had done this to me: Four days every other team in baseball was either off or playing at night, except for the little bears and their opponent. And all because the chewing-gum tycoon of Chicago wouldn't put lights in Wrigley Field. Not a bulb! Not a candle! Nothing except day games that always seemed to pop up just when you'd think a weekday was going to go by without hearing about Billy Williams' line drives.

This time I was so mad, I wanted to make believe P.C. never called and leave as planned. I couldn't. If it was the Phillies and Cubs, maybe, but Stewy and Sal were Giant fans, and I had to stick around knowing they'd want to bet the game. Sure enough, they both called in that afternoon and put fifty dollars a piece on the "Jints." I settled for a movie at the Beacon Theatre on 74th Street, a walk down Fifth Avenue, and a late dinner at Tad's Steak House. It wasn't much but by the time I'd bought a paper to check the score, I was soothed enough to get a good night's sleep. After all, the season couldn't go on forever and if the Cubs had won, a hundred bucks would make a nice consolation prize. Immediately, I flipped through to the Sports Section. There, buried under an article about a bowler named Billy Welu and an ad for trusses was one line. "Chicago Cubs vs. San Francisco Giants, postponed on account of rain." I wouldn't buy a stick of Wrigley's spearmint if I lived to be 3,000 years old.

After that, only the approaching All-Star Game break kept me going. It was a target—an oasis between Cub assaults. I would have thirsted for it even if I weren't losing money.

Baseball wasn't a smarter bet than anything else, like Stewy hoped, but it took time to learn how to book. For instance, the vig was different than in football or basketball, in that it was built right into the line. In baseball, the line was referred to as the point line and it came out daily, based on the opposing team's overall ability and further adjusted according to the scheduled starting pitchers. The line never came out in advance because pitching rotations were subject to frequent last-minute changes. A typical line on a game would be something like: Yankees, 6½, 7½ over Cleveland. This line and every other one used $5 as a base, and the first team mentioned—in the above case, the Yankees—were the favorite and the second team, Cleveland, was the underdog.

Winning or losing aside, the most important thing to a bookmaker was that the vig in each game was always there. It was simply the differential in the odds a bettor had to lay to bet the favorite against the slightly smaller odds received when betting the underdog. For example, if you bet the Yankees, you'd have to lay out $7.50 (7½) to win $5. If you bet Cleveland, regarded as the inferior team, you'd have to lay out $5 to win $6.50 (6½). No matter how much someone bet on the game, that price wouldn't change. If he wanted to win $50 on the Yankees, he'd have to put up $75; to win $100, put up $150, and so on. Conversely, someone betting Cleveland would have to put up $50 to win $65, a $100 to win $130, and $200 to win $260. Though the line on any given game would change depending on who was playing who and what pitchers were starting, this formula remained constant. So if a very good team like the Cincinnati Reds were playing a very bad team like the old New York Mets, the line might have Cincinnati 8, 9 over New York. Then it would take a $9 bet on the Reds to win $5, and a $5 bet on the Mets to win $8; $90 on the Reds to win $50; $50 on the Mets to win $80. A Cincinnati bettor would have to lay the 9 to 5 odds, which were steep, but a New York bettor was getting 8 to 5 on his money and that was a nice pay-off, too.

If all of that seems like a big edge, just remember BMs spend their summers thinking Bain de Soleil is an Italian relief pitcher. If that doesn't faze you, then rent a dingy room on Amsterdam Avenue, put in a phone, say goodbye to your family's cabana and wait until the Cubs are at Wrigley Field for a nine-game home stand.

I made it to the three-day All Star break, but I slid in slowly edging into the red. My customers weren't that smart, but they all liked to bet chalk, and for the first half of the season the favorites were tough to knock down. After the break—the National League won the game six to five while I slept—the second half of the season picked up where the first had left off. The good pitchers kept pitching good and in my first four days back, I was on the goose egg side of eight shut-outs. All I could do was wait and hope that some of the weaker teams began playing better ball. It just wouldn't happen. Case and Larry were laying 90 to 50 every day and winning. Even Tum and Stewy were ahead, and Sal, a chalk monster if there ever was one, hadn't suffered a losing week all season. I felt a little less snake-bit when I found out I had company, namely my whale-sized pal, P.C. himself. "In this game, kid, you want guys to bet chalk so they laying you odds and vig. Trouble is dis year the chalk ain't losing and if dat Woild Series don't get here fast, old Pot Cheese gonna be steam-rolled."

My theory was that there were too many "blue-chippers" around, blue chippers being exceptional pitchers whom everyone bet and bet heavy. I mean, it was nice having guys put up $110 to win $50 every time Juan Marichal faced the Mets, but it wasn't much good if Juan never lost, and he wasn't the only blue chipper. There was Bob Gibson, Don Drysdale, Jim Bunning, Dean Chance, and the best of them all—the pitcher bookmakers loved to hate: Sandy Koufax.

I never believed in a sure thing, but if anybody in sports history ever came close, Sandy Koufax was the guy. He made $10 ninnies into $100 plungers, conservative bettors into rubber-band-off-the-bankroll monsters, and when he was in his prime, even the bookie colony in Tel Aviv rooted against him!

There was a game that Friday when Los Angeles came into Shea Stadium to play the Mets that summed up Koufax. The line on it was Koufax 2, 2½ runs over the Mets. I'd never heard a price like it before, but P.C. explained it was a kind of defensive betting line bookmakers used as a last resort in emergencies. Koufax against the Mets was an emergency.

P.C. said the runs line was designed to stop chalk players, because if they wanted to bet the favorite, it forced them to lay runs instead of odds. Like in this game, a Dodger bettor could bet at even money but he'd have to lay 2½ runs. Then if LA lost the game outright, won it 1-0 or even 2-0, he'd still lose his bet. Only if LA won by 3 or more runs would he win. A Met bettor would get 2 runs and also be able to bet at even money. Then, if the Mets lost the game by 1 run, they'd win the bet; by 2 runs they'd tie, and if they lost by 3 or more, they'd lose. The vig was that the chalk player had to lay 2½ runs and the underdog bettor only got 2.

He added that the runs line wasn't used more often because it tended to cut down betting, because having to lay runs could usually stop a chalk monster from betting the favorite, but it wouldn't necessarily make him grab the other side. As a result, bettors often wound up bitching, not betting, and hanging up, and if it weren't for pitchers like Koufax, the runs line might never be used.

Well, after P.C.'s explanation, I had a renewed sense of pride in bookmaking. I mean, this runs gimmick sounded ingenious, and laying 2½ of them figured to stop chalk monsters if they were in tanks. Unfortunately, my customers drove Dodge Darts, plus they were stubborn, and I got $900 bet on Koufax, laying the 2½ runs, and zero on the Mets. Even Catch, who loved to bet underdogs, put $25 on LA, and by seven forty-five I was anxiously awaiting P.C.'s wind-up call. For the first time that season I hedged the limit with him, 500, held the other 400 myself, and tuned in Channel 9.

LA was up first. Double... error... pop out... walk... single... error... single... pop out... triple... ground out. Half an inning, 6 runs. It was five more than they needed. The Mets never got a man past second base, lost eight-zip, and got one hit, a scratch single by Joe Christopher who swung at a gnat and hit Koufax's curve ball by mistake. It wasn't all the Mets' fault. With the stuff Koufax had that night he could have pitched from center field and won!

The rest of the weekend was filled with more bad scores and even with the hedge money I got back from P.C., the three-day binge had cost me $950. Everyone was paid by Tuesday but my smile was smaller than usual and the baseball season seemed longer than ever. My sweet Knick memories were disappearing and my hopes for a new race horse were going with them.

August passed, slowly and unprofitably, featuring a Drysdale overwhelming of Philadelphia, a fourteen-strike-out Sam McDowell special against Detroit, and a Jim Maloney no-hitter leveling the Cubs. And as I was reeling an unexpected phone call from Sal early on Sunday morning shook things up. "Al, remember Guildo, that friend of mine you met in my office?" "Yeah," I said, sensing a strained tone in his voice. "What about him?" "Well, don't laugh, but it's not him I want to talk to you about. It's his wife, Lillian. She needs a bookie." "Sal, do me a favor and don't bother me with women. If she wants action, let her play canasta." "Okay, Al, if that's the way you want it, but remember I gave you first crack at a broad who cost her husband five grand last year." "Five grand?" I said, my ears suddenly unpuckered. "That's right, Al. Five big ones, not counting what she lost in Vegas where Guildo told me he had to drag her out of the Flamingo. She's got a real thing for gambling like nymphos have it for sex and Guildo's so pussy-whipped he gives her an open checkbook to keep her happy. You still want her to play canasta?"

The next night, I heard the husky, yet feminine voice of my first female degennie. "Hi, Al. This is Lillian Camilli. Can I have a line, please?" Quickly, the novelty of dealing with a woman wore off. I mean, Lillian kept sounding somewhat feminine, but she bet like a man and lost like a turkey. $60 parleys were her specialty, and the first week she went for $180 and followed up by dropping $240 the second. I never saw her, but on both Mondays I went to Sal's office and the money she'd lost was there waiting for me. I was beginning to think more women customers wasn't a bad idea. The promotional possibilities were limitless. I could have Ladies' Days when all females could bet at half-vig. Or use gambling wives to get their husbands involved, with slogans like: "The family that bets together stays together," but unfortunately, by the Wednesday of our third week together my enthusiasm for women degennies had cooled considerably. Lillian dropped $360 that Monday, then $300 more Tuesday, and Wednesday night I made up my mind to tell her I was cutting off our arrangement immediately. Open checkbook and pussy-whipped husband aside, she was giving off that unmistakable scent of disaster like maybe a female David Dale. Surprisingly, I didn't hear from her that night, or the next day. By

Friday morning I was thinking how glad I was that she'd quit gracefully, when the phone rang. It wasn't going to be quite that easy. Lillian was on asking if I'd meet her in an hour in front of Riker's Restaurant on 57th Street. She said to look for a woman with dark glasses and white kid gloves.

When I arrived, Lillian was waiting for me outside, and despite her ridiculous outfit, she wasn't a bad-looking woman. I mean, I expected her to be a cross between Smokey Burgess and Marie Dressler, but she was fairly young—thirtyish—had a good figure and a cute, if not pretty, face. "Al," she said, nervously, "Guildo took away my checkbook. I can't pay you what I lost this week. I'm sorry." "Lillian," I said, calmly. "Stop biting your gloves and relax. Pay me the money whenever you get it and go back to the PTA. Okay?" I began walking off, annoyed as hell for ever letting myself get involved with this crap. I noticed she was following me. "That's not what I dragged you down here to tell you," she said. "I want to make a deal. Just let me bet one $60 parley with you every day, and if I win, deduct it from what I owe until we're even. If I lose, I'll pay in other ways." I didn't really want to hear what was coming, but Lillian wouldn't quit. "Look at it this way, sweetie," she said, a la Mae West, "if I get lucky, you get your money, and if I don't, I'll do things that'll melt your zipper!"

This was getting sick and I was right there germing up Riker's window with her. And out-to-lunch married woman that she was, I kind of liked her, so, after a moment of silence, I said, "Lillian stop petting my coat. You got a deal."

Unfortunately for Mrs. Camilli, the next six days drew blanks. In four of the parleys she bet, both teams lost and in the other two, one did. I felt good and bad about her lousy luck. Good in the morning when I went up to her apartment on Riverside Drive to get a hand job and coffee, and bad at night when I was horny again and remembered wanton sex didn't pay the phone bill. I let this incredible situation continue, but after Lillian lost five out of the next seven days, I decided I had to call it off. The woman showed no signs of quitting no matter how many times I came on her couch. Her husband, Guildo, was big and strong, and who needed that, and on Friday when I walked into her apartment house I was determined to stop this madness. I had no choice. If it went on much longer we might have had a baby.

Lillian must have picked up on my wanting out, because as I strode through the lobby, I noticed her standing in a waiting elevator motioning for me to join her. "Al, listen," she whispered tensely while pressing the "Up" button for the twenty-fourth floor, "I know this is getting absurd but, please, let me go until Labor Day and if I'm still losing I'll quit." "Lillian," I pleaded, "enough's enough. I got your fingerprints all over my body. Forget the money you owe me, forget our deal. I can't come up here like this any more. I'm beginning to feel like I'm booking my way through a French film."

When we reached the twenty-fourth floor, the elevator doors opened and she looked numb. Hurriedly, I pressed the button for the lobby, but as we ground back down, Lillian began to get crazy. She dropped to the floor, unzipped my fly and put her hand in my pants. "Al, Al," she panted, like she was in heat, "don't cut me off. Don't do it! Next week we can start sleeping in motels." Was this really happening? Was I actually getting jerked off in an elevator by one of my customers? "Lillian," I literally bellowed, "I'm only a bookmaker. Would you pull yourself together. If Guildo ever found out, he'd kill us." With all my screaming, she wouldn't stop. My pants were down around my ankles, and she was alternately giving me a hand job with her left hand and trying to press the "Emergency Stop" button with her right. Then, just as we reached the lobby I tore myself away from her, grabbing my pants in the same motion. It was too late. As the door opened, an elderly couple was there and watched while I helplessly came all over the elevator railing, barely missing Lillian who was lying in a disheveled heap on the floor as if she'd been raped. I ran out, pulling up and zipping my pants together as I went, but even after I got through the revolving doors I could still hear the piercing screams of the couple in the lobby.

I made it home and spent the entire day hoping Lillian wouldn't call. When the weekend passed without my hearing from her, I felt better. When four more days passed after that, without Guildo coming by to gun me down, I finally relaxed. I might have laughed off the experience, but while I was busy being perverse my luck hadn't improved, and I was still doing a lot more withdrawing than depositing.

Then, out of the bleachers, at the start of the first week in September, on a steaming hot Monday night, I began winning baseball games. The action wasn't heavy, with both New York teams out of pennant contention, but I was winning eight and nine out of ten games a day and by that Thursday I was ahead $600. For a BM who hadn't won two weeks in a row since June and was still in business only because P.C. was around to hedge with, this sudden sizzle was more than welcome.

By close of vig on Friday the action remained slow. My luck remained phenomenal. I won $400 more that night, which made me plus a grand for the week. Saturday brought news of the Phillies sweeping a double-header, the Mets won, Kansas City won, a trio of blue chippers lost, and I made another $750. Sure, I thought, as I added up figures that night: Stewy—$265, Solomon—$390, Max—$80, Catch—$115. Now I hit a good shoot after I'd had my football jersey dry-cleaned, begun doing wind sprints, and was re-signed to booking football.

Still, going into Sunday I was flying. Another day didn't figure to get me ahead enough to resume my Kentucky Derby quest, but it would have made for a nice winter coat. One of the scheduled games that afternoon was Philadelphia at Cincinatti.

P.C. gave me the line at a pick which meant the BMs

rated the game a toss-up. All in all, it looked to be a very dull contest on a day filled with them. So dull that forty-five minutes before it started, I hadn't written one bet on it. But then in the space of thirty minutes I got calls from Catch, Case, Tony, Sal, Larry, Solomon, Stewy, and Max, and everyone of them bet the Phillies. Amazing. At one forty-five, closing in on batters-up time, I had $1,100 bet all one way. I knew the boys were trying to get even for the week, but why this game? The teams were reasonably equal. It wasn't on television, and I didn't think they'd sent Tum out to Crosley Field in his cab to fix it.

I mean, I knew Stewy and Larry and Tony sometimes discussed games with each other before they bet but they usually wound up arguing and bet against one another. I decided it was just a weird coincidence, but as I sat waiting for P.C. to call I did some quick figuring and realized that weird coincidences aside, this seemingly meaningless game was very important. Even if I hedged off $500 I stood to blow $600 of my own money if the Phillies won and, worse, it would have stalled my late season burst of momentum.

By five of two I was working on the fingernails and by two I was into the cuticles. P.C. hadn't called me for twenty minutes. He was never this late. The game was about to start. I had to do something so in a cold sweat I flew out of my apartment and didn't stop running until I got to 76th and Columbus. No P.C. up the block. No P.C. down the block. I could feel the perspiration seeping through my shirt. What was wrong? He'd been here an hour ago and I knew he hadn't left early to get a good seat for the ballet. After I rummaged through the hotel lobby and didn't find him, I slumped down on the curb outside and gave up. I didn't know what had happened but I was holding $1,100 on the visiting team in a game that started eighteen minutes ago.

That night, at eight o'clock, with my heart in my mouth, my hands trembling, and still no word from P.C., I made myself walk to the newsstand at 72nd and Broadway. I bought the *News,* walked under a street light, opened it to page 83 and read the following: "Tommy Helm's single in the ninth inning drove in Tony Perez and gave the Cincinnati Reds a 10-9 come-from-behind victory over the Philadelphia Phillies."

I didn't read the rest of the article, but I stared at the box score for at least a minute.

Philadelphia 4 0 0 0 3 0 2 0 0– 9
Cincinnati 2 4 0 0 0 2 1 0 1–10

It was beautiful.

The next morning, P.C. called me from St. Vincent's Hospital to tell me he'd been taken there suddenly after having felt some sharp chest pains around one o'clock Sunday afternoon. "Sorry, if I hung ya up, kid, but there was no phone in the ambulance. Don't worry, though. The doc says it was a midget of a heart attack and I'll be outta here in a coupla days."

By Wednesday, I'd collected $3,300 on the week and looked back to see that in the past seven days I'd won nineteen out of twenty-three heavily bet games. With all my bitching and moaning and sweating, I'd finished out the baseball season a couple of grand ahead. A week later, P.C. seemed good as new. A month later, I'd made another $1,500 in big shoulders, and by late November my small band of customers' action was down to a trickle. Then I turned the trickle over to P.C. and got on the phone to a surprised Joe James at Tropical Park in Miami. "Keep your eye out for a goodie, Joe," I said. "I'm coming back in the saddle."

Chapter 12

The cheapest horse at Tropical Park was open lengths better than the finest horse ever to set a hoof in Sunshine Park (now called Florida Downs). Still, I let five weeks pass without buying one. I mean, a lot of them looked good but so did Knight Charger and he was stumbling around a silo with Farmer Brown's kids on his back.

Forgetting about mystery, I finally decided to go for a $5,000 claiming horse named Mr. Grey who, from what I'd seen of him and read in the form, looked like a sound, reliable plodder. Joe agreed, and before the horse ran his next race, he claimed him for me. After forking over the money and signing the necessary papers, we went out to watch Mr. Grey's last race in the silks of his ex-owner. (A horse can only be claimed out of a race before it is run. If the horse wins any part of the purse, the money goes to the guy you've claimed it from. But if it breaks a leg, bleeds, or comes down the stretch doing the cha-cha, there's no refund.) Six furlongs later, we were back in the barn. With us was our newly acquired five-year-old gelding, who'd just run sixth, looked bad doing it, and was limping. Joe had to call the vet. I was busy punching my fist into a bale of hay.

When the vet showed, he poked around Mr. Grey's

puffed-up right front ankle and said it was nicked slightly but would take only a couple of weeks to heal. Considering how fragile horses were, the diagnosis was a relief. In fact, with Joe's great hands doing the caring, Mr. Grey's ankle doing the mending, and my once fair, but now failing, bankroll doing the bill paying, we were ready to race again ten days later.

We entered him in an $8,500 claimer, and I didn't have to bother telling the jockey to take it easy. Mr. Grey had no shot running against this field, and I merely wanted to use the race to see how well the ankle would hold up. It was a six-furlong sprint and we broke out of the gate on top. As the horses approached the half-mile pole, Mr. Grey was visibly shortening stride, a sure sign he was tiring. He faded to finish a tired but snug fourth and that was better than I'd expected. I picked up a little piece of the purse, 5 percent for coming fourth, the horse was standing up, and his ankle looked good as new.

The problem now was that I'd gained a horse and lost a track. In a few days Tropical was closing, Hialeah was opening, and there was no way Mr. Grey could do anything in Flamingo land except run up feed bills. I mean, Tropical was tough, but Hialeah was brutal. That was because racing people thought of Hialeah as *the* place to be in winter, in the same way Sarotoga was *the* place to be in August. And since it was *the* place to be, most of the big Eastern stables shipped their horses there and almost every race was incredibly tough. As a result, if I ran Mr. Grey for what he was worth, about $5,000, he'd either get claimed or never win, and if I ran him for more, I'd have to get a jeep so I could pick him up and get him off the track before the start of the next race. With all that in mind, I couldn't help but agree when Joe suggested I ship Mr. Grey along with his small stable to Raceway Park in Toledo. "The purses won't be as big, but a piece of a little pie is better than no piece of a big one." Who could argue with logic like that?

So, in February, we left warm, beautiful south Florida

and vanned up to cold, miserable Ohio. By the time the meet began, Mr. Grey looked ready to tear down buildings, but I was content to let him keep working out for just a bit longer so he'd get used to his new surroundings and be perfect his first time out. In the meantime, I was helping Joe train a couple of horses for a friend of his, and although neither one of them could run a lick, it was good experience. Then, on a Tuesday morning, no more than a day or two away from wanting to run my horse, the racing secretary—the guy at each track who runs the racing program from top to bottom—called me into his office and asked if I would run Mr. Grey that afternoon. "I'm not trying to mess up your schedule, but we need one more entry to fill the seventh. Can I put you in?"

A racing secretary's always a nice guy to stay on the right side of, so I agreed, got a jockey, and helped saddle Mr. Grey for the race. It was a half-assed handicap—kind of a small-track stake race—and the short field of six horses was terrible. I thought we had a big shot to win it. "What the hell!" I said to Joe, when we broke third and moved up to second down the back stretch. "I might as well win my first race some time." At the far turn Mr. Grey took the lead effortlessly. As he began to pull away in the stretch, Joe and I got up from our seats and strutted down toward the winner's circle. Okay, it wasn't the Kentucky Derby, or even the first at Monmouth, but a win was a win. Then, like Tampa all over again, it happened. I glanced up to see Mr. Grey not fifty yards from the finish wobble for a moment, stumble, and almost come to a complete stop. As the field brushed by him, he hobbled home, crossing the finish line in last place, his right front leg quivering in the dirt. I wanted to kill somebody—the jockey, the racing secretary, myself—I didn't care who! All I knew was that my horse was limping back to the barn after running at half speed, at a cheap track in a race I hadn't wanted him in. If somebody had given me $100 and a tank of gas, I would have chucked everything and gone back to the city right then and there. Even Joe was shaking his head at my incredibly bad racing luck as he led Mr. Grey into his stall and told me to call for the vet. I was just starting to ask the lady on the track switchboard to page him when I heard Joe's excited voice, "Al, hang up! Hang up! And come here!" He pointed into the stall. I looked. Mr. Grey was standing firmly on all four legs. I thought I was seeing things. I opened the stall gate. Mr. Grey came prancing out, acting positively frisky. I felt his right leg, the very same right leg that looked like a stick of melting licorice ten minutes ago. There was no swelling or soreness or cuts. "Al," Joe said, "he must have just taken a bad step. His leg looks fine." The next day we had a vet x-ray the leg to be sure we weren't missing anything. The results were negative. Mr. Grey was solid as a rock. "Joe," I said, "the financial possibilities of this situation are boggling my mind."

A few weeks later, I entered him in a race just to see the form's comment. Beside Mr. Grey's name was the terse remark, "Returned Lame." The chart of his last race showed: "3-3-2-1-4-7^{31} ." I was getting hot flashes. Nobody in North America would bet this horse unless he ran against a herd of elephants. Immediately, I scratched him from the field. I'd wanted to play this business straight but the temptation to bend a little was overwhelming. This was more than some apple in a garden; this was the whole tree and there was just enough hustler left in me to take a bite.

Running him back at Raceway Park was out. For what I had in mind I needed a different track, one small enough to let me on the grounds but big enough to make fun of me once I got there. Joe said Hazel Park in Detroit was perfect. It was semi-major league, opening in a few weeks and only a couple of hours van ride away. At first, he was planning on joining me when the Raceway meeting finished. Then I let him in on the inner workings of my mind. The next day he gave the two horses I was helping him train back to his friend suggesting he donate them to a merry-go-round, put his three-horse stable in a van, and came along for the ride to the rain and soot of the Motor City.

By early May, Stage One was well underway. Mr. Grey was working out regularly, but always under a tight wrap so nobody would notice. In the meantime, Joe and I were busy making sure everyone on the backstretch thought we were complete bimbos. We'd parade around the barns dressed in starched overalls and black loafers, like two plow boys who'd got all duded up on a Saturday night. Sometimes when I'd spot a horseman I'd pop a chaw of chewing tobacco in my mouth and strike up a conversation. I'd let the tobacco juice slowly dribble down my cheek as we talked and if we were near our barn I'd point to the stalls and say, "Them nags might not be in shape now but watch out when we get them to a-runnin'." Between my sounding like a Bronx-bred Tex Ritter and Joe standing behind me reading a Super Boy Meets Jimmy Olsen comic book, we moved quickly on to Stage Two.

That was when we set out to meet and greet the racing fans of Detroit. What we did was enter one of Joe's horses, Navajo Chief, in a $10,000 claiming race. The program read:

J. James—Owner-Trainer

A. Talcum—Asst. Trainer

Tops, Navajo Chief was a $6,000 horse. With a silver bullet up his ass, maybe $6,500. He went off 60 to 1, ran last all the way, finishing so far back, you'd have thought he'd run in the Arc de Triomphe, and even with the extra oats I gave him, he stayed depressed for days. I was sorry for the horse but it was a perfect introduction to the fans.

The third, and final, stage was set. On the following Friday I gave Mr. Grey his last workout, letting him out a notch to be doubly sure he was super-fit, and then Joe entered him in a seven-furlong $2,000 claimer, carded as the third race Saturday afternoon. The horses didn't come much cheaper here. It looked impossible to lose. Joe and I were prepared. We dug up $900 and tucked it in the pocket of my

Sweet-Orrs. On the way to the barn early Saturday, we picked up a copy of the day's form and flipped it to the magical page of "expert" selections and comments. "I can't believe it," my voice was cracking. "Joe, we're 25 to 1 on the morning line." He gulped. "Listen to this," I said, reading the various handicappers' remarks: "Mr. Grey—not today. . . ." "Mr. Grey—Dull Ohio Invader." "Mr. Grey—Rumored Lame." A real "expert" would have known the horse was a steal at 3 to 5.

An hour before post time we'd pulled ourselves together and were busy getting Mr. Grey ready for the race. To make him appear sore, Joe was wrapping bandages around his front knees and to make him look sloppy, I was rubbing a thin film of dust into his coat. When we finished, the three of us—Joe, me, and the horse—ambled into the paddock and, I swear, we looked like the last survivors of the Civil War.

Forty-five minutes later, we were saddling Mr. Grey and the tote board was flashing his odds at 35 to 1. We darted a couple of peeks across the horse's back but neither one of us could speak. Then, our jockey approached and the sight of his tiny body snapped me out of my daze. He was a twenty-year-old kid named Karl Korliss, one of the top ten riders at the track, and he wasn't what you would call real enthused. I took him off to the side. I didn't want to let him in on what was happening but I didn't want him to fall off either. "Karl," I said, "listen to me and listen good. This horse can't lose. Forget how all of us look and I promise there'll be a piece of cake in this for you." He eyed my overalls, Joe's loafers, Mr. Grey's knees. "Mr. Talcum, just let me ride the horse and I'll see what I can do."

Two minutes later, Mr. Grey's odds were holding steady at 35 to 1. But as I stood with Joe gaping at the numbers, I heard a voice. "Talcum, James, I want to speak to you fellows, please." It was the state racing commission's veterinarian and he was standing by Mr. Grey, shaking his head and making notes on a memo pad. The other horses and jockeys were making their way onto the track, but he was planted in Karl's way so he couldn't mount the horse. "I'm sorry," he said, firmly, "I can't let a mess like this run here." Sure. Ten minutes to go and I'd blown it. "He's not as bad as he looks," I whined. "I swear he'll be okay." The vet eyed the bandages. "Well, I'll take a quick look-see at his knees, but if they're as bad as I think I'm going to scratch you out of the race."

As he stooped down and undid the wrappings, we stood watching helplessly as a dozen compact balls of cotton popped out and rolled onto the ground. The vet slowly straightened up. Karl looked stunned. Joe and I looked defeated. The vet winked. "Better give your boy a leg up and get this nag moving," he said, slyly. "I wouldn't want any of us to miss those real nice odds!"

Joe and I didn't waste time saying thank you. Instead, we ran to the $50 win-and-place window, bet the whole $900, and when we got back to our seats a minute before post time, the crowd was buzzing. I guess it was because the odds on the five horse had dropped from 35 to 1, to 12 to 1 in a single flash. Hell, as the field entered the gate you could still hear the buzzing and now it was joined by the crinkle of papers being rustled. It was the sound of entire sections of Hazel Park degennies leafing through their forms to see what they'd missed.

It was too late. The gate sprung open and before my binoculars were focused, Mr. Grey was in front. At the quarter pole he had six lengths. At the half, he had ten, and was widening. By the top of the stretch, he could have stopped for a hot dog and coffee and won. But luckily, Karl had a brain in his head. I mean, it was obvious we had pulled a fast one but there was no point rubbing it in, and through the last eighth he kept trying to ease the horse up. I can still see them coming to the finish line with Karl pulling on the reins so that Mr. Grey's head was turned nearly straight up like he was bird watching. With all that we won by eight lengths and the horse was almost strangled in the bargain.

You better believe buzzing and crinkling gave way to booing and murmuring after the race, but there wasn't a helluva lot more anyone could do. Everything we did had been tricky but legal, and the eight grand Joe and I won made up for the racing secretary warning me that if I pulled any more shit, he'd throw me off the grounds. He didn't have to worry. I'd made my score; now all I wanted to do was build an empire.

To get the empire rolling, I started Mr. Grey a week later in a $7,500 claimer. It was a good field but I thought we had a shot to win. If I was right, the purse money added to what I'd made would put me in a position to claim a real nice horse. If I was wrong, I'd run him again, and if he was claimed I'd use the money to get another horse. He went off nine to two. I bet $500 on him. He ran fifth and nobody claimed him.

I ran him three more times in six weeks. All $7,000 claimers. He came fifth once, and eighth twice. I lost $500 betting on each race and nobody claimed him. Joe said running out of the money four times in a row wasn't Mr. Grey's fault—that he was in shape and had a heart the size of a medicine ball and that I was stubbornly and stupidly racing him over his head. He wasn't a $2,000 horse and he wasn't a $7,000 horse. He was a $5,000 horse, just like he'd always been, and my thinking any different was holding up the show. He was right, so on the 10th of August I ran him in a $5,000 claimer. I bet $1,000 on him, $500 win, $500 place. He went off 5 to 2. Mr. Grey must have sensed he was back running against horses he could beat, because he went right to the lead. Down the backstretch he was still in front and Karl wasn't pushing him. The empire was rolling again. Unfortunately, this wasn't a dogmeat-filled $2,000 claimer and a quarter of a mile from home the seven horse, a solid 4-to-1 shot named Fact-Finder, came charging hard down the middle of the track. Inside the sixteenth pole we were still in front but Fact-Finder was in a drive and our length lead was being gobbled up. It was down to a neck when Mr. Grey suddenly realized he was in a horse race. As Karl whipped him furiously from the right side, he responded with a surge but as he strained to regain a half length lead, he bore in slightly toward the rail. There was only twenty yards to the finish but Mr. Grey was so tired he kept veering nearer the rail, and despite Karl's desperate efforts to straighten him out, an instant later he hit it.

I never saw Fact-Finder go by and the motion of the other jockeys steering their horses to the far outside was a blur. My eyes were transfixed on the horrible sight of Mr. Grey and Karl lying in the dirt. An ambulance came. It took Karl away on a stretcher, conscious, but with a broken collar bone. Then, a small van drove out to get Mr. Grey. He'd broken his neck and he was dead, and unclaimed.

At 3:00 A.M. I was alone and drunk, standing in front of Mr. Grey's vacant stall. "I would have settled for a little empire, you know," I cried into the empty space. "I would have settled for any empire at all."

Then, I staggered back into the night. For hours, I sat outside in the damp air reviewing my life, and by sun-up I'd stopped feeling sorry for myself. I did it by thinking about bookmaking. About the Cubs, the Mets, the Giants. About its being my future occupation.

The thought didn't make me feel good. It just made me feel real.

Chapter 13

Give my parents credit. I'd been using their apartment as an annex to the Port Authority for years, yet every time I schlepped home, my room was waiting for me with the bed made and the carpet vacuumed. I didn't get a tearful "Our boy's back; God is good to us" welcome, but from a mother who could ruin salmon croquettes, and a father who couldn't sell pajamas at a sleepwear convention, a greeting of "The meshuggenah's here, Hymie. Get me the Anacin" was good enough. I mean, they were talking to a son who was about to make them accomplices before, during, and after the fact.

My very first morning back, I went over to 76th Street, and the sight of P.C. roaming up and down the sidewalk in front of his old stand was beautiful. "Hey, kid, good to see you," he said. I told him about my horse, asked how he felt, and asked if my customers were okay. P.C. didn't say much but as I babbled, he put his transistor in his pocket, put a beefy arm around me and walked us down the block. We didn't stop until we got to Central Park West and sat down on a bench. "What's a matter, P.C.? You don't seem like yourself!" "Kid, I've done a lot of thinking while you've been gone, real heavy stuff, you know, and now that you're back I want to talk serious. I'm sixty-three years old, Al. I'm tired. You know, I started in a wire room off Hylan Boulevard in 1930. The first thing I ever booked was the Schmeling-Sharkey fight. That's a lot of vig under the bridge, kid. Hell, before you was born I had lead pencil marks on my fingers and they still haven't come off. Look, I'm not too good at this reminiscing crap, so let me get to the point. Kid, you and me—we can help each other. I know you don't have much dough but you're smart, you're honest, and you're young enough to have a future in this business. I got a safe deposit box full-a money, two ex-wives to empty it every month, and a bad ticker that ain't getting any better running around the city. Here's my offer. I got forty, fifty guys bet with me regular. Half of 'em are people I've known forever and I'll take care of them myself, but I want you to handle the rest. You take their action over your phones, do their work, run the pay and collect, and I put up all the cash. I'll pay you $250 a week plus 5 percent of whatever my sheet drops and don't forget you get your bunch of Little League customers back. Is it a deal, kid, or what?" "P.C.," I said, without a second's hesitation, "tell me how soon I can start."

The next Monday was his answer and it didn't take long to see I wasn't being overpaid. Okay, it was September, with baseball hanging on, football in gear, the flats flatting, the trots clopping, and pro hoops and hockey warming up, but I got the feeling P.C.'s customers could keep my phones humming Christmas Eve. There was no "Ooh, ooh, I gotta tell ya about Frank T. Ace breaking at the wire," from Tum, or Case asking me if he could pay off a losing Knick bet with a stolen air-conditioner. I mean, these people were serious bettors, and the only thing they had in common with my ninnies was a larynx. Even Sal, my most consistent hitter, suffered. "Al," he said Saturday, "I got so many busy signals last night I felt like I was dialing my own number."

Deluged as I was when the first week ended, I was

creaming at the thought of making P & C rounds. The hell with being tired. I wanted to see if these voices I'd been hearing all week were coming from real-life, flesh-covered people. How could I not be curious? Sunday I'd got a line from P.C. on a Montreal Canadien-Detroit Red Wing exhibition hockey game. I figured there might be a little action but on a game where the coaches might play everyone from seventeenth-round draft picks to their general manager's nephews, I didn't expect to write $1,200 in business on it. It would have been less, but someone named Gus doubled his $200 Red Wing + 1½ goals bet after I told him the game was being played in Manitoba. I just crossed out the 2, substituted a 4, and kept my mouth shut. For all I knew, Gus was an Eskimo.

He turned out to be an Italian toy manufacturer, but in the months that followed I met characters who made his exhibition hockey bets look sane. I really thought some of P.C.'s customers had a big shot at making their last calls from a pay phone at Creedmore.

Take Jerry, the Arab, a big Syrian guy who owned an importing firm on West 13th Street. I'd heard of people who lived to eat or work but Jerry, the Arab, lived to bet. 12:01 to 6:01, seven days a week, always my first call. "Hello, Al, what's good today?" Obviously everything was, because he'd put money on anything breathing—$50 here, $75 there, and two or three hundred on his top games of the day. More amazing was he didn't do bad. P.C. told me Jerry bet close to $80,000 a year with him and never came out too far behind. "The guy's perfect," he said. "I make four, five grand a year off him in vig alone. It's like getting paid for living."

I liked Jerry. Every time I went to his office, his desk was covered with weekly tip sheets on basketball and football and the trotters and I'd thumb through them reading items like, "Go heavy on Texas Tech—Tough at home," or "Capelletti hurt. . . . Patriots don't figure to do much without him." Sometimes when I'd get there Jerry'd be busy on the phone and often he'd be talking to an exporter in the Middle East. While I waited for him to finish those part-English, part-Arabic conversations, I'd amuse myself by picturing Ali Baba on the other end of the line wearing a turban and reading from a tip sheet put out by Damascus Dan, saying things to Jerry like, "Dan's sheet says the Forty Thieves are a pretty good bet with the points. Let's throw 400 drachmas on 'em."

Jerry had a good sense of humor, too. He missed a week of action in late October when his wife filed suit for divorce and on his first call back, he said: "Al, tell P.C. to get a lawyer. Frieda's naming him and Arizona State as corespondents."

At least, Jerry was fun. A bettor named Phil J. was a different story. He was a young Italian kid who managed an appliance store in Harlem and had been P.C.'s customer for three years. Up to that fall he never did very well, but he never bet very much either, so it didn't matter. Then, about the second week I started working, he married the only daughter of a Mafia big shot and things got sticky. It started right after the wedding. Phil must have raked in a bundle of bulging envelopes and, boom, $25 bets were hundreds, $100 bets were two, and while the "I Do" and "Thank you, Mr. Telardi, for your generosity" were still echoing through the Kings Highway catering hall, he went from player status into the Monster League. He was betting college football and baseball and losing steadily in both. Finally, one night, I got a call from P.C. "Listen, Al, when Phil J. comes in tonight, make believe you're someone else." When I asked who, he said: "I don't care. Just don't take his bets." Well, an hour later, Phil called and I botched it. I chickened out of doing my Puerto Rican impersonation and let him bet the Yankees for $300.

My phone rang at seven-thirty the next morning. It was P.C. "You take a 60 times bet off Phil J. last night like I told you not to?" "What could I do," I joked, "tell him I was a recording?" P.C. didn't laugh. "Very cute. Very, very cute, kid," he said, calmly. Then he exploded. "Keep making with the yucks 'cause you're going to need 'em. Phil's new father-in-law called me at 6 A.M. That makes twice he's called me, Al. He said he don't like calling me, says he's too busy with other things. If he has to call again, I think I'm gonna give him your number." "Okay, P.C., but ask him if he can hold off until 8 A.M." Still no laugh. In fact, now P.C. was really angry. "Hey, I ain't fuckin' around. This guy don't make no third call and I'm telling you he says his daughter don't like gambling and I ain't about to get involved in a Wop family argument 'cause you think this is playtime. When Phil calls, hang up—understand?"

Boy, did I understand! Too bad, Phil didn't. For the next week he called me every night wanting to bet, and sometimes I could hear his wife sobbing in the background. "Phil," I said, the first few times, "do yourself a favor and stop gambling. I hear your new father-in-law is very unhappy about it." When he kept calling past Wednesday, I'd say: "Phil, please—I wouldn't take a twenty-five-cent bet off you on a potato-sack race. Goodbye!" When he didn't call Sunday I figured he'd got the message, but then Monday night he called in. "I just called to tell you creeps I got myself another bookie, so do *me* a favor, punk, and go fuck yourself!" I never spoke to Phil J. again, but I bet his father-in-law did.

There were others. Like Max Gaines, an old dress salesman who, one Sunday, left his wife sitting in their car so he could call me to get a bet down. That might not sound too memorable, but at the time Max was driving down the Gowanus Parkway on the way to his brother's house. When he noticed it was twelve fifty-five and the game he wanted to bet began at 1 P.M. he jerked the car off the road and up onto the highway divider, ramming his wife against the door in the process. Then he ran back 100 yards to a Texaco station and called me. He bet $150 on the Eagles, who lost 31 to 7.

After he told me this story Monday, I said it was too

bad he had gone to all the trouble considering that he lost. I'll never forget his answer. He said, "Trouble? What trouble? I was in the left lane anyway."

Or the guy called Pat who bet football for three, four hundred dollars a weekend. P.C. had asked me to handle his action, but he settled with Pat himself so I didn't meet or know who the guy was for eight weeks. I never did meet him, but one day Pat called in, started to make his bets and suddenly stopped, gave me his number, and said to please call him back in five minutes. I said okay but when I called him back I hung up right after hearing a deep Irish voice say, "Ham'side, Riely speakin'." If P.C. hadn't called me minutes later and told me Sergeant Riely was Pat and that he was a homicide detective who didn't care what I did as long as it wasn't murder, I never would have dialed that number again.

By November, I figured I'd spoken to or met close to every type of bettor in New York, but in the first week of that month, P.C. got a new customer, and dealing with him opened my eyes to a brand new world. I felt like Magellan.

The man's name was Eberly, Bob Eberly, and he was a WASP—a six-foot-one-inch, chiseled-featured, stock-brokering WASP. P.C.'s accountant (what a job that was!) referred Eberly to him and P.C. wanted his action but he was intimidated. "Do me a favor, kid," he asked before either of us had spoken to the WASP, "handle this Eberly guy for me, huh? Call him tomorrow and introduce yourself as my partner. He works on Wall Street for Merrill Lynch something or other. I forget the whole name. So here—take his number and find out. I ain't been to Wall Street since I got lost looking for the Brooklyn Bridge."

P.C. had every right to be intimidated. I was no pin-up kid, but the couple of suits I owned put me two up on him. Besides, I could sound like a Princeton man if I had to, and when I called Eberly the next day, my "Old Nassau" pennant was waving. "A pleasure to hear from you, Mr. Talcum," Eberly said. "My accountant speaks very highly of both you and Mr. Cheese. Shall we meet at my office tomorrow at three to discuss business?" Mr. Cheese! He said Mr. Cheese! I mumbled to myself when we hung up. Who was putting who on here?

I was dying to find out, and the next day at 3:00 P.M. I was ready, because the Al Talcum who showed up at his Wall Street address was wearing a grey double-breasted suit, a white shirt, a striped tie, and newly shined shoes. If I didn't look like I just left Cambridge for a tour of the Colonies, nobody did. Hell, with a smaller nose I might have passed for an earl, and when Eberly's secretary ushered me into his enormous, tastefully furnished office, I felt surprisingly comfortable. This was a first for me, but the bottom line was the same. Eberly wanted to gamble and I could help.

He was sitting at his desk dressed in a dark, conservatively cut suit, surrounded by four other men dressed exactly alike. The word here was "perspire," not "sweat," and then only at the New York Athletic Club after handball, and I walked in thinking what a long way this was from Jewish furrier country, and what an even longer way it was from Harlem's five-peso crowd.

I'm positive they were expecting to see a cigar-chomping, pinky-ringed slob wearing one of Seventh Avenue's flashier creations, and you better believe my outfit was a shocker. My vocabulary was a bigger one! I mean, pearls were flowing from my lips like I was an oyster, and as I talked to Eberly, with his associates listening, each letter was measured. "Bob," I said, "I'm sure you're familiar with most of the usual ground rules, but there is one I'd like to establish now. Normally, I settle each week with my customers but considering your—shall we say—position, I'd like to suggest that if you have an outstanding figure of less than $100 on Sunday eve, we simply carry it to the following week."

I must have sounded pretty good, because when I was done, I got Eberly's number, plus the numbers from the other four, plus handshakes all around like we'd just completed a corporate merger, and in a way, I guess we had. Still, I wondered how corporate the boys would have felt if they'd been in Ratner's with me two nights before. P.C. was there talking to a bettor in the back booth. "Marv," he said, "if you want me to let the sixty bucks ride, you gotta take your fork outta my cheesecake and get your face outta my blintz!"

Anyway, Eberly's associates turned out to be exactly what they seemed—neat. Oh, they'd bet all right but only on events you might say were "proper" ones they had an excuse to bet on, like $50 on a televised Giant game or $25 on the World Series or a friend's horse. They might have had other vices but as far as gambling went, they would never consider betting West Texas State for a nickel. Being used to less inhibited customers who might call and say, "Al—Barney. Give me everything hooked with everything and double the whole schmeer if Drake wins," they were quite a change of pace.

Bob Eberly, on the other hand, was the exception to the rule. He was pure and simply a degenerate WASP. He used the same cultured tone of his friends, the identical "this-really-is-beneath-me-but" manner, only he was hooked. I mean, Eberly was a card-carrying monster. He stuck to football but he more than made up for missing other sports. "Al," I'd hear every Sunday at exactly twelve forty-five, "I've decided to take Green Bay minus the six and a half for 500, Houston plus the nine for 500, Kansas City minus the three for 300, and the Jets plus seven for 200." After I'd repeated his bets back to him, he'd thank me and say goodbye. When he lost, he'd have an envelope waiting for me Monday morning, propped crisply on his secretary's desk. It always held the full amount.

He was good when he won money, too. Then he'd have me come into his office and thank me as I counted out his winnings. Occasionally, we had conversations and once I told him of a thought I had about stockbrokers and bookmakers. The way I saw it, people were risking their money in the market, hoping to get lucky by investing wisely through a broker who would handle their transactions for a fee. Since bookmakers did much the same thing, wouldn't it be interesting, I said, if bookmaking was legal and stock trading was illegal?

Then I told him how I imagined men riding into the city on the seven fourteen from New Haven with *Wall Street Journals* hidden under the *Times* Sports Sections. They'd arrive at Grand Central, duck into phone booths and call their brokers, "Hello, Hubert? This is Bucky," they'd say. "What do you have Monsanto listed as?" Then this gravelly voice would answer: "74-75," and Bucky would continue. "How about Pan American? What did that open at?" Hubert's voice would croak: "114-116 and I got AT&T 121-123, but if you want that price you gotta give me the order on this call." "Okay, Hubert. Give me 10 shares of Monsanto at 75 and 40 shares of Pan Am taking the 121." "Sorry, Bucky," Hubert would shoot back. "No odd lots on Pan Am. You want odd lots, ya gotta lay another point."

When I finished relating this madness to Eberly, he laughed and said, "I have news for you, Al. From what I see, bookmakers are a lot more honest than brokers, and there are times when I wish I could change places with one." We smiled at each other and I remember thinking how much I admired the guy. These WASPS were okay, I said to myself, when I left. Maybe it was something in the mayonnaise.

Aside from the customers, the season itself was give and take through most of November. Two good weeks, a bad one. A lucky game, an unlucky one. Nobody was getting rich but nobody was getting poor either. Then on the last Tuesday night of the month, I got the line for the coming weekend's pro and college football games from P.C. and by Saturday I had roughly the same amount of advance betting I always did. Saturday night the play picked up and I was beginning to write a lot of business on the Green Bay Packers who were playing the Minnesota Vikings on television Sunday.

Writing Green Bay business wasn't a novelty. In fact, if BMs used typewriters instead of pens, the G and B keys would have been obliterated long before 1966. In the Vince Lombardi era of the sixties, they'd become to football what Koufax was to baseball and the Celtics were to basketball—a blue chipper that was always bet and almost always won. For this game they were 7½-point favorites, which was less points than they were usually favored by. The spread was low because the game was being played in Minnesota and the Vikings were a good, tough club that could give anybody a battle when they played at home.

By twelve-thirty Sunday afternoon, someone peering over my shoulder would never have believed it. It was like the Packers were playing Erasmus High. Every ring had a Green Bay fan on the other end and when P.C. called to check in, I said, "We better make the Packer game 8 or we're going to need a shovel to get out." "They betting you that heavy, huh? What do you got it for—a dime?" "Try two," I said. "Okay, kid. I'm getting all Packer money myself. Make it 8 and if they take that, make it 8½. Last time this happened with them I started at 6, went all the way to 8½ and they still won 54 to 7. But you gotta try, kid. You know what I mean?"

(Usually moving a line does what a BM wants, which is to balance out very uneven betting. If the price on a hot favorite is raised a point or two, the chalkies sometimes skip the game, shop around for a better price, or even bet the other side. In the identical manner, heavy betting on an underdog can be swayed by lowering the points, like dropping the line from plus 3 to plus 2½, or if the short betting persists, even 2. A line can't be moved too many points either way or BMs can get middled or sided, which I'll explain later. In any case, changing the line isn't tricky or cheap or cheating. It's just how good BMs try and control the law of supply and demand. Bookies know about economics; they might not all be able to spell it, but they know it.)

I knew what P.C. meant but if Green Bay was eating their Wheaties, we were in trouble. I raised the line to 8½ before one-thirty, but this game was what I'd heard called "a buckshot special"—a game where even moving the line couldn't stop heavy one-way betting, and the only Viking money it drummed up was $50 from Catch who was experimenting with a new system based on betting underdogs at home.

To make matters worse, the game was the four o'clock thriller, which meant quitting time was 3:00 P.M. instead of two. At one forty-five P.C. called, "Kid, I hate to do this but I want you to make the game 9." I did. He called back forty minutes later. "Do any good, kid?" "Not for us. I got $1,400 more on Green Bay." "That's it. I ain't takin' anymore," P.C. said, in a huff. "Al, I don't want to do this either, but when we get off the phone, take 'em off the hooks. Not counting what you got, I'm holding four grand and there ain't a bookie left in New York I can lay it off with." "P.C., I got $1,050 on the game from my own sheet and you know I never hold more than 400. What should I do?" He moaned and hung up.

An hour later, I was in Catch's West Village apartment. He greeted me wearing his Viking sweatshirt. We gave each other a bear hug for luck and then sat down in front of his television set, and I mean right in front, like close enough to see the dits and dots. I know I was supposed to be a serious bookmaker watching a game that meant a grand to me, and God knew what to P.C., but sitting in that darkened room, with a ninny who chanted, "Roll, Big Purple!" after every Viking first down, I felt only part BM. The rest of me was all degennie, and if the Vikings had stopped falling down I would have been in Paradise.

For the first half, I stayed in the West Village. After the Vikings drew first blood on a twenty-seven-yard field goal by Fred Cox, it was all Green Bay. On defense, they went everywhere with Tarkington except back to the huddle, and

Willie Brown, the Packers' all-pro defensive end was in the Viking backfield so often he could have changed jerseys. Their offense wasn't bad either. It scored three touchdowns—a one-yard run by Elijah Pitts, a fourteen-yard pass from Bart Starr to Jim Taylor, and a ten-yard pass from Starr to Marv Fleming. So at the break, it was 21-3 and more than the room was dark.

The third quarter brought a ray of hope. Cox kicked two field goals, the Packers failed to score, and going into the last quarter, we were hanging in there at 21-9. It was give and take for the next ten minutes and I was thrashing around so much, Catch fled to a chair to avoid my flying elbows. The Vikings seemed to be outplaying Green Bay, and when Tarkington capped off a long, time-consuming drive with a thirty-eight-yard touchdown pass to Dave Osborn, the score was Green Bay 21, Vikings 16. Even a Commerce under-achiever knew that was "ni-i-i-c-e"! And the bookie in me took over. I wanted the game to end right there even if it meant watching Roger Mudd and the CBS news team for three hours.

Unfortunately, it didn't, and when the Vikings saw they had a chance to win, they went berserk. Their defense held off Green Bay and with less than two minutes left, they had the ball on their forty-eight-yard line along with plenty of momentum. On second down, Tarkington went completely bananas! Okay, I understood he didn't care about the game being a lock to BMs, but pitching the ball out to his fullback, Phil King, and having it lateraled back so he could attempt a pass, didn't figure to help anybody but the chalkies. I mean, if this play was sent in from the bench, it had to be from Green Bay's, and as the ball spiraled through the air I was on my knees praying someone on offense would catch it. My prayers must have got lost over the Great Lakes because Herb Adderly, a Packer cornerback, intercepted the pass and returned it to the Vikings' forty-five-yard line. I didn't know whether to give Catch a double-hand slap or resume atheism. I decided on the double-hand slap, because after what

Tarkington tried, we were lucky Adderly hadn't gone in for a touchdown and with just over a minute left in the game, Green Bay figured to be content to run out the clock.

The Packers moved the ball down to the Viking thirty-six-yard line but in the process, they forced Minnesota to call their last two time-outs. I was home free! There were less than twenty seconds left so now all Starr had to do was tumble over and the game would end. I was putting on my coat to leave as he walked slowly to the line of scrimmage, took the final snap, and handed the ball off to Jim Grabowski. "How about that?" I said to Catch as Grabowski looked for a soft spot to sit down on. "I guess Starr got tired of taking cleats in the face."

An instant later, Grabowski was inches off the ground when Ed Sharockmin, the Viking safety, came barreling into him and knocked him upright. Then as Sharockmin's charge carried him away from the play, Grabowski, like a muscular fart in a blizzard, began running slowly toward the Minnesota goal line. I don't think he wanted to go anywhere, but the entire left side of the field was empty and as he lumbered downfield, I fell, actually fell, down, and said, "Catch, there's nobody in the tube except him and the ref." The ref didn't make the tackle. Grabowski crossed the goal line untouched and Chandler kicked the extra point as the gun sounded ending the game. The final score was: Green Bay 28, Minnesota 16. None of our customers laid twelve.

Even with taking the phones off the hooks, P.C. was a pro. The $1,050 I dropped was invisible compared to what the game cost him, but when I met him outside the Brill Building Monday morning, my face was ashen and his wasn't beaming, but it looked better than mine. "It happens, kid," he said, handing me an envelope with the three grand he owed out to the customers I handled for him. "Happens all the time." Then he gave me another envelope with my $250 salary in it and said he'd loan me money if the game had wiped me out. I told him it hadn't and he waddled off down the block toward the jewelry district. He was three-quarters of the way when he stopped, lit his cigar stub, and padded back toward me. "Kid, ya can't get upset. Ya just gotta keep squeezing that juice."

Well, I got to "squeeze the juice" with P.C. for nine more months. We went through the rest of the football season, losing the first super bowl ever played en route (to who else but Green Bay!?), the basketball season, and most of baseball, and we were both doing okay when on a Wednesday night in the middle of that next September, I got a call from him. He said he was home, told me his Fordham Road address, and asked me to come over.

When I arrived, P.C. was sitting on a couch eating a TV dinner but the set was off and on the end table, where I would have expected to see a radio, there were four or five vials of pills instead. He looked okay, except for his horrible bathrobe. But no cigar? No radio? No TV? Something was wrong.

"Kid, you and me have been a pretty good team but I gotta break it up." "Come on," I said, but I already sensed he wasn't joking. "I saw the doc this morning, kid. He says I try and drag my ticker through another football season it'll be my last. I been ignoring him for years but this time he scared me enough so that I'm gonna cut down to five or ten guys and ease outta the whole thing before they bury me." "P.C., what can I say? Your health comes first. Nothing else matters." "Ah, kid," he said, cupping my face in his hands, "I still feel lousy you hadda get hooked up with a BM with a bum ticker. If I'd met ya twenty years ago, I woulda made both of us rich. Listen, I'll get in touch with everyone over the phone and settle with 'em myself. Meantime, here's a grand for ya and the number of a small bookie I know who'll help with them Little Leaguers of yours." Then we shook hands and I let myself out.

I guess I should have felt worse than I did, losing my job like that, but driving home I didn't think about me at all. I just hoped Pot Cheese would make it to a condominium in Miami Beach. An old bookmaker deserved one.

Chapter 1.4

I didn't forget about P.C.'s well-being, but with what went on after his unexpected retirement, I got a lot less concerned. First, I had to say, "Thanks, but no thanks," to most of the customers I'd handled for him when they asked if I would keep booking their action. Believe me, I would have loved singing "Autumn Leaves" with Jerry, the Arab, and Bob Eberly, but I didn't have the bankroll to take monsters like them on. Next, I realized the bookie P.C. arranged for me to deal with was unreliable. While I was trying to run my small sheet smoothly and professionally, hoping to pick up extra customers and build up a business, this guy spent the Boston-St. Louis World Series trying to get me into plumbing supplies. For two games he did half of everything right. In the first he gave me the right line on the wrong pitchers. In the second he got the pitchers straightened out, but I didn't get the good news until Yastremski was up. By the third game he must have bought a watch and the teams' yearbooks, because he called on time and had the line and the pitchers right, but going to all that trouble put him in a nasty mood. From then on whenever I laid off money on the same team his own customers bet, he'd get mad if they won and make some snide remark about not needing my $350 of aggravation.

Well, I didn't need his either, and as soon as the Series was over I drove upstate for two days of rest. It wasn't much of a break but it cleared my head, and driving back on the thruway, I decided the first thing to do when I got home was to have a talk with P.C.'s friend. I mean, there was no way I was going to make it through football with this clown screwing up and complaining, but before I got the chance to call anyone, I got hit with a bomb.

It exploded around 2 A.M. Tuesday morning when I walked through the door of the apartment. My mother was in the living room. Awake. She hadn't pulled a clock watch since my senior year at Commerce when I went out to play poker and returned home thirty-two hours overdue, so I knew she wasn't there to scold me. After an "Alfred, mine son," followed by a pillow pat and a "come sit on the sofa," I girded for what was beginning to look like a medium-sized touch, minimum, a grand.

Then my father came walking wearily out of the bedroom, right on cue. He embraced me and mumbled a sentence ending in the word "mitzvah." I sat down. In my family, an embrace and a "mitzvah" (the Jewish word for favor) figured to cost a lot more than money.

Sure enough, I got a one, two punch from my parents that made me feel like I was back at St. Nick's. The jab was my father had given up on his pajama business and wanted to retire. The left cross was his office had a lease with seven months to run and they wanted me, their "only" son, to take over the firm in the hope that my "fast mouth," as they called it, might sell enough pajamas to pay off their obligations, and bring in some extra cash.

I'd never seen my father's office but if a man who thrived on work like he did wanted to turn over a business to a son who thrived on not working like I did, this was trouble. Still, could I refuse? These were my parents after all, facing retirement on Social Security, Hymie's World War I disability pension, and a short stack of borrowed and saved money. Even tired blood was thicker than water. I couldn't.

Instead, I promised them I'd see what my "fast mouth" could do, and Wednesday morning made my first visit to the sixth floor of the dilapidated building on West 38th Street that housed Jama, Inc. At six o'clock I came back to the apartment.

When Screw-Up called minutes later to give me a line on the night's NBA action, I told him until further notice I'd only be booking weekends. I was too upset to lecture him on manners. When my customers called, I told them the truth but swore the inconvenience would be temporary. Everyone was annoyed; nobody quit. The minute I finished on the phones I walked out of my room wishing my parents hadn't left that afternoon for a short stay at my mother's sister's house in Roslyn. In fact, I almost called my aunt to ask for them. I didn't want to know how they were. I just wanted to thank them for sticking their "only" son with the biggest red flannel, button-up-the-front lemon I'd ever seen.

Jama, Inc. was everything I feared and more. My father had put in enough hours there to build the Golden Gate Bridge, but from first impressions it looked like he'd dug a tunnel to a bankruptcy proceeding instead. The entire firm seemed to consist of an outer office with a desk, chair, Rolodex and phone, plus a showroom full of unsold pajamas hanging on garment racks, some rusted sample cases, and some very blank order forms.

The longer I was there, the worse things got. Believe me, I wasn't happy being a weekend BM, but by the time I'd get home nights I was exhausted from being confused. I knew my parents hadn't handed me Jonathan Logan, but there had to be more than one salesman who called in a small order every three weeks and a mill in Taiwan that answered my letters with bills. There was more. Later in October, Hymie showed me the books: one-third illegible, one-third Yiddish, one-third numbers. Three-thirds red. In November I got a call from a warehouse in Long Island City saying I could arrange to have the 600 pairs of pajamas being held for Jama, Inc. at any time. All I had to do was pay a four-month overdue storage bill. Sure.

By December, I completed the task of calling every single retailer listed in the Rolodex. The ones I reached either put me on "hold" and never came back, or put me on "hold" and then bought a dozen pair. That was the good news. The bad news was three-quarters of the people I called were retired, missing, or dead. Luckily, the pajama buyer listed for John Wanamaker's in Philadelphia was still around. I say "luckily," not because he gave me a big order, but because he took a minute to explain what was going on. "Al," he said, "I've known your father and mother since the old days in the ready-to-wear business. I give them a small order every few months so they should know I'm still a friend, but their business was outdated from the day it opened. They had no capital, no energy, sometimes even no merchandise, and, Al, believe me, a few more old-timers like myself die off, there won't ever be an order to fill."

Hearing the bottom-line story on this nonbusiness was a mixed blessing. It was a relief to know the firm was beyond real help, because it made me stop feeling guilty about not being the 38th Street "messiah," but my relief wasn't going to pay my parents' bills or get them the extra money they'd hoped my "fast mouth" could produce.

I had a couple of ideas. Like buying fire insurance and starting one, or paying off the lease and bills and taking a walk, but neither of them were any good. I never took the arson thing seriously, and if I had given up I would have been out three grand in expenses and left home with 600 pairs of old pajamas and one pair of old, unhappy parents.

Still, I had to make some kind of decision. My customers were getting fed up with only being able to reach me weekends, and I was getting more fed up thinking about money I was losing by not being available. Then on the last Monday in December, I asked Catch to come up to the office so I could pay him the $130 he'd won the previous week. I hadn't let any of my friends up there before, because I knew they'd go hysterical if they saw me in a suit trying to sell children's pajamas to an old woman buyer who didn't want any. But I have to admit, I was wrong. Catch didn't even giggle. He just sat behind a buyer from Neiman Marcus making faces, and I wasn't even angry when the guy turned around to see Catch with a straw sticking out of each ear. I'm sure he hadn't planned on giving me a very big order anyway.

After the guy left for Dallas, Catch sat still long enough for me to tell him the general situation, and when I finished I asked if he had any bright ideas. "Forget the fire," I said, hearing his first one. "I already thought of that." He said he couldn't think of anything else so I paid him his $130 and walked him to the door. Just as he stepped through it, he turned around and said, "Why don't you just forget about selling pajamas and use the place for a joint? I'd rather lose money bookmaking than try and unload that shit I saw hanging from those garment racks." How many guys who put straws in their ears were that smart?

Well, at least I moved fast, if late. Within a few weeks I told the part-time model that she could go back to being a full-time hooker, informed the handful of buyers who ever stopped up there to call instead, had a second phone installed, and gave my BM customers the new numbers and old arrangements. During the last week in January, Jama, Inc. made close to $1,000; $840 of it from bookmaking. The next Monday I told Inga and Hymie the pajamas were moving slowly but not to worry because I was using the office to start a second business. Neither of them asked what kind.

By March, I was doing okay. The basketball season was running fairly hot and I was managing to pay the $300 a month rent, save a little, knock off a few neglected bills, and smile when I got home. The only problem was P.C.'s bookie

friend was acting up again. During football he'd been okay
but slowly he was falling back into his old habits, and I didn't
give up pajamas to give him a second chance at putting me
back in plumbing supplies.

So, I called P.C., hoping he hadn't left for the old
bookie's home in Miami. He hadn't. I told him it was impossible for me to operate with a guy who called twenty minutes
late if the Knicks were at home and an hour late if they were
on the road. He understood and said he'd see what he could
do. He called me back on the eleventh. "You consider getting
into an arrangement like ya had with me, kid?" I said I'd try
anything. "Okay, then I got somethin' cooking for ya. Eight-
thirty tomorrow night go to 218 East 64th Street, Penthouse
E. The guy's name is Freddy and he ain't a BM, but ya gotta
meet him 'cause he's a pal of the guy you might work for." I
thanked P.C. for his efforts. "I owe it to ya, kid. Just stay on
your toes. This could mean big money but the people involved are a little gamey."

"Gamey" was a new word coming from P.C., but it
didn't stop me from arriving at 218 East 64th on time. The
doorman was out hailing a cab so I breezed through the
lobby unannounced and took the elevator to the 32nd-floor
penthouse. I got out, followed the gold lamé arrows, and
found the door to the apartment unlocked. I let myself in.
The place was gorgeous, and empty. "Anyone here?" I
yelled. "It's Al Talcum, P.C.'s friend." "I'm in the bedroom,
Al. Make yourself a drink and come on in." I skipped the
booze but I found the door to the bedroom wide open and
strolled through it. The first thing I noticed was a guy lying
in bed wearing a pair of boxer shorts. He was listening to a
short-wave radio propped against the headboard, and the set
looked big enough to pick up the play-by-play of the Tokyo
Giants. There was a TV near the window tuned to a college
basketball game, and the floor was spotted with copies of the
New York Post, the *Philadelphia Bulletin* and the *Chicago*

Tribune. If this guy wasn't a BM he was doing a great imitation.

The second thing I noticed made me think he was also doing a nice imitation of a eunuch, because stretched out on the couch, her legs straddling "Joe Gelardi's Aqueduct Picks," was a beautiful, naked blonde, apparently and incredibly, sound asleep. I wasn't staring at Joe's longshot special when the guy in the bed looked up and said, "I'm Freddy Longo. Nice to meet you, Al. Be with you in a minute."

I stood in the middle of the room for a minute. It passed slowly and awkwardly into four, then five. Freddy was not acting like there was a naked lady on the couch. Freddy was not acting like there was an uncomfortable stranger watching her. Freddy was not doing anything. "Is it okay if I wait in the living room? It's a little stuffy in here," I said. "Sure. Fine, Al. Make yourself a drink. I'll be with you in a minute." As I left, the call letters of station KNOX trailed me out.

Twenty minutes later, Freddy appeared. He asked me who I had worked for, where I was from, and how old I was, and he made some small talk about sports. I must have sounded okay, because when I left he gave me a number and said, "I think you'll do fine, Al. Call before noon tomorrow and ask for Barry Squires. He'll fill you in on the rest." I never asked who the blonde was. I was scared Freddy didn't know she was there.

Besides, I was more interested in this Barry Squires and anxious to make a fresh start, I called him at 11 A.M. The first words out of his mouth were: "Whoever this is, you're too early. Whaddya think I get the line while I'm sleeping?" That was before I said hello. When I identified myself he said to come over right away and gave me the address of his apartment in the Forest Hills section of Queens. He hung up before I could say goodbye.

There was nothing scheduled in the afternoon except

for some exhibition baseball games, so I rushed over to Queens hoping I could make a quick deal with this guy and take off. I got to his place a little after twelve and the doorman asked my name, buzzed Apartment 6, and told me to go up. Some big guy was leaving as I arrived, and this time I wasn't greeted by an empty room. Instead, I walked in and saw the back of a guy sitting on a black leather stool in front of a huge bar. There were three phones on it. Barry Squires swiveled around and said, "Have a seat, baby. You're going to get a kick out of this."

I got more than a kick. In fact, just watching Barry Squires, just being in a room with him, was like nothing I'd ever seen or done before, and by two o'clock I couldn't take my eyes off the man. Part of it was how he handled the phones. I mean, I already knew about people betting exhibition games so I wasn't shocked at how often they rang, but Barry could hold a receiver to each ear, balance the third on a shoulder, and deal with all three callers at one time.

Then, there was his personality. He was constantly intense, and his normal tone of voice was a scream. Curse words were strung together without any clean ones in between. If the phones stopped ringing for a minute, he'd prowl around the room like a mad dog, snarling, "Fuck 'em, Talcum. If my wise guys think I'm going to move the price on that fucking Yankee game because they're betting this Bahnsen kid, they can curl up and die. I don't move a price for nobody unless I feel it—nobody." That afternoon he was too busy cursing and being intense to notice his open fly or the occasional Kent cigarette he'd light from the wrong end, but with his nice looks, cashmere sports jacket, and alligator shoes, he still reminded me of a flashy gangster.

When the phones stopped ringing after two, I got to talk with him enough to be called "baby" five or six times. Between "babys" he mentioned that P.C. and Freddy said I was okay and that he'd call in the morning to propose a deal. He kept repeating how much he needed someone reliable to take his action and do the work. Right before I left, he said: "It's a good thing I like you, Talcum, because if I didn't I might have had you killed just to get your joint." He laughed at his own lousy joke but not until he paused a moment to catch the stunned expression on my face. All of a sudden, I wanted to know what P.C. meant by "gamey."

Later, I went to see P.C. The story I got was that Barry Squires had been a big gambler in and around New York since he was twenty-five, winning and losing thousands of dollars week in and week out. Then, four years ago, he'd hit a horrendous losing streak betting baseball, and one Monday he realized he owed his bookmaker a very large sum of money. It was much more than he had and, in fact, much more than he had any chance of getting. Unfortunately for Barry, his bookie was an aging Sicilian who still believed in the Old World method of collecting overdue debts, a method that sometimes consisted of throwing delinquent customers in front of trucks on the West Side Highway and watching them disappear into potholes. Barry, not wanting to become part of the West 56th Street off-ramp, rented a U-Haul trailer, packed all his possessions into it, and drove it over to this bookie's joint in the Red Hook section of Brooklyn. He parked in front of the door, marched inside, and told the old man he was broke and that everything he had in the world was parked outside. The Sicilian didn't have much use for a trailer of crap but he knew a pair of big balls when he saw them. So he put his baseball bat away and gave Barry a job working for him as a runner (a runner being someone who gets customers for a bookie and collects a percentage of their losses in return).

His plan was to have his spumoni and eat it, too, because Barry figured to bring in plenty of business, and the old man could book it, pay Barry a tiny share when it lost, and deduct the rest from what Barry owed him. The plan worked out well for the Sicilian, but it did even "weller" by Barry. He turned out to be a better runner than gambler; and by the end of a year he'd brought in enough money to pay off his marker and made enough contacts to become a bookie.

Over the past three years, Barry had parlayed his flashy style, and more than his share of good luck, so that now he was a very big bookie. Keeping him big was also a growing number of friends and customers who were very high on black or navy blue Cadillacs, Havana cigars, and selected bars, restaurants, and nightclubs. Some of these people were straight businessmen who liked to gamble and hang out with a guy who could match them cuff link for cuff link, but a fat portion of them were, to quote P.C. word for word, "a little connected with organized crime. You know what I mean, kid? No shoulder holsters, but no Mary Poppins either."

(I followed what he meant but talking to me about OC and bookmaking was like discussing "The Untouchables" while I watched "Captain Kangaroo." I heard the words. I just didn't pay attention. I knew bookmakers in New York worked in one of two ways: There were independents, like Jo-Jo and P.C. who worked for and by themselves, using other BMs only to get lines from and hedge with; and there were BMs who worked for betting offices. These offices were run and financed by organized syndicates, and physically they consisted of joints scattered around the city, each with phones and a clerk to answer them. An office might have anywhere from 20 to 200 BMs to deal with, and the arrangements varied. Some guys called in all their action, getting a salary, and risking nothing but the office's money if it won and receiving a percentage if it lost. Others simply paid a fee to get a line—which originated with professional odds-makers in Las Vegas and varied slightly from one office to another. Still others worked on a salary/percentage deal where they laid off what they wanted to from their own sheet and handled customers someone in the office hierarchy wanted handled—like a guy who wanted to bet and had cash but no bookie. Whatever the case, if you made book and laid off action, some of it was going to wind up in the hands of OC somewhere along the line, and if you couldn't accept that fact you couldn't be a clerk, runner, or BM.)

"So what?" I said to P.C. "I know the facts of life. Hell, you're the guy who told me some of them." "Okay, kid, just stay on your toes. As far as I know Squires don't do nothin' 'cept make book, but he's still a little gamey." That's what I loved about P.C. Whenever I asked him a question he'd tell me a long story that had nothing to do with the answer.

The next morning Barry called and made his offer. He said he'd start me at $300 a week and pay the office rent and the phone bill. For that he wanted me to deal the line he'd provide to everyone (his and my customers), help check the work, and "remember who was boss." Then he said I could either book my own customers' action and lay off whatever I wanted to him, or let him book it—for which he'd give me a percentage of its losses. I told him my sheet was almost all ninny and said for a guaranteed hundred dollars over and above the percentage I'd be glad to let him call them his own. He said only if I did their P & C. I said that would cost twenty-five more. He said fine, start tomorrow. I agreed and Barry ended the conversation with, "Baby, you won't ever be sorry. All you're going to be is rich." When I hung up I'd gone from being a BM and a "kid" to being a clerk and a "baby." As I'd come to find out, with Barry Squires labels didn't matter.

I spent the baseball season swamped with action. There were days so frantic, so incredibly busy, I came close to wishing I was a struggling pajama prince again. Of course, I regained my senses every time Barry paid me with some of the crispest $100 bills this side of Chase Manhattan. And it didn't hurt when I got enough pictures of Ben Franklin to slip a few to my parents, or when he gave me four months' rent and told me to renew the lease. In short, I was satisfied, but if I was satisfied, Barry was wild with joy.

With me working for him, and with him seeing how

really superefficient, bright, and reliable I was, he was free to indulge in his favorite passions. One of them was riding around New York in his red Eldorado with the top down and the radio blaring, making U-turns on Madison Avenue, hitting ninety on the F.D.R. Drive and parking in spots so illegal cops wouldn't use them to stop for coffee. Another favorite was taking hookers with him wherever he went, which, most of the time, meant the "Copa," Manny Wolf's, or 1407 Broadway. I was with him and a hooker on one of his 1407 trips. He parked the Eldorado between a fire hydrant and a loading zone, told us to tell anyone who asked that he was a doctor making an emergency call, and left. I spent the thirty minutes he was upstairs—paying and collecting money from coat and suit salesmen—praying no police would come by. Barry might have had the balls to tell one he was a surgeon and the hooker was his nurse, but I didn't.

Before the baseball season ended, I could see that his fuck-the-world attitude was one reason he was a big bookie. P.C. had told me he was a wide-open hold-all-you-can type BM, but when the mood hit, Barry was more than just wide open. He'd take $500 bets in the street. He'd let guys bet more money than they could afford, and sometimes he'd even call me and say that if someone wanted to bet a game I didn't have a line on, I should make one up and give it to them. I got pretty good at knowing when he was having a fuck-the-world day. The tip-off was when he'd call to check how things were going and I'd say something like, "Nothing's being bet superheavy outside of the Pirates over the Phillies. If you hedge off a few grand on that, we'll be sitting pretty." Then, if I was right, he'd scream, "Hedge? Hedge?" into the phone so loud I'd have to hold it away from my ear while he made the word sound like an insult to his manicured nails. "If I hedged off money every time I was supposed to," he'd rant on, "I'd still be running around Red Hook buying green noodles for Sam Bianni." It wasn't my style of bookmaking, but it was his money, and at least I got a treat just thinking about football. If Barry had these moods, then he might win enough money to buy out Wellington Mara or lose enough to jimmy open a vending machine.

My two co-workers weren't bad, either. One was a guy I talked to ten times a day. He'd give me the line at noon and six, call me back with changes, and often tell me to have Barry get in touch with him "at he knows where." He also called at two and eight every day and had me read him the bets so he could copy them down. When I'd worked for P.C., I never gave in complete rundowns until the following morning, so one day I asked the guy why Barry operated this way. He said it was done in case of a bust, because then the cops would confiscate the work, and without a second copy, we wouldn't know who bet what—which I soon found out was only part of the reason.

Well, his mentioning a bust didn't scare me, but for months I figured this guy was some kind of underworld character calling from a secluded hideout. When I finally met him in late August, I found out that not only wasn't he a gangster, but he was Sydney Squires, Barry's own father, and the hideout he was calling me from was a phone booth on Queens Boulevard. It seemed Sydney had a weakness for Del Insko "hotiolas," owed Barry $1,700 because of it, and was working for his son and bookie to help pay off the debt.

The week after I met squat, irritable Sydney, Barry gave me a peek at his father's opposite number, a towering, tough-looking slob named Tony Gulmo. He said Tony was his right-hand man, which I assumed meant Tony scared delinquent customers with it. All I ever saw him do was drink beer and try and pick up hookers for Squires Jr. with lines like, "Hey, honey, if I throw ya a twenty will ya sit on my friend's face on our way to de Bronx?"

Considering the cast, it was amazing that the star didn't get out of control until World Series time. I guessed it was Barry's way of seeing off the season, but it was also a good way to drive his clerk crazy. In the first game of the Series,

St. Louis, with Bob Gibson pitching, was favored 6½, 7½ over the Detroit Tigers, who were starting Denny McClain. (Remember, this is with football season raging, featuring days when I could have used a second mouth and a third hand.) Anyway, forty-five minutes after I began dealing, Barry called. He'd already spoken to Sydney so he knew what line I had. I told him the betting was evenly divided. "Fuck that divided shit, Talcum," he screamed. "Make the game 7½, 8½ Cards, and take Tiger money till your pen bursts. I don't give a fuck how much they bet. Nobody's beating Gibson today."

At first I thought he was kidding, like with that "If I didn't like you I might have killed you just to get your joint" joke he cracked the first time we met, but he hung up without a snicker. Make the Cards 7½, 8½, and he was serious. Get the Rolaids. I mean, I'd heard about BMs jobbing lines, but Barry had the kind of customers you didn't do it with on a whim. A lot of them were $1,000-a-game and up bettors and they didn't sound like assholes either. In fact, I would have laid odds most of them were pretty close to being professional gamblers, and P.C. told me those kind of guys used BMs like shopping carts, wheeling down aisles until they found one with a price they thought was out of line and then jumping all over it. Well, I would have won my bet and P.C. would have got a gold star for knowing his gamblers, because twenty minutes later, quoting 7½, 8½, Barry got six grand on the Tigers. From four people I might add, none of them named Tum or Stewy. Then we got another $1,800 bet on Detroit in slightly smaller chunks. When Barry called me before game time, I told him what had gone on and added that I thought he was out of his mind. "Talcum," Barry said, nasty like, "I don't want your advice. I don't listen to your advice, and I don't pay you for advice so don't give me any. Okay?"

If he did pay me for it, I would have made $1.40 that week, because St. Louis won the opener plus two of the next three games. Each day I'd get the line—which usually came out around 6, 7 Cardinals—and soon after Barry would call. No matter who was pitching or what was being bet, he'd tell me to make the line anywhere from 7, 8, to 7½, 8½ St. Louis, and the Havana cigars would come puffing in on Detroit. Even with a $2,000-per-cigar limit, and with the Tigers winning once, Barry must have cleared $15,000, and he was moved enough to apologize to me on the night before the fifth game. "Baby," he boomed through the phone, following a pattern where I was "baby" when he was happy, "Talcum" when he wasn't, and "Talcum-Baby" when he was undecided, "you gotta realize something. Nobody makes book like Barry Squires. I know I don't do the smart thing. I know I break all the rules, but when I feel something click inside, I'm flying too high to need anything but a parachute. Stick with me, baby, and I'll make you my protégé." Then he said, "How much am I paying you?" Before I could answer, before I could blink, he added, "Whatever it is remind me to put a hundred on top of it Monday. A protégé got to live right."

I got my raise but Barry's click went bye-bye. The Tigers, down three games to one, and losing the fifth, 5 to 2, rallied, and pulled that game out like they had their own click. I kept jobbing the line down to the bitter end, but not even an obedient protégé and a clicking master could stop Mickey Lolich's strong pitching, and the Tigers won the sixth and seventh games along with the world's championship plus $18,000 of Barry's money. He wasn't what you'd call gracious in defeat. While Detroit celebrated their incredible comeback on NBC, I sat in his apartment, wedged between a sweating Sydney and a burping Tony, watching him stomp around roaring, "I'm not paying nobody!" He'd pause periodically to give Al Kaline's smiling locker-room face the finger but all it took was a Gillette commercial to renew his harangue. "And if anybody don't like it they can sue me for their fucking money." I heard those last words through the door I closed behind me.

Despite his threats, Barry paid everyone off without being taken to big claims court, and I figured the bath he took would temporarily dunk, if not drown, his suicidal instincts. I was wrong. Not only was I wrong but I was about to watch a man spend three months defying and overwhelming the laws of nature, bookmaking, and Alfred Talcum, because Barry Squires hit a lucky streak like no other I'd ever seen.

He ran so hot for so long there were weeks I needed potholders just to hold the phone he called me on, and there were a couple of games I booked, watched, and read the box scores of, that I still haven't forgotten. One was in Cleveland and the teams involved were the Browns and the New York Giants. The Browns opened up as 13½-point favorites on Tuesday. By 1 P.M. Sunday, the line hadn't changed and I had about $13,000 bet on the Giants and close to $10,000 on Cleveland. (In the regular football season Barry's customers bet up to $30,000 on a pro game, and, believe me, Barry was a big bookie, but there were and are a lot bigger ones.) The Giants weren't getting bet because they weren't good. In fact, they were terrible, but Barry had a few customers who had trouble forgetting the days of Tittle to Shofner to the playoffs. So those memories plus 13½ points produced $13,000 in Giant money. Cleveland, on the other hand, was a really good team and I wasn't surprised when Barry called me at 1:15, asked how the betting was going, and then told me to make Cleveland 15-point favorites. The only problem was that moving the line in this game didn't do anything but get a few guys to try and middle us. (In a middle a bettor tries to win both sides of a game. In this case, it was possible if someone bet Cleveland laying 13½ and then bet an equal amount on the Giants taking the new price of 15—if Cleveland won by 14. It was an enormous long shot, but if the middle wasn't hit, the only risk was dropping the 10 percent vig on the losing bet.)

I got surprised at 1:55 though, when Barry called to see

if his jobbing-the-line antics had stirred things up. The second after I told him the betting hadn't swung to the Giants, that in fact it was dead even, he said, "I'm too high on Cleveland to settle for the vig in this one. When Sydney calls tell him to bet five grand on the Brownies for me with he knows who." For once, I appreciated his habit of smashing down the phone without saying goodbye, because if he hadn't, I might have hung up myself. Barry wasn't a BM. He was a gigantic degennie. I relayed his very ill instructions to Sydney. All he said was, "If it wasn't my own sick son, I'd never believe this." Then I gave him the work. The guys who played for a middle missed by a mile, and the ill BM who bet $5,000 watched Leroy Kelly lead the Browns to a 41-10 massacre of the Giants. I did the final figures for the week. There were three guys in the pay column and sixty-one in the collect.

Then there was the famous New York Jet-Oakland Raider game around the third week in November of '68 when the network cut away to a special on something called "Heidi" with less than fifteen seconds left to play. We'd dealt the game with Oakland as a 6½-point choice and finished with $12,000 more on the Raiders than the Jets, maybe two grand of which Barry laid off. When the game went off the air, the Jets were ahead 32-29, and like most everyone else in New York, I thought the game was over. Barry certainly did, because he called me a few minutes later and moaned loudly about it, which took a lot of nerve considering it was the first big game he'd lost in weeks.

I didn't hear from him again but after I went out to get the late paper and brought it home to check the scores and do the work, I couldn't wait for him to call. The Oakland-Jet game hadn't ended when NBC split, and in the last nine seconds, while Heidi was romping in the Alps, Oakland scored two touchdowns. One was by Charlie Smith and the other, the one that made the final score 43-32 Oakland, came when—are you ready?—Preston Ridlehuber picked up a Jet fumble on the kick-off and leaped into the end zone. Finally, a little past midnight Barry called, and assuming that he'd heard the final score, I simply said, "That Oakland-Jet game was some incredible thing, huh?" "Talcum, just read me the pay and collects you got so I can check them against Sydney's." He sounded a little drunk, which usually made Barry nasty no matter how many hookers he laid or games he won, so I began to read him the figures without comment. "Carl collect 900; Abe collect 750, Patsy collect 1,100, Carmine collect 1,600." As I went on, Barry started to snap out the word "What?" after each figure, and by the tenth or eleventh one I gave him, the "What's" were firing out of his mouth like rifle shots. "Whaddya mean we collect 1,400 from Irving?" he said a monent later. "Sydney makes it we owe him 820, and none of these other figures check either."

For a second I didn't know what was wrong. Then I realized Barry and Sydney hadn't heard the Oakland score and were counting the game as a loss. I read him the article on the game—twice. He still didn't believe me. "Stay there, Talcum-Baby, I'll be back in a minute." He must have called Darryl Lamonica to check, because it took him ten minutes to phone back but when he did, he was a believer. "Baby," he said, "remind me to give you an extra fifty this week. You're almost as good a clerk as I am a bookmaker."

Well, I thought I was a better clerk than he was a bookmaker. I mean, I was beginning to think he might have been the luckiest BM alive as his hot streak blazed through December, but I was still the glue holding him together. Barry wouldn't admit it, of course, but Sydney told me that before I showed up, his pay-and-collect figures were often wrong or occasionally lost and that a lot of customers would have quit if they still had to listen to his foul mouth on the phone.

By the end of the month I at least had Barry's trust, because around Christmas, Sydney, Tony, and he went off on a few 48-hour benders, leaving behind the number of a guy I could get a line from and hedge with. I say "trust" because that week Sydney told me the main reason Barry used to always insist on having him copy the work off me after each session: He'd been afraid I was going to cheat—that if Sydney didn't keep tabs on me, I'd make deals with customers to change their losing bets into winning ones, splitting the profits, like three other clerks he'd fired for trying the same thing.

Of course, even though he trusted me and seemed to sense I was sincere when I said the thought of cheating never entered my mind, Barry always kept expecting, almost hoping, to find crumbs of dishonesty. When he'd return from those days spent licking teased hair and guzzling Johnny Walker Red, he'd say, "Come on, Talcum, let me hear the numbers I missed. I swear I won't shoot you unless I lose over a million on Buffalo." I'd ignore him and read the figures, but as straight as I sounded, he'd throw in teasers like, "Get to the good stuff, Talcum. Go ahead and ram me up the ass while I'm bending over. What did Tum hit last night, a nine-team parlay or an 8-7 exacta for four grand?" When I'd finish giving him a bottom figure of collect five or six thousand dollars, Barry would shut up, tell me to remind him about another raise, and hang up.

I saw out 1968 at a party in Barry's apartment on New Year's Eve. I was making $650 a week. Penn State was about to make us nine grand by not covering a 7-point spread in the Orange Bowl, and I was drunk.

I was also watching Barry, Tony, and Sydney dancing naked in the middle of his very expensive all-white rug. It would be the last time any of them would feel like dancing for a very long time.

Chapter 15

I guess I should have known what was coming. Maybe not all of it because some was unpredictable, but a helluva lot more was inevitable. Thinking back, I'd say it started with the '69 Super Bowl between the New York Jets and the Baltimore Colts. Barry always got psyched for special games and this one had him sky high. He loved the Colts, hated the Jets, and, for a clincher, despised Joe Namath. When I heard it was because they'd met in a bar where Namath had called Barry a "greaseball," I got out my Baltimore helmet.

Sure enough, Sydney called me at six Tuesday night quoting Baltimore as 17-point favorites, and Barry called ten minutes later telling me to make them 18½. In two days we got over three grand on the Jets and less than $500 on Baltimore. It was baby advance action, but it was also a trend every bookmaker knew would continue. The AFL had yet to come close in one of these championship games. The New York papers made the Jets sound overmatched, and while other BMs were moving the line up to stop the NFL flow, we'd moved it just to make the AFLs go faster.

On Thursday, Barry said to keep the line at 18½. I mentioned that we had twenty grand in on the Jets already and asked if he'd like me to make house calls so I could pick up the Jets fans' action in person. I thought it would add a nice touch to take the money a father was saving for his son's tuition face-to-face rather than shoving political science behind the goal posts over the phone. Unfortunately, Barry had been drinking breakfast again so I got my usual, "I'll make the fucking game pick-em if I get drunk enough, Talcum." And since most BMs had the game up to 18 Colts, our price easily pulled in another $7,000 in Jet money by Saturday. I thought Baltimore was a winner, but to me it was what I called a "sure" game. If the Colts won 73-14, everyone would say, "Sure, they win by 59. The Jets got nothing but Namath's big mouth." And if the game turned out to be a squeaker, everyone would say, "Sure, Baltimore only won by 3. Who'd you think they were—Green Bay?"

My views aside, with fifteen minutes to game time Sunday we had close to $40,000 on the Jets against $9,000 on the Colts. It was, by far, the biggest game I'd ever booked for Barry and when he called minutes later, I gave him the late betting, said I'd try to get out of the joint and over to his place in half an hour, and asked how much he'd hedged off. When he said, "Not a fucking penny!" I decided to watch the game at home. If he'd given Al Kaline the finger for eighteen grand, I didn't want to see how he'd carry on with Namath for twenty-two more. Anyway, late in the first quarter, the game was scoreless when the Jets fumbled a completed pass away to Baltimore on their own twelve-yard line. Here it comes, I thought, but on third down, Earl Morrell overthrew his receiver in the end zone and a Jet cornerback picked it off. I took the phones off the hooks. Barry knew the numbers here and until the Colts started imagining Alan Ameche was back, I didn't want to hear his voice.

Baltimore had another great scoring opportunity in the second quarter when they got a first down on the Jets

sixteen, but they blew it again. Then New York took over.
Matt Snell scored a touchdown on a short run before the end
of the half; Jim Turner kicked a couple of tweezers in the
third period, and going into the final fifteen minutes, we
needed 32 points to win. We got 10, only 7 of them our way.
It was tough finding something to be happy about after
laying 18½ points and losing outright 16-7. I managed. I just
thought how lucky it was to have the East River between
Barry Squires and myself.

Well, a $30,000 payout didn't erase all the profits from
the long shoot Barry had been on, but it at least made him
behave through the first few months of roundball. Then, on a
Thursday morning in March, Barry phoned me at home to
say he'd taken on a new customer named Archie Ilescu,
casually remarking that Ilescu lived in, and would be calling
from, New Orleans. "Louisiana?" I asked. "Not Connecti-
cut," he answered. "Or New York either," I said aware that
taking out-of-state action was a federal offense. I still didn't
think of bookmaking as a serious crime, but the letters FBI
made the thought stir around. I began grumbling. Barry
reacted. "Talcum, for the money I pay you'll take action
from Argentina, if I want." I double grumbled until he gave
me some straight answers as to why we were getting involved
with Ilescu.

He started by saying that Archie Ilescu was a very big
gambler with a reputation for losing big and paying fast. He
said "very big" meant up to five dimes on an NBA game,
which he agreed to handle on the condition that all bets were
to be made a day in advance. Ilescu went along with the
condition, Barry added, because he knew most bookies
wouldn't take that kind of action unless they'd get a day or
so to lay part of it off, and because he loved Barry's offer to
take him to the Latin Quarter and get him laid by a showgirl
when he came to New York.

I don't know what Archie would have done if he heard
why Barry was going to all this trouble, but when Squires

told me the rest of the story, I stopped bitching. In fact, if what he'd heard about Ilescu was true, I was going to buy a white suit, because we figured to wind up with this guy's plantation.

By Monday, Barry had arranged to have a betting office give us the line on the pro games a day early, and at noon Sydney gave me the night's slim college stuff plus Tuesday night's NBA card. Barry called later to tell me Ilescu might call that night and said if he did I was to phone him at home right afterward. He added, "And don't forget what I told you. Raise the price a point on every game this guy asks about."

I assured Barry I hadn't forgot what he'd told me about "playing faces," as he called it, and hung up to await my first call from west of Riverside Drive. (With Ilescu, "playing faces" meant moving the line up because the word was he always bet chalk. But in general, "playing faces" referred to what a BM would do with a line when he had a customer who constantly bet the same way—favorites, underdogs, lucky teams—and/or he knew the customer was too stupid, stubborn, or naive to realize he was getting a price the bookie adjusted accordingly. Of course, most bettors aren't quite that dumb, and some bookies play it straight even if they are.)

Anyway, this Archie called around seven o'clock, asked for and got Tuesday night's line, and said he wanted the Boston Celtics over the Cincinnati Royals, laying 8. If the way a guy said, "Make it for five big ones," meant anything, he sure as hell didn't sound like he knew the right line was 7.

I called Barry immediately and told him what Ilescu bet, and nothing else unusual happened until the next day, when Sydney told me not to deal the Celtic-Royal game. Now, I'd been told to limit betting on certain games before (P.C. called them "circle jobs," and said BMs did it when a key player was injured and might or might not play or when a game was relatively meaningless—like exhibitions or late season contests between out-of-contention teams), and I'd even been told to take games off the board completely (when there was loose talk about fixes and betting coups that never seemed to materialize), but this was the first time Barry Squires had done anything except book every dollar he could get.

Well, that night a few degennies asked why the game was off and all I could say was nobody had bothered to tell me. That was the truth until eight o'clock when I asked Sydney what was going on. He said Barry took the game off because he wanted to concentrate on it. Then he said Barry needed to concentrate so much because he'd spent the whole day trying to middle Archie Ilescu.

I figured Barry had done something sick. I mean, I knew he bet money on games he booked. I'd heard him job lines. I'd seen him go weeks without hedging, and I'd listened to him talk about Ilescu like he was *the* golden goose of all time, but trying to middle his own customer wasn't just sick, it was impossible. It was like me KO-ing Sugar Ray, Mushy marrying Grace Kelly, or Dean Neely turning gay. And I swear, if Sydney hadn't been an eyewitness, I never would have believed it.

He told me how he'd watched Barry whip into action on the phones that afternoon, calling bookies he knew everywhere until he found a few in Cincinnati who quoted the Celtics as 5-point favorites. (The price was lower because bettors in Cincinnati tended to bet the Royals. I mean, the "Queen City" was their home town and the Big "O" + 5 wasn't bad no matter where you lived.)

So he bet his own five grand on Boston, laying only the five, and, Sydney said, Barry then began pacing around the apartment. He kept muttering that if Boston won by 6 or 7—the middle—he'd take the $5,000 he'd win from the bookies and the $5,500 he'd collect from Archie, and throw a party to end all parties. "Hell," Sydney added, "Barry said he'd have a little bash if he just sided the guy." (A side being if the game ended with Boston winning by 5, leaving Barry even with the bookies but owed by Archie, or if the game ended with Boston winning by 8, which would leave Barry even with Archie, but owed by the BMs.)

As usual, it all sounded good until I heard the score. Worse, I was the one assigned to meet Barry at Henry Stampler's to slip it to him, and when I spotted him at the bar there around eleven-thirty, I broke the news as gently as possible. "Barry, the Royals won by 3. I heard it on the radio before I left my apartment." He winced. He lost the vig to the bookies and made it back from Ilescu. He didn't say a thing about giving up middles and sides. Discouraged, but not stopped, Barry foamed at the mouth through March trying to bop Ilescu. He never came close, but if nothing else, the phone company was getting richer. Then, approaching NBA playoff time, Ilescu called in a five-grand-er on a Wednesday night. He bet his package on the Los Angeles Lakers over the Knicks in the Garden, and he laid 6½ points.

A minute later, I told Barry what Ilescu bet. By Thursday afternoon he was hard at work calling bookies in LA. This had become a personal vendetta and he was going to hit a side or middle with Ilescu or die trying. It was a little after 4 P.M. when I entered the picture. It happened as I was listening to a radio in the office, killing some time until six. A sports report came on over WOR. "At the Garden tonight, the Knicks take on the Los Angeles Lakers in their last meeting of the regular season. Late word has it that Jerry West, the Lakers' All-Star guard won't be in the line-up due to a slight muscle pull suffered in last night's Laker win in Baltimore." Wait a second, I said to myself. Jerry West's not playing? Ilescu's got five grand on Los Angeles laying 6½ and West's not playing? I called Barry. "Listen," I asked excitedly, "what prices have you been hearing on the LA-Knick game?" "Lousy ones," Barry snapped. "The books out there all got it 6½. I'll wind up laying it off at my own price like some kind of asshole." "Well, I'm not," I said, proudly,

"West's not playing tonight. I just heard it on WOR. Why don't you forget about laying it off at all?"

West didn't play that night. Elgin Baylor did. He scored 43 points and the Lakers won 129-103. The next day Squires sent Ilescu five $1,000 money orders. Then he called him personally and told him to take a walk into the Gulf of Mexico. . . . I couldn't wait for baseball.

You can bet spring fever didn't mean pretty girls, blooming flowers, and falling in love to Barry Squires. What it did mean was speeding down Queens Boulevard, buying a paper, and checking scores. We were on a bad streak and if some bookmakers wanted to unwind on the Jersey shore, Barry wasn't one of them. Instead, he took on customers from three vacationing bookies, and as a result I wound up with a third phone in the office and a summer basking in the warmth of a Seventh Avenue skylight. "Don't worry about it, Talcum," Barry would say each time I mentioned my lack of free time, "if we don't start winning soon you can take off the rest of your life."

We rallied all through June, but with Barry out $70,000 since January and into loan sharks pretty heavy to boot, he needed a game breaker. It came on a Sunday in July. I was in a little early that morning knowing it would be a busy day. Summer Sundays were for picnics, human beings, and sane bookies. For Barry, myself, and the kind of hard-core gamblers he had on his sheet, they were for Cleveland at Orioles. At least, I'd have company, I thought, as I looked out the window into the deserted streets of New York and saw Pluto get out of a taxi. This was the fourth weekend in a row he'd been working with me and it was a good thing Barry let me hire him. On Saturdays and Sundays he came in handy and at fifty bucks a day, he was a bargain.

I'd met the kid through Catch and his real name was Irving Koenigsberg. I don't know why I dubbed him Pluto. I just thought the name fit. He was pale and had red hair parted in three directions. He might have been six foot one, but he couldn't have weighed more than 130 pounds, and when you saw him at a distance, he resembled a skinny carrot. When he came in that day, he was wearing his regular outfit of Bermuda shorts, yellow tee shirt, and sneakers without socks. I smiled at him and nodded a hello. I was already too busy on the phones to talk. The Mets were at home for a twin bill against Atlanta, and from noon to one o'clock when game one started, the only conversation we had was when Pluto said, "Hey, Al, I got Dominic on the phone. He wants to know if he can bet $50 on Koosman and if it off to some trotter running tomorrow night." "Take whatever he wants," I yelled into the showroom. "Just remember to write it down."

We stayed around, and busy, until three o'clock, normal on days with lots of doubleheaders, and after Sydney called to get the work, we got up to leave. I didn't get the door open six inches before I saw five serious-looking men standing on the other side. Each had short hair, and a badge attached to the lapel of his Robert Hall suburban jacket. We all stood there staring at one another for a second when one of them said, "Step back inside, please. We're police."

I'd gathered as much when nobody said "trick or treat," but as they poured in the office like they expected to find Bonnie and Clyde inside, I was shocked. Was this happening? Was I really getting busted? I mean, come on, fellas—I thought—who complained? Through my daze, I heard the "step inside" guy say he was Lieutenant Dorsey and that Pluto and I should sit down on the couch and stay out of the way. Then I noticed Pluto was already on the couch, only he wasn't sitting on it. Instead, he was standing on the cushions with his hands raised over his head mumbling, "I give up," over and over again. I sat down next to him and Dorsey said, "You can put your arms down, son. We arrest people for bookmaking. We don't shoot them."

In a few minutes, Dorsey told three of the cops with

him to leave, and after they had gone he and one other detective continued rummaging around the office. Occasionally, they'd look up to see Pluto sprawled on the couch in a near coma. Once, Dorsey walked over to me and said: "Does he need help or is this some kind of act?" I told him that he'd be okay and the lieutenant walked away laughing.

Nice as Dorsey seemed, he was still a cop and minutes later he was busy again. He asked us our names, made some notes, and holding up the two legal pads full of the day's action, said sternly: "You know if there's over $5,000 in action here, this is a felony rap. That's serious, boys."

Since I had more than five dimes bet on the White Sox-Tiger second game, I didn't comment on the charge.

At least Dorsey said it was okay for me to put on the radio while he filled out some police forms. His partner was even more casual. When I tuned in the Mets game he said, "Who do you need, kid?" I was about to tell him the Braves but Dorsey gave him a dirty look and he walked away. It was 4-4 in the seventh inning when Dorsey got up and motioned for Pluto and me to follow him and his partner out. As we were leaving, I noticed Dorsey reaching under my desk and pulling out the telephone wires, a procedure I'd heard was mandatory in gambling arrests. "Lieutenant," I said, as he eyed my third phone, "I know what you're supposed to do but I run a real business from this place. Would you please leave me one phone? If you want, I'll have it hooked up to a loudspeaker at police headquarters but, please, I'll be ruined without it." "Okay," Dorsey said, and the four of us walked out the door.

We must have made some sight filing down the street. The lieutenant was in front, like the lead float in the Rose Bowl Parade, Pluto and I were wedged in the middle like POWs, and the other cop was in the rear, keeping a few feet behind so he could get out of the way if Pluto fainted. We weren't handcuffed, which was against regulations but Dorsey was good like that. I guess he realized the worst we could do was whip out a radio and poke him with the antenna, and when we got to his unmarked car, he stopped. "Okay, fellas, I have to take you to the 18th Precinct for booking now, but if you want to grab something to eat tell me and I'll let you pick it up. It's the only chance you'll get until tonight. You'll never be able to eat the slop they serve at the Tombs" (the Tombs being the Manhattan House of Detention).

"What?" I screamed at Dorsey. "The Tombs! We're going to the Tombs? That horror I read about in the *Daily News?* There? What the fuck for?" For the first time all day I was upset. I mean, I didn't know what was going on but I'd figured we'd be booked at a precinct and released. The Tombs was a different story. "Let me tell you something, Talcum," Dorsey said, sounding like a cop again. "I know you think this isn't serious, but bookmaking is illegal. You've committed a felony and thinking different don't change the law." "Would you knock off that felony crap?" I screamed, really worked up. "People run around this city killing their fucking neighbors with machetes and you're telling me I'm a felon because I booked action on a few lousy games. Come on, Dorsey, why don't you arrest the fucking ballplayers? They're playing the goddamn games, I only booked them." Unfortunately, Dorsey was in no mood to debate the Penal Code on the corner of 36th Street so he ignored me and put us in his car for the ride to the 18th.

(Dorsey was a nicer than average cop but he didn't have many reasons not to be. For a bull, the gambling squad is a plum of an assignment. They seldom get hurt and never get killed, because BMs don't carry sharp pencils, much less deadly weapons. Also, there's little pressure on them from the public and press who are more concerned with violent, more visible crimes, so unless there's a big syndicate bust or a police-protection scandal uncovered, they can do twenty years and retire without breaking a sweat.)

The booking was quick and painless. We were finger-printed, had mug shots taken, and answered questions for the cops who typed out reports. One rookie type must have thought I was a friend of Meyer Lansky, and he kept asking me if I had a nickname. "You got to," he said, when I swore I didn't. "All you guys got nicknames." To shut him up I said, "Okay, some people call me Big Alfred Palfred." Without blinking, he typed it on my sheet.

The charges we were booked on were "Possession of Illegal Gambling Paraphernalia" and "Promoting Gambling in the Second Degree." On the ride to the Tombs I said, "Lieutenant, what do you have to do to get charged with 'Promoting Gambling in the First Degree'? Walk around New York with a gun telling people to bet on the Phillies?" I was going to ask him about the gambling paraphernalia too, but I decided against it. After all, he had $20,000 in evidence sitting in his briefcase. I didn't know how serious that really was but ribbing Dorsey about it didn't make sense.

When we got to the Tombs, we were rebooked. A cop told me it was to make sure we were the same two people arrested. We were led to a detention cell to await arraignment. The walk was an experience. I mean, I'd read and heard this place was no palace, but I never imagined it was this disgusting. The halls were littered with junkies lying unattended on the filthy floors. There was a stench in every corner of the building, and some of the cells were jammed with five or six prisoners each yet they looked small for two. I felt a little better when we were put in an unoccupied cell. I figured Dorsey had arranged it but whatever the reason it was a nice surprise. If Pluto got lodged in one of those cramped jobs, with a murderer or three for company, he might have passed away altogether. As it was, he was still petrified, so to cheer him up I started a sports trivia quiz. The kid really knew his stuff, too, but I was tough. And for an hour, names like José Tartabull, Jerry Lumpe, Tobin Rote, and Pete Pihos flew around the bunks. I was unbeatable when it came to boxing and I finally won the championship when Pluto couldn't come up with Jersey Joe Walcott's given name (Arnold Cream). Hell, I was feeling so good when he gave up that I momentarily forgot about being lodged in the Tombs with a cellmate ready to hang himself.

Suddenly, I heard footsteps in the hallway. A moment later, a guard appeared. He had Barry Squires and Tony Gumpo with him. "Talcum, how you doin'?" Barry asked. Then Tony slurred, "He's okay, boss, but I think Irving's had it."

Instead of putting Barry and Tony in the cell, the guard told Pluto and me to come out, and all four of us were escorted to an empty cell, big enough for ten, fifteen, men. I was still wondering why we weren't getting the sardine treatment like everyone else when I saw Barry slip a $50 bill into the guard's hand. That solved the mystery.

"Okay, we got busted," Barry announced after we were inside. "I've been busted before. I'll probably get busted again, but it don't mean shit. Talcum," Barry said sharply when he noticed I wasn't perking up, "I said this is bullshit." "Please, Barry, cut the pep talks and just tell me what's going on. All I know is one minute I was making book and the next I'm raided. What'd you do? Kill a hooker?"

"All right, Talcum, I don't blame you for being pissed. Just let me tell you the whole thing in a nutshell. Dorsey's been on my ass for years and every once in a while he pops in to let me know he's around. He don't take money. He don't ask me to get him laid. He's a freak. You know—honest and whatnot—but he's no ballbuster. When this shit comes to trial he'll get his rocks off if I get a nickel fine, and you and Irving figure to get off with a $50 touch. Believe me, that felony speech Dorsey makes is written on his sleeve. I know guys in Brooklyn been popped thirty times and if they got ten days, they'd appeal."

Barry's speech made me feel better. Hell, he'd sounded so convincing, Pluto had quit wheezing.

An hour later, we all seemed more relaxed but Tony

couldn't sit still. When one of the guards said we might not get into night court for a while, he gave the guy a $50 bill and said, "Bring me back a couple of roast beefs on rye, a pastrami, some cole slaw, a pickle, and a six-pack of 'Bud' and you can keep the change." The guard said okay and after he finished writing down the order, he strolled off. Then Tony told Barry he'd booked a big trotter bet Saturday night, and screamed down the hall, "Hey, you—get me a *News* with last night's trot results and there's another ten in it for ya."

Forty minutes later, the guard returned. Tony gave him the extra ten, inhaled his food without offering anyone a bite, and for dessert, ripped open the paper. When he saw the horse he booked a $100 win bet on had finished second and paid $26 to place, he let out a sigh of relief that almost blew Pluto through the bars.

Tony was chugging down his fifth Budweiser when another guard came to take us up to night court. The courtroom was overflowing with pickpockets and drunks so we waited while the judge waded through one mess after another. It was close to 1 A.M. when our case was finally called. As each of our names was read, we walked to the bench accompanied by Herman Baum, Barry's lawyer, and pleaded "Not Guilty." The judge set bail for Barry and Tony at $250, and released Pluto and myself on our own recognizance. Barry paid his bail by peeling five $100 bills off a roll big enough to post bail for Leopold and Loeb and on the way out he said, "I told you, Talcum. This legal-beagle stuff ain't diddly shit!"

When we hit the street, Barry told Herman to drop Irving off on his way home and, putting the kid in Baum's Cadillac, said, "Don't worry about a thing, Irving. Herman wouldn't let you in his car if he thought you were a criminal." Then he hailed a cab for the three of us and we sped off toward Queens. "There's work to do, Talcum," he said, "and you're the only one I got to do it."

It was past two when we got to Sydney's place in Flushing, but his wife had coffee brewing and fresh danishes laid out for us. She poured the coffee and went to wake up Sydney. He stumbled into the kitchen a minute later wearing his pajamas. When he saw us, he took off his top, wheeled around, and pointed to a manila envelope taped to his back. "The second the operator told me Talcum's phones were disconnected, I knew you guys was busted," he said, peeling off the tape. "So I put the work in here in case they came looking for me." We all got a laugh out of that but as Barry, Tony, and Sydney sat around giggling, I got busy. I sat down on the living room floor surrounded by the thirty or so pages of work and went through it, checking the bets against the scores listed in the newspapers we had bought on the way over. By 6 A.M. I was finished (on top of everything we lost $2,180), and got ready to leave.

Everyone had fallen asleep so I crept over to the couch Barry had fallen out on and nudged him awake. "Listen," I said, "I did today's work and left the figures on the kitchen table. I'll call you tomorrow with the totals for the week." Then I walked tiredly to the door. Barry ran after me. "You don't have to call me tomorrow, Al," he said, warmly. "I want you to take the day off and freshen up."

I was too wiped out to ask what he wanted me fresh for.

When I got home, I took the phones off the hooks and slept until seven o'clock that night. When I got up I was still woozy. I had a headache. I thought about the work I'd taken from Sydney that had to be finished and the degennies who were getting an out-of-order recording in the joint and busy signals here. I went back to sleep.

The next morning I did the work, called my personal customers to tell them what happened, and told my parents I wouldn't be using the office much anymore. Then I got a call from Barry. I said I had the figures done and he asked me to bring them over to his apartment so we could talk over a few things. I went there, but he did all the talking. "Talcum, I been asking some questions. From what I hear, I think you got busted on a wire-tap Dorsey put on your phone after he found out you were working for me. I don't know how he found out. It could have been he overheard some shmuck we deal with mouthing off in a bar, or maybe a piece of shit tipped him, like that guy Henry I took on last month; you know the motherfucker still owes me four dimes? But whatever, things are just as cool as I told you in the can.

"Listen, Talcum, they busted me and Tony in the street. We had a few betting slips in our pockets so they charged us with possession of gambling records. That's a bullshit felony but it don't mean nothing. If this was serious, and I told you it never gets serious, don't you think the cops would have known about Ilescu, or busted the betting offices I deal with, or tore my apartment apart? And what you got charged with—the 'Promoting in the Second Degree' shit, and 'Paraphernalia Possession'—they're like big misdemeanors. You didn't hear anyone book you for conspiracy or have your door broken down, did you?

"Anyway, I'm telling you all this to clear your head because now that Dorsey got his collar, I'm going back to making book. He knows I'm not about to stop, and as long as I don't send a singing telegram to his captain announcing my reopening, he don't give a flying fuck! All I care about is finding a good joint. I got Tony looking for one, and if you want in, nothing changes but the phone numbers. You want out? That's cool, too. I'll still pay your legal expenses with Herman and they'll be no hard feelings."

If Barry made things any clearer, I'd need sunglasses. What he was saying was that getting busted was a pain in the ass, but it came with the territory, was no big deal, and if you wanted to make the kind of bucks we did, you had to put up with it.

"I guess you got to pay dues everywhere you go," I said, and he nodded his head like I'd got the message. I had. I couldn't make $600 a week pumping gas, so in exchange for Barry's agreeing to pay the rent on Jama, Inc. until the end of the year, I told him he could tell Tony to stop looking for a joint. After all, I had those two phones in my bedroom and I didn't know any pajama buyers who'd pay my telephone bills.

For a guy on an unexpected holiday, the week was tough. Wednesday and Thursday I went around settling with my regular crew, apologizing for being late, giving out my, by now, familiar home numbers, and assuring them they could start gambling again Friday. As happy as they were to get their Talcum security blanket back, most weren't completely satisfied until I gave a play-by-play account of my bust from the second Dorsey made his Dick Tracy entrance right through to when I left the Tombs. The story didn't scare anyone (there's no law against betting, at least none that's ever enforced), but they all seemed fascinated by it. Tum almost drove me crazy all by himself. I spent an hour with him Thursday answering question after question, but when he wouldn't stop bugging me about how it felt to be finger-printed, or if I had a copy of my mug shot on me, I started to get annoyed.

Finally, I just turned my back on him and walked away. He followed me out of the coffee shop we'd been sitting in and I guess he kind of summed up everyone's fascination with crap like that when he said, "Hey, Al, I don't mean to upset you. It's just exciting to have a criminal for a bookie."

Well, after a week of making book, my "criminal self" noticed a few changes other than numbers. For one, Barry was calling me from phone booths instead of his apartment, and for another, I was spending a lot of time thinking I was being tailed and an equal amount wondering if my phones were tapped. At least, I admitted being paranoid. Each time I asked Barry to tell me how okay things were, he'd say: "Talcum, nobody's tailing you. Nobody's tapping the phones. Just make believe Dorsey's been transferred to the Mounted Police and deal the goddamned line, huh?"

Since the summer moved along without a pop, I stopped annoying Barry. By August, I'd quit peeking over my shoulder, and soon after, I quit thinking the static on my phones came from Dorsey's tape recorder. Instead, I was concerning myself with the important things in life again, like how to beat Tom Seaver on the days his fastballs looked like Bufferins.

Then, in late September, near the end of a -$6,000 baseball season, Pluto's and my case came to trial after a month of delays. Baum had held it off by requesting three or four adjournments, and whenever the judge cared enough to ask for a reason, he'd say I was indisposed. Herman wasn't lying. I was indisposed and Barry was the indisposer, because he wouldn't let me take a day off until the case was scheduled on a no-game afternoon.

I was a little late in arriving at Criminal Court, and as I entered the room, Pluto was already there, huddled in a meeting with Baum. Not having seen the kid since the bust, I gave him a big hello. About a minute later Baum asked the judge to dismiss the "paraphernalia" charge, and his request was granted so fast I'd thought he'd asked if we could get a drink of water. "Herman," I said, "I can see why there's no jury but if it's this easy, what do they need a judge, an assistant DA, and these other flunkies for? Come on, move we make the other charge 7½, 8½. If the court wins, they get Pluto, if we do, we get eighty-five bucks. Either way, the city saves a fortune."

Herman laughed but said he had a better idea and asked the judge to dismiss the "promoting gambling" charge on the grounds that the police had no justifiable cause to enter my place of business. With that, the assistant DA, who looked to be a real eager beaver, maybe a year out of law school, bolted out of his chair. "Your Honor," he said, "the police had every justifiable cause to enter Mr. Talcum's offices, and I'd like to call the arresting officer in charge, Lieutenant William Dorsey, to testify to that fact."

The judge denied Baum's move for dismissal, and the court clerk asked Dorsey to take the stand. Then the kid from law school asked Dorsey to tell the court why he thought there was justifiable cause for entry, and I had to admit the lieutenant had come up with some pretty solid stuff. Dorsey opened with, "Mr. Talcum's comings and goings had been under surveillance for three weeks preceding his arrest. The investigation was first initiated two weeks prior to that when my office received an anonymous tip from an informer who said Mr. Talcum was working for a known gambler and bookmaker named Barry Squires. I found little evidence to support the latter allegation but in observing Mr. Talcum's daily schedule, it became obvious he was involved in an illegal gambling operation." (Baum later told me Dorsey probably had wire-taps connecting me with Barry but that he just didn't want to waste everyone's time by playing the tapes. In other words this case wasn't being treated too seriously.)

Especially not by the judge. He told Dorsey he had four cases to hear before lunch and asked him to hurry up. I remember the kid prosecutor looking shocked but Dorsey didn't do anything but read his notes faster. He gave a condensed rap about having observed me engaging in known bookmaker habits such as exchanging money in the street, making P & C rounds, and other routines, which, he said, "I won't take the court's time to mention."

Then he got into how he thought he'd accumulated sufficient evidence to obtain a search warrant for 246 West 38th Street, and as Dorsey kept droning on about standing outside the door of Jama, Inc., I noticed the few spectators we had attracted were gone and the bailiff was reading *Time* magazine.

The judge noticed also, glanced at his watch, and said, "Lieutenant, if you don't finish soon I'm going to let the defendants go and arrest you." "Okay, okay," Dorsey said, still reading from his notes but at a mile-a-minute clip.

"Both Mr. Talcum and Mr. Koenigsberg were on the telephone for over an hour. They were taking sports bets and I heard comments like—and I'm quoting now—'You can't bet the Oriole game, Milton, it started twenty minutes ago,' and 'Okay, Carmine, you got the Yankees laying 6½ in the first game for a nickel and if they win you want Detroit at a pick for a dime.' "

After the judge gave Dorsey a come-on-already look, the lieutenant finished in thirty seconds by saying how Irving and I had been cooperative and, in his opinion, were merely salaried clerks in a gambling operation now under investigation.

"Dorsey must like you guys," Herman whispered to me as the judge said, "Mr. Baum, I'll tell you what. Have your clients plead guilty and I'll reduce the remaining charge to loitering with intent to gamble and fine them $50." I was already shaking my head "yes" when Herman turned to us. "Let's grab it before that DA takes out his law books and gets technical. It'll give you a line on a yellow sheet but it's like getting one for jaywalking."

Herman paid our fines, and ten minutes later we were out on the street. Even Pluto was smiling, but when I asked him if he'd like to help me book the World Series, he said definitely not.

A week later things didn't go quite as easy for Barry and Tony. The cops didn't have much evidence against them but it seemed like they wanted Barry's ass. I guess they knew he was a big bookie and that he was "connected," and Herman said he was sure someone over Dorsey's head was after more than a shake-up.

In fact, when Herman found out the DA's office wasn't going to follow the almost routine procedure of reducing a felony charge in a gambling case to a misdemeanor, he told Barry and Tony to keep their mouths shut and proposed a deal minutes after they showed up in court. At first, the detective in charge of the case balked, but then he consulted with some guy sitting next to the assistant DA and gave his okay. So Barry and Tony pleaded guilty to the original charge and they both wound up getting six-month suspended sentences and $1,000 fines.

I watched this mini-drama unfold from the first row, and it was obvious by the sullen expression on Barry's face that things had gone rougher than he'd expected. I mean, Sing-Sing it wasn't, but this was his fourth bust and up to now he'd had two dismissals and a $100 fine.

Of course, he recovered in time to head into the tail end

of September refreshed, and if he had any lingering resentments, they were probably trampled by spiked football shoes, the New York Met-Baltimore Oriole World Series, and the betting avalanche accompanying both.

The Mets being in the Series was really something. They'd been clowns for so long, most New York bettors had a difficult summer accepting them as pennant contenders. For years, they'd been watching Marv Thronberry dropping pop flies, Charley Neal hitting beer vendors with his throws from third base, and Craig Anderson giving up home runs to hitters like Dal Maxvill, and it took month after month of Seaver and Koosman pitching, Cleon Jones hitting, and Tommy Agee fielding to finally convince them the Mets were for real. But by Series time the doubters had become believers and I had a feeling the Met fans were ready to send it in.

I'd never seen Barry behave as well as he did during the week preceding the Series, and I was hoping he'd given up clicks for good. He got me a little anxious when he made some comments about the Mets being overrated but with his luck on a very extended vacation, he let me deal the first game at the 6½, 7½ Baltimore-on-top price most BMs were using. We got nine grand bet on the Mets against $2,500 on Baltimore, and still behaving, Barry hedged off $4,000 in Met money. (That figure didn't represent any formula. Barry laid off action according to how his luck was running, how many times he got laid the night before, and in games he had an opinion on, whom he liked.) When the Orioles won the opener, beating Tom Seaver, he had the excuse he needed to let out a notch or ten. "Fuck it, Talcum," he roared the next morning, "not only ain't I not hedging any more Met money off but I am jobbing the line starting right now." Sure.

A week later, after the Mets swept the next four games, I figured out that if I had bet $500 against Barry every time he'd heard a click and jobbed a line since January, I could have been retired and living on the French Riviera. Since I hadn't, I was stuck on East 53rd Street consoling him at a table in P. J. Clarke's, as he poured Scotch down his mouth, neck, and silk shirt until closing time, when he left with a little booze seeping through his socks.

Squires was teetering. We didn't talk about it much but I knew he was staying in business only because New York City was the loan shark capital of the world. Unfortunately, when Barry's luck didn't improve through the next month of football, even his Triple-A credit line couldn't make ends meet.

The first serious signs of the shorts came late in October when I started to get my salary piecemeal. A couple of hundred Monday, another bean Wednesday, if I asked, and another hundred Friday if we were having a good week, with a promise for the remainder. I was still getting the office rent but I paid my home phone bills and didn't make an issue of it. I mean, it was obvious Barry was suffering. The Scotch was Inver House instead of Johnny Walker or Chivas Regal, and the shots were singles not doubles. The Eldorado wasn't washed every day, and the shirts weren't being thrown out as soon as the collars frayed. In plain English, Barry had simply stopped living in the "anything goes" style that got him into this mess in the first place.

Two losing weeks in a row early in November made the shorts shorter. I fronted the money to pay my own customers both times, which didn't bother me, but when Barry asked me to help make rounds for him, I ran into some flack. He didn't get the pay money together until Wednesday, and his customers screamed pretty good about getting paid late after years of having Barry jump down their throats if losses weren't settled by Tuesday.

We survived that blitz, thanks to Dallas losing a game Barry held eleven grand on, and going into the third Friday in November we were hanging tough. That afternoon, I was in the Jama, Inc. office, a stop I'd been making a few times a week so my parents would believe my story about trying to start a legitimate business, when the phone rang. None of my customers knew I was there. I picked it up figuring it was a wrong number. "Alfred," the voice of my Aunt Mildred said, "please come home right away. Your father's had a sudden stroke."

I was stunned, not surprised. My father hadn't been healthy since long before his retirement, and since then his mental and physical condition had slipped further. I got to the apartment in fifteen minutes. When I walked inside, he had already passed away. Thankfully, my aunt was still there, and after the doctors, and the hurriedly called for emergency ambulance left, she stayed behind to make things easier for everyone.

My mother seemed to be holding up all right but she was heavily sedated, and when Mildred said it might be a good idea for Inga to stay at her house for a while, I agreed. She called her husband to have him come pick them up, and when he arrived, she said they'd take care of all the funeral arrangements and that I should come to their place later that night. Then they left, leaving me sitting alone in the living room feeling a strange mixture of guilt, sadness, and a little relief.

I didn't stir for a couple of hours, but at five o'clock I called Barry and told him the news. "Al, come on, you don't have to ask about taking time off. I just wish there was something I could do to help." There was almost no emotion in his voice. I understood. Barry's feelings were buried under 100 times as many box scores as mine, and I knew before I called that he was the kind of guy who could feel bad about a tragedy one minute and in the next think about having sixty customers vainly trying to reach a grief-stricken clerk. Still, I thanked him for the nice words, and when he asked, gave him the number at my aunt's house. He said he'd probably lose a lot of business but he'd try to reach a few guys from phone booths to salvage something from the weekend. Then he said he hoped his already pissed-off customers wouldn't think he couldn't afford a full-time clerk. He meant it as a joke.

Late Saturday afternoon, he slipped me another joke, only this time it wasn't even sick-funny. "Al, I'm sorry to call you at your aunt's. Believe me, I know about grief. I've had deaths in my family. I was just wondering, and it's okay if your answer's no—hell, I'm the first guy to send flowers when a guy's old man dies—but I was just wondering if there's any chance you might work tomorrow. I'm only asking 'cause you know the spot I'm in. It's a big spot, and you never know, Al, Sunday could be the turnarounder kind of day to get us right back on our feet. Whaddya say, baby? You wanna win one for the gipper, huh?"

"Goddamn it, Barry," I said, hoping my aunt couldn't overhear, "my father's funeral is at one-thirty tomorrow. What do you want me to do—put a phone in the hearse? If you're so desperate, deal the line yourself and let me go to the cemetery in peace."

"Take it easy, Al. I'm only trying to do what's best. You know I can't work the phones, not after my last bust. Come on, you saw them make Tony and me sweat like pigs. If either of us got popped sitting direct, we might have to serve that six-month bullshit." I asked why Sydney couldn't do it. Barry said since the trial he was scared of phone booths. I suggested he offer Pluto $10,000 to come in. He said twenty wouldn't be enough, and he was right.

"Barry, do what you can. I'll call you Monday. Stop boozing for twenty-four hours and you might understand." There was an awkward pause. Then Barry said he had a good idea. "Let me get a couple of guys to come up and take over for you at one o'clock. You'll get a lot of the heavy stuff booked, my people will pick up the rest, and you'll get to see your dad off in plenty of time. That's fair. Right?"

Maybe my feelings were only buried under half as many box scores as Barry's, and if I spent much more time with a guy who could make a son think his father's funeral was a bon voyage party, we'd soon be even. "Okay, Barry, don't say another word. I'll work tomorrow but if you don't have these people at my apartment by one sharp, I'll call Dorsey and turn you in myself!"

I got up extra early Sunday. Instead of dealing in my shorts, as I usually did, I showered, shaved, and dressed. At eleven-thirty I was at my desk decked out in a black suit. Hopefully, I'd be able to tear out of my place at one, jump in my car and devour the West Side Highway fast enough to reach the funeral chapel in Washington Heights on time.

The first hour went smoothly. I got the line, told customers why I was leaving early, and accepted sincere condolences between more sincere Kansas City Chief bets. By 12:45, I was sweating through my white shirt. Five minutes later, while I'm in the middle of taking $600 on the Lions laying 3½, the doorbell rang. I completed the call, did the off-the-hooks trick, grabbed my car keys, and ran to the door. As I opened it, I said: "I'm glad you guys are here." No I wasn't!

Standing in the hallway were two men. The bigger of them was dressed in a brown suit jacket worn over a white polo shirt with light brown pants and white socks—droopy white socks. The smaller one was wearing a blue cardigan sweater covered with lint, a pair of dungarees ripped in both knees, and a nylon jacket with the words "Funzi's Pizzeria" over the front pocket, and some of Funzi's tomato sauce crusted on his chin.

If they didn't have the wrong apartment I almost wanted them to be undercover cops. Then the polo shirt said: "Glad to meet ya, Talcum. I'm Ralph. This here's Joey. Barry filled us in on the operation so go ahead and enjoy your funeral." When Ralph turned to his friend and, in the exact tone of voice Ollie used on Stanley, said, "That's right, ain't it, Joey? Talcum don't have a thing to worry about." I asked them to wait outside for a minute and ran back to my room.

I got Barry on the phone and said he was the biggest schmuck I'd ever known and that if this was his idea of a joke we were finished. He said they were two goons who worked for his friend in the trucking business but were the best he could do on such short notice. "Al, they've been told what to do. My buddy vouches for them, so please get your ass outa there and quit worrying about them eating your bedspread."

Reluctantly, I walked to the door, let the two of them in, explained telephones had to be put on hooks before they could ring, and left.

Speeding madly, I got to the chapel twenty minutes late and was greeted by my relatives' dirty looks. I ignored them but saw my Aunt Mildred crooking an angry finger at me from the back of the room. I made my way over to her. Her voice was quivering with emotion. "Alfred, I've been humiliated in my life but never like this!" I said I was sorry about being late. That wasn't it. "What happened, Aunt Mildred?" "What happened? What happened?" she repeated in a voice rising through much of the small chapel. "What didn't happen? Five minutes ago I called to see if you had left the apartment and whoever you have staying there answered the telephone. . . ." "Why don't we talk about this later?" I interrupted, trying to head off everything. My relatives and I hardly ever spoke but none of them knew I was a bookmaker and I wanted to keep it that way. "No, not later, Alfred, now! I want to talk about this now. I was polite. I asked for you nicely. I said it was very important and he hung up. I called again and, do you know what I got for my trouble? I got a man tell me—your aunt, your mother's sister who is paying for this funeral—that I was tying up the phone and if I didn't get off the line I'd get a meat hook shoved up my . . . my . . ." "I know where, Aunt Mildred, I know where!"

I made up a story about letting a friend sleep off his hangover at the apartment. I apologized, squeezed her hand, kissed her cheek, and, finally, got her in a seat for the service that was almost over.

That was the "coming attractions." At two-fifteen, as the service was coming to a close, the feature started. Vincent Price should have been in it. I was sitting in my seat, still embarrassed, thinking 50 percent about my father and 50 percent about getting back to work, when I heard a commotion coming from the rear of the chapel. I turned to see what the fuss was. A rush of fear shot through me. Standing thirty feet away, poking his finger at my Uncle Max was Ralph. "I ain't putting one on," I heard him say to my tiny, high-blood-pressured uncle, who was holding a yarmulke in his trembling hands. "All I want is to talk to Talcum, Al Talcum. Okay, buddy?" Ralph went on as the color drained from Max's face.

Well, with Max and Mildred ready to join my father in the coffin, with my mother pretending not to have heard a thing, and with thirty relatives watching out of the corners of their eyes, I ran to Ralph and, in a panic, grabbed him by the soiled lapels of his jacket and pulled him into the foyer. "Ralph," I said through clenched teeth, "you're supposed to be answering my phones. What the hell are you doing here scaring the shit out of an eighty-four-year-old man?"

I must have really looked and sounded vicious, because Ralph held his temper even though he could have killed me with his thumbs. He said—almost whimpered—that the phones had gone dead, that him and Joey had run to a phone booth to call Barry and that he'd told them to drive here to tell me so I wouldn't worry if I called home and got an "out-of-order" answer. Meanwhile, the service had ended and my relatives were filing past us on their way out. When my mother passed us in tears, Ralph put the yarmulke he'd been holding on his head, but he did it so quickly it slid to one side like a cap on a drunken sailor. I was too numb to laugh and too shocked to be angry and if I wasn't outside in a minute to join the funeral procession to the cemetery, I'd blow what little dignity I had left. "Ralph, I shouldn't have got mad like I did. This wasn't your fault. All I want is for you to drive back to my apartment, leave the work you did in an envelope, and put the key under the mat."

Ralph promised to do everything I asked and I ran to the parking lot where the procession of cars was lined up ready to leave. The door to the lead limousine was open and I climbed in, taking a seat between Aunt Mildred and my mother. As the car slowly pulled away, I was debating whether to apologize or explain or simply not say anything, but before I could decide on which, I saw Ralph jogging alongside the car. Desperately, I lunged onto the lap of my grieving mother and began frantically turning the knob to close the rear window. Too late. In the instant it took me to react, Ralph had stuck his head through the open space and as I stared blankly at his reddened, protruding face, he gasped, "Al, I forgot one thing. Barry wanted me to tell you he needs the Oilers for his fucking lungs!"

Well, my mother decided to live with Aunt Mildred permanently and most of the people who were at the funeral never spoke to me again. Considering what had happened, I couldn't blame them. In fact, I was so appalled by it, I made a promise to myself: When the Super Bowl was over I was jumping off Barry Squires' merry-go-round.

Quitting wasn't easy. From the weekend following my father's funeral through the first few days of January 1970, Barry hit a winning streak. That's right. A winning streak— something we figured extinct, like a woolly mammoth or Frank Tripuka. The run was no chippie, either. It ran through the NFL playoffs, plus the post-season College Bowl games, and in that time, we made $45,000.

Super Bowl week almost pulled me apart. My smarts were telling me to ignore the streak and quit like I planned, but Barry's money juices were at high tide busy drowning my good sense. Back and forth. Back and forth. One day thanking him for buying me a $200 custom-tailored suit, the next cursing him under my breath when I'd think of the bust and

and it wasn't until after the trial, when the Feds learned Barry hadn't been upset enough to stop booking Mormon monsters, that the feuding stopped.

As Herman went on, I was trembling. Although everything he was saying came as a complete shock, there was no question it was true. Herman Baum had been around the gambling scene in New York for years and he knew the kind of people who could find out stuff like this. I was wondering how fast you could become eligible for parole on a ten-to-twenty stretch when he noticed my glazed eyes.

"Al, let me tell you where you stand. First of all, forget about Barry. The Feds pulled him in today and they're holding him on $15,000 bail. It's tough to get in real trouble for bookmaking but he asked for it. He was careless. He got mixed up with the wrong people. He did everything a man could possibly do to put himself behind a government eight ball. The second thing is you have nothing to do with his situation. The Feds wanted Barry Squires. They got him and they're happy. As far as they're concerned, you're an ex-clerk whose name they already lost in a file. As for Lieutenant O'Gorman, if I were you I'd send him a thank-you card. He charged you with the same garbage as Dorsey did and the worst that can happen will be a $100 fine, maybe two, if the judge notices it's your second offense.

"Okay, then, that's the facts. Call me when your case comes up and I'll represent you for no charge." "Thanks, Herman," I said, speaking for the first time in an hour. "I thought I was in a helluva lot more trouble." Herman didn't say a word. Instead, he pulled his wallet out of his inner suit pocket, flipped through it and took out a business card that read:

HERMAN BAUM
Attorney-at-Law
MU-4 3000
01
02
03

"Al, I've been a lawyer in New York since 1935 and I've represented hundreds of bookmakers. The only ones who ever get screwed are guys like Barry. The big mouths, the wisenheimers, the ones who want to make a thousand dollars a minute and tell the world it's two. You don't go to jail for being a bookmaker. You go to jail for being a shmuck."

With that, Herman put his card in my shirt pocket. "If you know what I'm talking about, use it to pick your teeth. If you don't, keep it handy. You're going to need it all your life."

A month later, my case came to court and I was found guilty of both charges and fined $200. A month afterward, Barry was tried in federal court and found guilty of everything from not having a federal gambling stamp to income tax evasion. He got three years and if it weren't for Herman, it would have been eight.

After a long fight, Barry Squires was finally going . . . going . . . gone!

Chapter 17

On the losing side of the ticket, Barry left me with an apartment with no telephones, a raided business office with one phone connected and two others impounded, a pack of angry relatives, a couple of busts, a budding ulcer, and a full-blown case of paranoia. The flip side had a bunch of new Talcum laws of gambling filed under the heading "How Not to Make Book" (including ones on not jobbing lines, not getting drunk before playoff games, not soliciting customers farther away than Oyster Bay, and everything else a person could learn by doing the opposite of anything Barry said). Also, there was the money I made and saved and there was meeting Herman Baum. But both sides considered, my first quick look back left me feeling like a ballplayer who hit thirty-eight home runs while his team lost the pennant by forty-two games. I was good but where was it getting me?

So in February, down to one phone, and too bust-happy to jump right back into action, I began dealing with life instead of spreads. It wasn't easy. If I took a walk in the street and passed a ringing phone booth I'd have to fight off the urge to grab it, to get the line. I had to stop thinking of music on the radio as an interruption between sportscasts or a movie theater as a place to hang out when there were no day games. I wanted to try reading newspapers from the front page instead of starting with the box scores in the back, and most of all, I wanted to begin regarding people as more than potential customers. Even I knew you couldn't get much from life if all you cared about was whether they bet chalks or shorts.

Some of my habits changed, but it was a nip-and-tuck battle. Certain days I wanted to forget about self-improvement, and firfd a joint, and on others, the thought of action took a back seat while I drove off to the Bronx Zoo. Then, in the spring, I began feeling more at ease, and the main reason was a girl named Jennifer Barnett. Our relationship broke out of the gate like a snail, but considering I'd always thought roses were for Kentucky Derby winners, just crawling was a treat. After all, I'd been a big favorite to be involved with a Barnett that April, only it figured to be Dick, not Jennifer.

We met in a West Side Chemical Bank where she worked as a teller. The first three or four times I saw her, I never said anything except, "I though my balance was higher," but she was so friendly that on my fifth trip I struck up a conversation. When she didn't bite or scream or push the silent alarm, I even took a shot and asked her out for a lunch date. She accepted.

It was the best time I ever had in a Horn & Hardart. Jennifer told me she was twenty-two years old and had come to New York from Philadelphia to see what the big town was like. She was attractive and honest, and when she talked, it was about parks and museums or her apartment in the Village and the antique shops she spent her spare time browsing in.

We went out often over the next month or so and the more Jennifer opened up, the better I liked her. For a young girl from a Catholic family, she was pretty hip. Like on the night I told her I was thirty and had never been in love and she said I might make it to sixty unless I let her in my apartment to make some.

Well, after that remark one thing led to another and by the summer she'd forgotten about West 8th Street espresso and moved in with me to try some 79th Street corned beef. I can still remember the moment of truth, the first instant when I realized this relationship was major league. It was when Jennifer threw her luggage down in the doorway of my parents' old bedroom and said, "That's a neat bed. Let's sleep in here."

In the short time I knew Jennifer, I had never lied to her. Of course, there were a hundred things I never told her, one of them being that I was a bookmaker. Whenever she'd asked about what I did or how I made a living, I'd always mouth a sentence ending in "poker player" and change the subject. But now, with her wandering around a four-and-a-half room apartment with no telephones it was time to level and level I did . . . after the bags were unpacked.

I hit her with both barrels, from Jo-Jo through Barry. The busts, the trials, where the phones were, if I could get some (when a BM gets busted in his own home or apartment it's possible to renew service legitimately but only if you're a good boy and the police approve your request), and how I felt about bookmaking. I dealt with that last item by saying, "Jennifer, I want to spend the next few months getting to know you and having fun. After that, it's football season and if things work out, I'm going to be booking it." She didn't flinch.

I rewarded her faith with a dazzling June and July. As a matter of fact, for a thirty-year-old bookie who couldn't dance, didn't dress well, hated parties, and thought foreplay was what the Celtics called to shake Havlicek free for a jumper, I put on quite a performance.

We had breakfasts in the park, lunches at outdoor cafes and dinners with wine. I smoked grass at her friends' parties on East 6th Street and said getting stoned made me think of the beach in winter while all it really did was make me want more Fritos. We visited her parents, went to the track, took a five-day trip to Quebec. Hell, I even promised to use the hamper for dirty clothes instead of for old issues of *Sports Illustrated*.

In mid-August we were still going strong. Jennifer had stopped complaining about the walk to the corner to use the phone, and after we made love, the last thing I wanted was for her to disappear. But there was one nagging problem that wouldn't go away. It was what to do with that costlier than ever pajama company.

For six months I'd paid the rent, made believe the lease didn't have a year still to run, and didn't multiply eighteen times $300, but I had a limit and $5,400 was it. So in desperation I put a "For Sale" ad in the Business Opportunity Section of the *Times* and began coming to the office for a few hours on weekdays, hoping someone would nibble.

I wasn't going to hustle callers. I was long past the point of thinking Jama, Inc. could be sold for any real money. All I wanted was $100 for the furnishings and the lease taken off my hands.

The first week the ad ran I got nine calls. Six were from Jennifer, one was from Elliot Shadman, an old customer of Barry's who wanted to know if I was making book, one was from a woman who hung up when I told her my interest was in selling the business, not buying office supplies, and the last one, on Friday, was from a Chinaman named Peter Chin. We spent a minute or two in conversation, little of which I followed because he spoke in a thick accent, but my ears were good enough to pick up the "sweet" words. Like, "Mr. Talcum, this business proposition you offer sound very interesting. Be in my office, please, 9 A.M. Monday and we discuss further, yes?"

Was I ever in Mr. Peter Chin's Mott Street office on Monday morning, and in an hour the price for Jama, Inc. went up, oh, maybe fifty times over. It wasn't that Peter was stupid. He might not have even been a Hall of Fame turkey, but he didn't have to be either for this hustle. You see, Mr. Chin thought of himself as the Orient's version of the flim-flam man. He was a type I'd seen over and over in poker games I'd played in on Canal Street. These self-styled Chinese wheeler-dealers were tough on the fortune cookie circuit but I knew their whole set-up. They'd own a Chinese restaurant that did a good business and on the side they'd run a little fan-tan game in a basement on Bayard Street. Then there was the shoe store that never showed a profit, unless you included the sales from the "hot" jewelry hidden in the slippers, and a bar that didn't need to sell liquor because it had a back room with a crap table and a roulette wheel that sold losing.

The problem with these would-be Chinese millionaires was they never knew when to stop. I didn't know if it was from seeing too many George Raft movies, or a burning desire to build their parents a retirement home on Formosa, but they loved to gamble, loved to feel money, even if it was just passing through their shrimp toast, and they had a need to collect businesses like little kids collect baseball cards. As a result, for every money-making scheme they had, there was a costly farce to match, and in the end they wound up with $9,100 a week coming in and $9,000 going out.

Well, weaknesses like those figured to play right into my hands, and by Friday, Chin and I were meeting regularly. He was such a special treat I didn't mind the trips downtown. Each morning I'd walk in and see him sitting at his desk. He was about five feet four, plump, and wore thick glasses under slick-backed black hair. He wore a different suit every day, but he managed to look dumpy early and his ties always had stains on them. By the time I'd sit down, he'd usually be going through the mail, opening the letters with checks and throwing everything else into the garbage. When he noticed me, he'd say, "Excuse me, Mr. Talcum, but the pressures of business are great. Must make telephone calls." And he'd start on the phones. The calls were all the same, only the names changed. "Mr. Weinstein, I have labor to pay. I have overhead. You no send money, Mr. Weinstein, you no receive merchandise." Or: "Mr. Quigley, I receive your letter. No understand why you not want do business. Think over offer, please. Possibly reconsider and call me, yes?" I never heard what the people he was talking to said but it must have been upsetting because after most calls he'd hang up and make a wheezing, whining noise that sounded like an outboard motor. I always knew when a call was super-aggravating. Afterward, he'd slump back in his chair, make that Evinrude sound, pop some kind of pill in his mouth, turn to me, and say, "Mr. Talcum, so sorry for delay. Over now. Please tell me more about your business, yes?"

Then I'd go into my routine. "Look, Mr. Chin, I told you the whole story. My father died and left me with what seems to be a solid money maker, but I'm a horse trainer, like I told you, and all I want to do is sell it for a fair price and go back to Tampa." I thought it was a great story. It made me sound innocent, sincere, and honest, and, to a man like Chin, who spent his life being attacked for pennies and nickels, fighting with unions and bill collectors, and dealing with people who would sell their souls for a chance to make a buck seventy-five, it figured to do the trick.

Unfortunately, this was the third time I'd told it and Chin was still holding out. I had to make him bite. "Well, Peter, I wish you were more interested because I'm sure someone with your energy and know-how could make a go of it. The firm certainly supported my parents in style for many years." As I opened the door, Chin sat up and smiled. "No need to be hasty, Mr. Talcum. Tomorrow I come to your office and if pleased with what I see, make offer."

Naturally, I'd hoped Chin would buy my act without coming uptown, but I couldn't stop him, so the next morning I was there to greet him. I had a few tricks up my sleeve to distract Chin, hopefully enough to make him forget things like books or sales receipts, and as soon as he walked in I handed him a list of 100 department stores. "Look this over, Peter. My parents did business with every store on there." I didn't mention how long ago. Chin took a seat and began murmuring. "Hmm, Bloomingdale's. I buy all suits there. Good store do business with." The phone rang and I ran to pick it up knowing it was Jennifer calling per my instructions. "Murray, how's everything at Strawbridge & Clothier today?" I said loudly so Chin would hear me through the showroom door. "I can't give you 1,400 pieces of No. 786, Murray. It's a hot item. Wait on it and I'll ship it to you first thing Monday."

When I hung up and walked out, Chin was smiling. "Mr. Talcum, you busy. I like that, but must ask why office so bare and only one phone? Surely for business like this, one phone less than sufficient." I pulled up a chair and sat down with a heavy sigh. "Mr. Chin, my father was so devoted to his work that when our family doctor ordered him to stay home and rest he had most of the office equipment shipped to his house. Do you know, he died in his bed taking a reorder from Arnold Constable? Mr. Chin, they just don't make businessmen like that anymore, do they?"

He was still shaking his head in amazement when there was a knock at the door. I excused myself, walked across the room and let Case in, winking, to let him know everything was going according to plan. "Mr. Talcum, my client has agreed to meet your price," Case said, opening the briefcase he'd stolen for the occasion. If you'll sign this letter of agreement, I have the check already made out." "This is very embarrassing, Mr. Daniels," I said, glancing back at Chin who was straining to hear each word. "I have a prospective buyer with me right now and I don't think it would be fair for me to make this deal without first hearing his offer. I'm sure you understand." For a moment, I thought Case was going to blow everything by dropping to the floor in hysterics. Thankfully, he took a deep breath, said he'd call me tomorrow, and went running down the hall with his arm wedged in his mouth.

From the door, I could hear Chin doing his motor sound, but when I came in it stopped and he smiled again. "Mr. Talcum, I very interested in business, but before make offer must talk to silent partner. You come my office tomorrow and if silent partner say all in order, I make offer on spot, yes?"

It looked beautiful. I mean, Chin had a silent partner like I had a racing stable, and if he was thinking of using an I-want-to-buy-business-hope-silent-partner-agree story as leverage, that meant he was actually ready to be reeled in!

The following morning I got to Chin's office fully prepared. I had a story made up about my father's lawyer misplacing the books, in case Chin remembered he hadn't seen them yet, a plane ticket made out for an afternoon flight to Tampa sticking out of my coat pocket, and a copy of the lease clutched in my hot little hand. The lease was all I needed. Between Chin's phoning his nephew with a scheme to finance smuggling illegal aliens into this country from Hong Kong and repeated attempts to bribe a building inspector into leaving his mice-infested restaurant alone, he made the first move.

"Mr. Talcum, I tell silent partner $5,000 fair offer your business, but he cautious man, only agree to $3,500. Silent partner won't go penny higher, Mr. Talcum, but we prepared to pay cash and have contract written up for you to sign, yes?" Beating down my natural impulse to haggle for another grand, I hesitated for effect and walked to Chin's desk. "I'll tell you the truth, Mr. Chin. I have an offer for more than that amount but I think you're the kind of man my father would have wanted to run business. It's a deal." Then, I signed Chin's contract, which was nothing more than a piece of blank stationery with a typed paragraph stating that the business was legally mine to sell, handed over the lease and key, and took a wrinkled envelope from his outstretched hand.

I began to count the money as Peter picked up a phone to make a call. Thirty-three hundred dollars was inside. I counted a second time. There was no mistake. That envelope was $200 short! I was thinking how you just couldn't trust anyone nowadays when Chin placed his hand over the phone's mouthpiece, swiveled to face me and said, "So sorry about missing 200 dollar, but must deduct for payment to friend in phone company. Very expensive to restore service for raided premises but sure you understand, Mr. Talcum, that sometime small investment bring large return."

With that, Chin nodded his head, as if to dismiss me, and through the most subtle victor's smile I ever saw, said, "On return from Tampa, please feel free to visit old office. Items will be on sale there you find nowhere else in city. Perhaps we do more business then, yes?"

Old luxury buildings were out, because I worried doormen might get suspicious of my unusual hours. New high rises were a no, because the walls were too thin. Every time I thought about a hotel I pictured a maid coming in my room daily to make the bed, only to find it was never slept in. Nice brownstones tended to have friendly, intelligent tenants, and with a cozy three apartments to a floor I didn't need a sociable neighbor to invite me over for a pre-dinner martini. After all, how many times could I say "No thanks Clifton, the Yankees are at Cleveland for a twi-nighter"?

Well, with all those real and imagined fears I might never have found a joint if I hadn't realized the perfect place for me. A place with no doormen, maids, or martinis. Where I wouldn't have to worry about how thick the walls were, because my neighbors didn't figure to speak English, or if they did, wouldn't care enough to listen. A tenement.

Two days later, I found a room for rent on the fourth floor of a corroding West Side dump, paid the slumlord—who lived on the East Side and acted like he didn't care if I was Professor Cohen or a professional assassin—two months' rent and got busy. First, I had two phones put in. I was a little nervous that the guy who came to install them might ask why I needed two lines in an eight-by-twelve-foot room, but the only question he asked was if I thought he could get back to his truck without getting mugged. Next, I moved in a desk and chair, a small radio and television, a mattress for naps, pillows for the phones, and enough pens and pencils and legal pads to last for years. Then I met my fellow tenants who were easily as "out to lunch" as I'd hoped, and I was set. Hell, if I was a cop I wouldn't have driven down this block, much less walked into one of its buildings unless I was getting combat pay.

Luckily, none of the local snipers tried to shoot a BM disguised as a professor, and I began making book from there in time for the last week of exhibition jokes. After that, it was all gravy. The BMs Herman had introduced me to were okay. My customers were as honorable as I thought they would be, and even after Brady Keyes, a Pittsburgh Steeler cornerback, cost me two big games in a row by tripping over his feet attempting to play pass defense, I didn't lose control.

I mean, the sight of an upside-down football player didn't thrill me, but now that I was back in action, running things my way—like an honest businessman, like a guy who put into practice every bit of sound advice he'd ever gotten, and avoided making every mistake he'd ever seen—I knew I could handle anything that happened on a playing field. There'd be good days and bad, cigar games and streamers, hot streaks and cold ones, but I'd been through all of them before and I knew that as long as I had the vig, a good BM to deal with, and no cops at my door, I was here to stay.

Feeling permanent like that was nothing to shake a stick at either. It helped me to stop living from one opening day to another and by the end of football, it had eased my mind enough to remember I had a real love affair brewing with what's-her-name, you know, the one in the apartment.

While I was busy squeezing the juice that season instead of choking it, Jennifer was busy making it tough for me to get this stupid word "marriage" out of my head. Not only was she still all the things that made me love her in the first place, but more importantly, she seemed capable of actually living with a bookmaker. That's not an impossible feat but it's about as difficult as, let's say, spending a couple of weeks in Sherman Plunkett's jock strap. I figured the divorce rate for BM marriages had to be at least 80 percent and it would have been higher if most bookies didn't have their homes, cars, property, and anything else they didn't want the IRS to know about, listed under their wives' names.

Still, having four out of five Mrs. BMs winding up in Reno wasn't bad. I didn't know the exact grounds most of them used, but if the judges heard a few off-the-record gripes almost any one would do.

Desertion figured to be a biggie. After all, a bookie's

wife could spend 300 days a year—weekends included—patiently waiting for her husband to get done dealing the line at 8 P.M., only to get a call telling her to throw dinner out, because he had to go to New Jersey to pick up a delinquent's postdated check.

I'm sure mental cruelty was right up there, too. A wife could testify about being able to go on vacations only during bookmakers mating season and the quicky All-Star baseball game break. Or the agony of nights struggling to get to sleep with the "brrppiinng" sound of her husband's adding machine in the background, finally dozing off after swallowing an almost fatal number of sleeping pills, and then, being jolted out of bed at 3 A.M. when a degennie called to get a score he'd missed.

And complaints about sex could have got some fat settlements, because as much as BMs liked it, they liked sports reports even better. In fact, if a BM's sex life was brought up he'd lose either way. If his wife told a judge about trying to make love while he listened to Howard Cosell giving good scores, and said that good scores made him too excited to think of anything but money, he'd get hit with an alimony figure that would gobble it up. Worse, if she claimed his hearing bad scores got him so upset he'd roll off the bed and consumate their union on the bottom of the mattress, he'd be lucky to get left with his pen.

Well, I was more considerate, less crazy, and had better aim than most bookies, but I had plenty of faults, and through December I never stopped expecting Jennifer to tell me she was leaving for a better life with the Abominable Snowman. Amazingly though, right after the first of January, the girl finally convinced me that she just wasn't going to crack.

It happened on a freezing cold Tuesday night while I was taking basketball action in the joint. I say "freezing cold" because in my excitement over renting this place I forgot that broken windows and steamless radiators made

New York winters unbearable. I'd beat off frostbite up to then, thanks to a portable heater and an overcoat I never took off, but this night was the worst yet. A damp, bitter wind was blowing in off the Hudson and I was so cold that my nose was running onto the work, smudging the ink, partially erasing a few bets.

As if I wasn't miserable enough, at a little after seven, the electricity blew. The heater shut off, the radio stopped, the lights went and there I was, jogging in place to keep from turning blue, and lighting matches each time the phone rang so I could see what I was doing. About a minute later, I heard some confusion out in the hall and the voice of one of the hookers from the whorehouse on the first floor. She was screaming, "Professor Cohen! Professor Cohen! The electricity's out all over the building. What should we do?" Meanwhile, I was standing there with a lit match taking a bet and I couldn't even grab my other phone much less answer her. By then the Spanish guy who lived next to me must have been out in the hall, because he kept a lot of animals in his apartment and the floor was starting to smell and sound like a zoo.

I had to do something. I mean, I was supposed to be a professor, so as soon as I got done with the call I was on, I threw the phones under some papers I had on the mattress and opened the door. Mistake. Mrs. Pop, the madam, came charging into my room with six of her hookers followed by Señor Maderos and three of his German shepherds, and everyone but the dogs was holding matches or candles. "Cohen! Cohen!" Mrs. Pop shrieked, "we're scared to stay here in the dark. What should we do?" I said I didn't know but in an hour I'd go look for the fuse box, and while I was telling her that, Maderos was walking around my place with the dogs following him, the hookers were looking everywhere for the student I was supposed to be tutoring, and I felt like I was hosting a house party at a nudist colony's kennel.

A minute later, Mrs. Pop said, "I'm not spending the

night in the dark. Roxanne, go and call the police. That's a good idea, isn't it, Cohen?" "Oh, tremendous idea. Just great. Best one I've heard in years, but please don't call them," I said. "There's a lot of health violations in the building. They might make trouble or steal something. You know the police. Why don't you just go back downstairs and wait? I swear I'll fix everything by a quarter after eight."

Thank God, that got Mrs. Pop to tell Roxanne to forget it, and then this eerie candlelight procession filed out of my joint, I got the phones from the mattress and started to deal the line again. I held out for another ten minutes but by then I was down to my last few matches, so I called Jennifer. "Honey, the electricity is out and I can't leave for forty minutes. Please grab a candle and matches and get over here." She said okay, but by seven-thirty, I had no matches left and was already writing down the bets in huge letters, one call to a page, hoping I' wouldn't make too many errors. About five minutes later, she arrived and as I went to open the door, I remember thinking it was lucky she'd showed up when I wasn't on a call. I mean, that hall was dangerous in broad daylight.

Anyway, the second I got up to let her in, one phone rang and I groped for the receiver. I picked it up and heard Stewy say hello. "Listen," I said immediately. "I'm having some trouble here. Call me back," and I started to hang up. Before I got the receiver off my ear, he began pleading like only a degennie in mortal fear of not getting down could. "Okay, Al, Okay, sure, whatever you say, but can you give me one line now? Any line? What's Duquesne? What's David-son? Gimme anything. I just want to hear a price." "Stewy," I snapped, imagining one of Maderos's beasts eating Jennifer, "Duquesne's favored by 11½. I got to go," and in the instant it took to hang up, Stewy said, like it was all one word—like they'd be the last he'd ever speak—"Thanks Al gimme the Dukes for thirty times I'll call you tomorrow goodbye."

Well, after I got off I ran across the room to let Jennifer

in, told her to light the candle, and for the next twenty minutes sat at my desk taking bets while Jennifer stood by my side, silently, except for two sounds. One was the clicking of her chattering teeth and the other was the plip-plop of the dripping wax. At five after eight, I was finished, only there was one more thing I needed her for. She came through again. Sure, I found the fuse box but Jennifer had to put the fuse in.

Two weeks later, we got married by a judge in Far Rockaway, Queens. For our honeymoon, we drove over the Marine Parkway Bridge, stopped on Flatbush Avenue to pay off a customer, and ate dinner at a seafood place in Sheepshead Bay. After all, a guy had to treat his wife right.

Adjusting to the thought of being a married man took more time than I thought. I knew I wasn't single any more but I was busy, and what I was busiest at was finding out that making book in the 1970s called for some adjustments all its own.

For one thing, there were a lot more teams around. (In fact, there were a lot more leagues around, and expansion had got so out of hand bookmakers ignored the American Basketball Association and didn't know what the hell the World Hockey Association was. To this day, there's never been a line on a WHA game, and BMs in New York usually deal lines on ABA games only when the Nets play on TV.) Since in the Big Apple more teams meant more fans, which meant more bettors, the already-established leagues' expansion was more than enough to keep BMs hopping. Of course, the increased action wasn't necessarily bad—unless you lost it—but even a medium-sized bookie like myself had to learn to live with Monday night football, the Philadelphia Flyers - 1½ goals against the New York Islanders, and seeing less and less of his wife and cat.

Another 70s "treat" was a new breed of customer. I called them space age degennies, and after Jennifer got me to start unraveling my mind twice a week on a shrink's couch, I understood the first one I came into contact with surprisingly well. He was an art dealer named Timothy J. Mentally he had a lead on me. I mean I was just beginning to learn that Vietnam wasn't an apprentice jockey or that the Black Panthers didn't play for Florida A&M, but T.J. had his own problems. One of them was dropping ʼacid or mescaline almost nightly and betting with me after he was tripping his brains out. The shrink told me T.J. needed love and stability, and besides he was a good friend of Catch's, so I allowed him to bet games, often both sides at once, even though I knew he'd call back within the hour and ask me to disregard everything he'd said.

I let this go on until the '71 football season when I was forced to propose a deal. I said he could go wild Monday through Thursday, but if he called during weekend rush hours, whatever came out of his mouth counted. T.J. agreed, and except for a "Give me Denver minus the 8 over the Patriots for a hundred and the Patriots plus the 8 over Denver for a hundred" one Sunday, he never slipped.

In fact, he might still be a customer if it weren't for a system he dreamed up in May of 1972 when he was ripped on hash oil. As T.J. tried to explain it—after he gave up drugs and gambling—his system was based on the reaction of baseball players' glands to hot and cold weather. He thought a player going from a cold climate to a warmer one would feel lethargic and play accordingly, so every time a team like Montreal would go to Los Angeles to play the Dodgers, he'd bet LA. Conversely, whenever San Diego would travel to San Francisco, he'd bet the Padres, thinking the cool weather would stimulate their competitive juices. I never went back and checked the records, but I'd guess he dropped around $1,400 in April and I had to figure that lame-brain theory had a lot to do with it.

A twenty-eight-year-old research analyst I met through Bob Eberly was another type spawned in the 70s, only this guy was no psychedelic fish. I called him "Paul the Bomb," and what he did was use a computer to figure out who and how much to bet. If there was anything I didn't believe in it was theories or systems, and to me computers were just one more gimmick with nothing going for it but nuts like Paul who thought they could outfox the future. Six months and something like sixty winners out of ninety bets later I hadn't changed my mind, but I was beginning to hate the sound of his voice. "Hello, Al, this is Paul. Tonight, I'd like Creighton minus 7 for a hundred, USC minus 8 for three hundred, and Temple plus 9½ for five hundred. Thank you." I kept waiting for Paul's computer to either screw up or short-circuit and electrocute him, but I cracked after he made six winning $500 bets in a row during the first three weeks of the '72 football season. The very next Sunday he called, I dropped my usual professional air. "Paul, before you say a word I want you to know that Bob Eberly told me about the computer you're using. I don't care, you understand, I just want you to know I'm aware of it." "It's no secret, Al," Paul said, totally unruffled. "As a matter of fact, I think now I can predict scores as well as results." I gave Paul the line and didn't say another word until after he gave me his action: A $500 bet on the Oakland Raiders laying 8½ points against Buffalo. Then I said, "Paul, for laughs, why don't you tell me the final score so I can start doing the work right away instead of waiting until tonight?" "Sure, Al," he said seriously, "Oakland should win 28-10 on a dry field, 17-7 on a wet one."

Would you believe, Oakland won 17-8 in a driving rainstorm, and coincidence or my thinking Paul was a quack aside, he became the first customer I cut off since Lillian Camilli.

Like most things, the changing 70s weren't all bad and if its good points didn't outweigh disasters like Paul the Bomb and his Univac or the Texas Rangers playing baseball on Sunday nights, it at least offered some advances to make bookies smile between Seattle Supersonic games.

The advent of all-news radio stations, like WINS and WCBS in New York, was one. For years, getting scores had been a constant problem. Newspapers were good but they never had all the results until the next morning or afternoon, so you'd wind up with a phone in one hand taking one day's action, and a pen in the other figuring where you stood from the day before. Television stations seldom gave more than home team results, and radio had always been annoying. Forget Jocko's old streamers. Now there were nights you'd have to sit up and get bombarded by loudmouthed disc jockeys, acne medicine commercials, and "Top 40" songs only to get some ass saying that instead of the 2 A.M. sports recap he was going to play the newest single by some horrors called "The Bee Gees." As bad as they were, sometimes getting a sports recap was worse. Like when a hung-over all-night DJ would announce: "In that big basketball game down south, Kentucky romped over Tennessee, 87-94."

What the all-news radio stations did was give a sports report at a set time, and they were complete, accurate, and professional. It wasn't long before the names of newsmen like Charles Scott King and Spencer Ross became household words to the bookmakers and degennies of the 70s, and to my kind of people, they had it all over Russ Hodges and Mel Allen.

The growth of the off-track betting corporation (OTB) was even nicer. The guy who ran it, Howard Samuels, claimed it took an enormous amount of horse betting away from bookies and shifted it to the state-run OTB betting parlors. That was hardly the case.

To begin with, bookies hadn't handled heavy horse action in twenty-five years, and the few customers who bet the ponies with us weren't about to switch over to OTB. Bookies extended them credit, convenience, and a policy of "If-you-won't-mention-my-taxes, I-won't-mention-yours." OTB, on the other hand, offered them long lines, computer breakdowns, and tax forms for big winning bets. I'll admit OTB would pay off on any odds while bookies wouldn't (standard practice is to limit pay-offs on horse action to 30 to 1 for straight bets, 75 to 1 on daily doubles, and 100 to 1 on exactas), but then OTB didn't handle bets parleying a guy's winnings from the sixth at Belmont on to Weber State + 7.

In fact, OTB not only didn't hurt BMs, it helped. The state did so much advertising to promote horse action that lots of people who never bet before decided to see what it was all about. They started out risking two dollars at their neighborhood OTB shop and some of the folks who liked how it felt raised the ante. Soon two dollars was five and ten. Then the Jets looked sweet against the Bears, the OTB was closed Sundays, and friends were asked if they knew a bookie. Six weeks later, thanks to dreamy Madison Avenue ads that made the Big A look like the Garden of Eden and gambling a virtue instead of a sin, BMs had fresh, new business.

Well, through all the changes, good and bad, I kept dealing the line day in and day out. I fixed the joint up with an air-conditioner for summers, a new, bigger heater for winters, and boards for the windows; and tacky as the place was, it was okay by me.

After all, I was still there in January of 1973, which made it three years since I'd last seen the inside of a police car. My sheet had grown to where I had thirty steady, if not spectacular customers, plus fifteen spot players, and I was grinding out enough money to feel secure whenever I remembered Jennifer was seven months pregnant.

Hell, after so many years of ups and downs, it was a pleasure to have finally built a business that took care of itself. Only there was one more short gauntlet to run. It looked shaky for a week, but the guy waiting at the end of it was going to make everything worthwhile.

The Knicks caused it, only it wasn't the same Knicks I'd won my first horse from. They'd come a long way since their days of picking number one draft choices with an ouija board, and starting seven-foot centers who couldn't dunk, guards who

thought they were Pinkertons and forwards who wore ortho-
pedic sneakers. They'd become good, very good, and in the
70s they single-handedly made pro basketball into a heavily
bet, network-televised sport which was quickly replacing
baseball as the second biggest action game in New York. I
could handle them going from doormats to world champions
okay. I could even appreciate the talent of Walt Frazier,
whom I considered to be the best basketball player I'd ever
seen—and believe me, by this time in my life, athletes were
just numbers—but what was killing me was what a jinx the
Knicks had become.

Since 1970, they were the one team in sports who not
only won when I didn't want them to, but had the balls to
lose on the rare occasions I needed them to win, and in the
winter of 1973, I got hit with the terrible news that I wasn't
the only BM in New York who hated their collective guts. I
found out during the first week in February, when I got a call
at home from Charley M., the spokesman for him and his
partner, Louis, the two bookies Herman had introduced me
to two and a half years before.

"Listen, Al," Charley M. said on a Tuesday night. "This
Knick team's busting my chops something awful. Last Thursday, I got four grand on them and all I heard was Marv Albert
for forty-eight minutes: 'Frazier, a twisting jumper.... Yes!
Reed, a reverse dunk.... Yes! Bradley, a running hook from
the baseline.... Yes! And he's fouled.' Two nights later I got
pounded with Milwaukee money, Albert does beer commercials, and the Bucks win by 17. I'm sorry, Al, but me and
Louis talked it over and we're going to take a break till we
get back on our feet."

"Charley, come on, you can't leave me hanging like this
in the middle of the season. Reed's screwed me so many
times since '70 he could carry my wife's baby, but you don't
hear me giving up, do you?" "Al, I'll look around for another
BM to help you out but I'm leaving for Puerto Rico Saturday
while I still got the plane fare."

Some business, huh? I spend three years making book like the Swiss make watches and in one swoop two BMs and five guys in hot pants put me back to holding every penny bet and dealing a line copied off the back page of the *Post*. By the following Friday I hadn't found one BM to deal with, and the pressure to hook up with a betting office or a Barry Squires type was growing. They weren't what I wanted, but making book like I was back on 86th Street wasn't either.

Come Saturday morning I decided to try and finesse it through the weekend, but my mind was made up. First thing Monday I was going to hook up with anyone who'd have me and references would have to wait.

I still remember sitting in the joint that morning with Charley and Louis gone, thinking that a real bad two days without a hedge to cushion the losses could wipe out a month of slow, steady winning. The thought made me nervous. Worse I felt annoyed and upset about being in this ridiculous situation, even if it was temporary. Then the phone rang for the first time at 11:35. I had the paper in front of me and I picked up the receiver slowly, like I almost hated to do it. "Talcum," a half-whispered voice said, "my name's Waldo Dorsohp. Charley M. tells me you need a sharp line."

Mickey Mantle probably thought his future looked made when Casey Stengel pointed to the center field monuments of Yankee Stadium and said, "It's all yours, kid. Come to me or Joe D if you need any help," but Mickey had to clout a few hundred home runs to be sure. With Waldo Dorsohp on my side it took me a month. The guy was thirty-three years in coming, but the wait was cheap at the price.

The biggest problem in talking about Waldo is knowing where to start. There's the funny stuff, like the overcoat he never takes off even in the dog days of July and August, because it has specially sewn-in pockets to keep all his pads, pens, phone nmbers, sports schedules, and rolls of dimes. And the crushed tan golf hat he wears out of habit, despite the fact it looks like a hippo's been sitting on it for two or three years. And the toupee to cover his bald head and keep betting slips under. And the time he simultaneously put his foot through the picture tube of his television set and a fist into the mouth of his third wife. (Of course, it was only after watching the Chicago Bulls blow a 24-point lead to the Knicks, so his old lady understood.) There's even the code names he uses for phone booths, himself, me, his 150 customers, days of the week, spots to settle, and enough other people, places, and things to have created a language all his own. But so what?

I could have just as easily started by talking about the bookmaking stuff. How he's a fifty-year-old independent BM who's made book every single day of his life since the age of eighteen. That some days he works out of phone booths and other days deals from his three joints. That he gets up to seven separate betting lines daily. That he takes hedges off me on buckshot games 99 out of 100 bookies wouldn't touch. That he has two runners working for him who make more money than most pro quarterbacks. I could even tell you that he booked $18,000 on a Fiesta Bowl or that he's never been arrested. But so what?

You see, the second biggest problem in talking about Waldo Dorsohp is knowing when to stop. So all I do now is simply think how lucky it was for me to have met him and feel good that he played a small part in the most important night of my life. . . .

It started at 5:45 P.M. on a Friday in March. I hadn't been in my joint that day because Jennifer had asked me to stay home with her. She was very pregnant. But, I was there that night, and when the phone rang I automatically said, "Hiya, Kaplan,"—Waldo's code name that week—and he said, "Jesus, Hammil,"—my code name that day—"You got me worried this afternoon. I thought for sure you got busterooskied." After I explained my absence, Waldo simply said, "Yeah, baby's are tough; here's what I got. Wake Forest 7, Tulane 9½, Utah State pick-em, Villanova 3—no forget 3. I hear Kraft got 'em up for this game. Make 'em 3½ until you get some Penn action."

He stopped for breath, went on to give me the lines on about twenty more college baskerball games and a few pro ones, and hanging up said, "Watch that South Carolina game-ski, I think 6½ is a bad line, but deal it till Whitey tells me different." Whitey was one of the people he got his lines from. Last week his name had been Soupy.

Anyway, by seven o'clock Waldo had called me four

times. Once to say he "needed St. John's *big*," once to say his customers were "all taking the chalkerooskis," and twice to say "Hammil, you got anything to hedgeoffski yet?" The only call I reacted to was his last "hedgeoffski" one, because for no good reason, I was getting a ton of money bet on Citadel, who were playing Richmond and were 1½-point underdogs. I laid off a nickel to Waldo and he said he'd call back as soon as he got to his next booth. (He always worked from booths on Fridays.)

At 7:30 I picked up a ringing phone and assumed it was either Waldo or a customer. It was Jennifer. "Al, I think the baby's coming. Please hurry up and come home." I had been mentally preparing myself for this moment for weeks, so to calm her down, I said, "Honey, just relax and I'll be right there," and for once in my life I couldn't have cared less about leaving the joint early. In fact, the only reason I answered the phone when it rang an instant later was that I was certain it was Waldo's 7:30 check-in. If I wasn't there, he'd figure to panic, forget about the baby, and spend the night thinking I was busted and he was next. "They still bettin' you Citadel, Hammil? I'm gettin' loaded up on Maryland myself, so if you get action that way, move the price up a half pointski." I said, "Waldo, I'm sorry, Kaplan—whatever the hell your name is this week—I don't have time for anything. Jennifer thinks the baby's coming and call me later at Lenox Hill Hospital if you want."

With that, I ran out of the joint and didn't stop until I got home. Sure enough, when I burst in the apartment Jennifer looked ready to give birth any second. She was in too much pain to be nervous, but I was a wreck and wasted a few minutes looking for her suitcase. When I found it on the bed where I'd left it, we went downstairs and got a cab. By the time we arrived at Lenox Hill, her doctor was waiting, and they rushed her off to deliver the baby while I went to a waiting room filled with guys who looked like they had a month's pay riding on a game they were losing 49-zip.

Meanwhile, as much as I was caught up in the excitement of becoming a father, I hadn't completely forgotten that I was also a bookmaker, and for that night, one who hadn't hedged anything except for the Citadel nickel. Luckily, there was a guard in the hall, sitting at a desk listening to a radio, and every fifteen or twenty minutes I'd walk out there hoping to hear a sports report. I remembered the eight games I needed the most—three for a grand, four for around $1,200 and the Citadel thriller for two dimes—and every other trip or so, I'd catch a partial score. By 10:00 I was hearing finals, and six of the big eight were in. I'd won all of them. By 10:15 I still had no news from the delivery room but I'd made one more trip to the hall. I was seven for seven. This was some night. Not only was my wife giving birth to our baby, but I was making a fortune.

By 10:30 I was really jumpy. There was still no news from upstairs and even though the guard was gone, I was walking out into the hall just to relieve the tension. About five minutes later a nurse came into the waiting room and asked for Alfred Talcum. When I told her that was me, she said I had an emergency phone call and could pick it up at the floor's main desk. In the same instant I picked up the receiver and heard Waldo's voice, I saw Jennifer's doctor at the other end of the hall, waving for me to come over to him.

For a moment I just stood by the desk watching the doctor wave and listening to Waldo. "Hammil, I had some *big* night. Ten, fifteen dimes in scratcherooski, Hammil." I started to nod my head at the doctor, as if to say I'd be right there, and while Waldo babbled on, I could feel this piece of bookmaker inside me being gently replaced by this newcomer, this thing called fatherhood. "Waldo," the exiting bookmaker piece said, "just tell me what happened in the Citadel game," and when he answered, "They won outright 87-81. Hammil, I'm telling you the shortski's went wild tonight," the newcomer had me down to that doctor mighty fast. "Congratulations, Al," he said, "if you're interested, a lovely woman upstairs just had a beautiful baby girl."

Instead of waiting for an elevator, I raced up the stairs,

two at a time, and didn't slow down until I found Jennifer's room. She was still under the anesthesia, but I wanted very much to tell her I loved her so I walked over to her bed, and kind of brushed her forehead with a kiss. Jennifer opened her eyes and although she was foggy, she could tell it was me. "Al," she asked weakly, "how's the baby?" and I told her the doctor said she was perfect. "I'm so happy. You know I was hoping for a girl," Jennifer said, and knowing she needed her rest, I gave her a hug, got up to leave, and promised I'd be back in the morning. As I bent down to kiss her goodnight, Jennifer whispered, "Okay, darling, but while you're home think of a name you'd like for our daughter."

I said that I would and as I reached the door, I hesitated for a moment, turned around, and walked quietly back to the bed. "Jennifer, I have a great idea." My wife looked up like she could barely hear me. "Tonight for the first time in my life I won every game I needed." Suddenly Jennifer sat up a little straighter, still half-asleep, but looking as if she didn't want to miss what was beginning to sound like a bookmaker special. "I was just wondering if we could name the baby after one of the teams. You know, like call her Citadel," I said, hoping she'd know I was kidding. "You see, I needed them for two dimes," I began to explain, but by mid-sentence Jennifer had fallen flat on her back, and as weak and as out of it as she was, she managed to reach out and put a pillow over her head. "Listen, honey, it's not that ridiculous," I went on. "Down South a lot of girls have strange names," but a second later Jennifer just nudged the pillow off her face, laughed, and told me to let her go to sleep.

Well, I thought it was pretty funny myself and riding down in the elevator I laughed out loud. Citadel Talcum, could you imagine anyone ever doing something as sick as that? Of course, I thought as I got into a cab, I'd heard worse names. It did have a certain ring to it, and as the cab passed through Central Park, I sat back in my seat thinking about having a daughter named Citadel. I mean it was a big underdog to get by the wife, but who knew, it had a little shot.

Talcum's Terms

Ace, Frank T.: An old trotter famous for almost always winning or losing races by a nose.

Accommodation Game: A game a bookie will take action on as a favor to his customers. Example: New Utrecht High School versus Erasmus High School—WPIX-TV—Saturday morning. If ninnies wanted to bet it, I'd make it 2½ Erasmus, have a good time.

Action: The act of gambling. What every bookmaker wants to be in, every ninny likes to be in, every deginnie needs to be in, and every sicky must be in.

Adjusting the Line: What a BM does to even out heavy one-way betting, as in making a heavily bet 9-point favorite 9½- or 10-point choices. Referred to by Waldo Dorsohp as "adjustskis."

Albert, Marv: Radio announcer for New York Knicks and New York Rangers. Disliked by many bookies for his habit of screaming, "Yes, and he's fouled!" after a Walt Frazier 30-foot jump shot cost them a lot of money.

Automatics: Customers who never miss a day of action.

Bell, Hugh: A retired harness racing driver.

Betting Line: What a bookie gives his customers before they bet sports. It's based on points in basketball and football, goals in hockey, and odds in baseball. Also known as the "line," the "prices," or the "spread."

Betting Slips: Small pads of paper some bookies use to write action on.

Big: The term used to describe the heavily bet team of the day as in, "I need the Mets big!"

Big Shoulders: Football.

BM: Bookmaker.

Bookmakers Mating Season: The period of time (late March through early April) after the NCAA basketball tournament and before opening day of the regular baseball season; often used by bookies to take vacations. Sometimes a bookie may have to cancel plans when angry Grapefruit League bettors threaten to go to the airport and lie down under the wheels of his plane.

Bottom Line: The cold hard fact or facts about a situation as opposed to bullshit. The real story.

Breeze: The beginning of a winning streak, as in "feeling a breeze."

Buckshot: A game in which one team is bet very heavily.

Bulls: Police officers. Referred to by Waldo Dorsohp as "bullerooskis" or "coperooskis."

Bust Happy: Bookie paranoia due to multiple arrests in short period of time. Imagining that all phones are tapped and that old nuns sitting outside of Yankee Stadium are gambling detectives in disguise.

Chalk: The favorite.

Chalk Monster: A bettor who loves to bet favorites.

Cigar Game: An easy win. Example: Betting on the Boston Patriots, getting 14 points, and watching them beat Oakland 49-7.

Clerk (pronounced "cloik" by many bookies): A guy who takes action over the phones for bookmakers who don't want to do it themselves.

Cover: What a team does when it's favored by 6 points and wins by 7 or more. Referred to as "covering the spread."

Creedmore: A mental hospital in New York City.

Dancer, Stanley: One of the better harness racing drivers.

Dealing the Line: Quoting the betting line. Usually done over the telephone, sometimes two or three at once.

Degennie: Human being almost always in action. Characteristics: Would much rather watch last two minutes of Fiesta Bowl than be raped by Brigitte Bardot. Has no idea that Green Bay is actually a city in Wisconsin. Can sit blindfolded in the trunk of a car and without getting lost, give directions to any racetrack or sports stadium within a 25-mile radius of his home.

Delinquents: The people who populate disabled lists.

Dime: $1,000.

Disabled List: What a bettor goes on when he has to pay his losses on an installment basis.

Dog: The underdog, the team regarded as not likely to win. Also known as the "short."

Exacta: A wager where a bettor has to pick the winner of a race and the horse who runs second in order to collect.

Flashes: Final or partial sports or race results. Usually received by radio, television, newspapers, or word of mouth. Recently available by phone, thanks to special service set up by New York Telephone Company. When you see a guy standing in a phone booth for over two minutes without his lips moving, you'll know he's getting flashes.

Flats: The thoroughbreds.

For My Lungs: A phrase a BM uses when the outcome of a game is very important, as in, "I need the Jets for my lungs!" Differs from *big* game in that bad score might result in BM turning himself in to police.

1407 Broadway: An office building in New York City's garment center. It is the headquarters for many of the country's leading clothing firms. BMs regard it as a shrine because it probably contains more bettors per square foot than any other building in the world.

Freebie: A free day for a BM due to lack of action. Most appreciated in baseball season when freebies are as scarce as inside-the-park homers.

Furniture: An elaborate code devised by Waldo Dorsohp wherein he substituted pieces of furniture for words he was afraid to use when he thought the coperooskis were listening, as in, "I got to borrow a sofa" ($1,000), or "Drop off an armchair ($500) tonight." I finally convinced him to use a new code after spending a football Sunday saying things like, "Waldo, I have three sofas on the end tables (Lions) from Detroit. Can I reupholster (hedge off) two armchairs?"

GA: Gamblers Anonymous. Where you go when HFC has a Wanted Dead or Alive poster with your face on it.

Getting Down: Giving a bet to a bookie, who then writes it down and repeats it back to the customer to make it official.

Going Wide: The first signs of strange behavior. Also known as "very wide." Going "out to lunch" usually follows.

Grapefruit League: The exhibition baseball games played during spring training. Occasionally BMs have to put up with Degennies who want to bet the Cubs "B" team against Arizona State at Tempe.

Heat: What happens when the police get serious about busting bookmakers, as in, "the heat's on." In New York, just a little bit more frequent than undercover witch hunts.

Hedge: What a bookmaker does when he lays off part of his action with another bookmaker, in an attempt to minimize his risk. Referred to as "hedging."

HFC: Household Finance Corporation. A loan company many gamblers are acquainted with.

Hitters: Bettors who seldom wager less than $100 and never more than $400.

Holding Everything: The opposite of hedging (also the opposite of sanity). What a bookie is doing when he keeps as much action as he can take. Referred to as "wide open."

Hoop Freaks: People who love to bet basketball.

Hoops: Basketball.

Horrors: Anything a bookie finds incredibly revolting. Examples: Booking thousands of dollars on the Detroit Tigers with each customer stipulating that Mickey Lolich has to be the starting pitcher, hearing Detroit lost 11 to 1, and then finding out Woody Fryman started. Having a delinquent settle his debt with a postdated check from the First National Bank of Bombay.

Hotiola: A horse bet down from 10-1 to 9-5 in the last two minutes before post time. Hotiolas have a tendency to make hotiola bettors tip over track snack bars after running fifth in a seven-horse field.

Insko, Del: Another harness racing driver.

Jamaica: A housing development that was once a thoroughbred racetrack in New York City.

Juice: See Vigorish.

Knockout Shot: The term a BM uses after losing a buckshot, for your lungs, or big game, as in, "That Giant game was some knockout shot."

L++: Found on upper right-hand corner of front page of New York Times. Indicates latest edition of paper, which will include West Coast final scores and the last race from Yonkers Raceway. Unessential for Eric Severeid. Very essential for BMs.

Laundry Lister: A bettor who gets down on lots of games.

Often takes so much time his bookie lights a cigarette, and takes his other phones off their hooks on hearing his voice.

Laying: Betting the favorite, as in "laying the points" or "laying the odds."

Laying It and Loving It: Betting the favorite and betting it heavy.

Lock: A sure thing.

Lunched: See Out to Lunch.

Monsters: Customers who bet the maximum a BM will take. Anything under a $500 wager is gumball money.

Monticello Raceway: A harness track nestled in the Catskill Mountains, where thousands of tourists visit their money every summer.

Morning Telegraph: A newspaper filled with statistics and articles on thoroughbred race horses. Frequently found hidden inside copies of the *Wall Street Journal* or *New York Times*. Occasionally found ripped into shreds in subway cars. Also referred to as the "Telly form," the "racing form," or by real degennies as the "Bible."

Need: The expression used by a BM when he's asked about a game. As in having $15,000 on Syracuse and $18,000 on West Virginia, and saying, "I need Syracuse."

Nice: A good feeling. Example: Winning any game in the last 30 seconds after losing it for 59½ minutes. If the game is won in last 5 seconds after losing it for two hours, just plain "nice" becomes "nnnniiiiicccccceeee!"

Nickel: $500.

Ninny: A small bettor ($25 or less), but often a degennie at heart. Characteristics: Asks whom *I* like before he bets. Worked for father and was fired. Loses regularly, thank you, but never for more than a $100 a week.

OC: Organized crime.

Out to Lunch: Crazy. (A person who isn't in a padded cell but should be.) Examples: Anyone who leaves Belmont Racetrack and without thinking, boards the degennie bus for Yonkers Raceway. Betting $100 on a greyhound because he has a nice bark. Also known as "lunched."

Overtime: What any basketball game (or championship football or hockey game) goes into when it ends in a tie during regulation time. Usually, the result is a "puker" or "steamer."

Parked Outside: What happens to a trotter who has to run outside of other trotters because he's not fast enough to get the lead.

Paying and Collecting (P & C): What a bookmaker and his customers do every week, usually on Mondays and Tuesdays. For a BM, process entails walking, waiting, and (depending on his customers' luck) either plenty of money or plenty of "pay later" stories. Also known as "making rounds" or "settling."

Players: Customers who rarely bet less than $50 or more than $100. The majority of my clientele and most bettors.

Plunkett, Sherman: One of the sloppiest and fattest pro football players ever to make it in the NFL. Often had jersey out of pants before taking the field.

Popped: Arrested. Also known as "pinched," "collared," or "busted."

Puker: A game that's impossible to lose, but you do.

Rikers Island: A New York City prison where courts occasionally send bookies in the futile hope that they'll be rehabilitated. More BMs have drowned trying to swim back to Manhattan phone booths than have been even slightly helped.

Roundball: Basketball.

Runner: A person who finds customers for a bookie and gets a cut of their losses.

Sheet: All of a bookmaker's customers, as in "I got forty customers on my sheet."

Shoot: What a BM is on while a winning streak is in progress.

Sicky: A bettor who crosses the line between being a degennie and a degenerate. Bets on everything and always for more than he can afford. Is capable of betting $5,000 on a weekend, yet takes family to Blimpie's for Sunday night dinner.

Sitting Direct: Having a joint as opposed to working out of phone booths.

Spot Players: Bettors who aren't in action every day.

Squeezing the Juice: Making money from vigorish.

Steam Job: A tough loss. Example: Getting beat in the

bottom of the ninth inning on a checked swing double by a relief pitcher hitting .078. Also known as a "steamer."

Suburban Jacket: A type of outer jacket worn by gambling detectives. Usually accompanied by white socks and short hair.

Sure: The word I use to sum up my reaction to not totally unexpected disasters, but nevertheless particularly annoying ones. Example: I'm stuck $1,800 in a poker game. It's the last hand and I'm dealt 10, jack, queen, king of spades and the 3 of hearts. The man to my left opens for the maximum bet. The three guys between him and myself each raise. I borrow money, raise everyone, and take one card. Then I put it in my hand, live through another round of betting, and slowly squeeze it out. . . . It's the 2 of hearts. . . . Sure!

Taking a Shot: Betting or booking more money than usual.

Taking the Points: Betting the underdog in basketball or football. Also known as "getting the points."

Tapioca: The state of having had money, not having any left, and owing some.

Tapped or Tapped Out: Having no money.

Taste: A portion of something valuable, usually obtained illegally.

Turkey: Someone a bookie can always count on to give him a niiiice feeling. Example: Anyone who ever bet against Sandy Koufax.

Tweezer: A reference to the number 3. A field goal in football. A 3-point play in basketball. A home run with two men on in baseball.

Vigorish: The percentage edge a BM has on his customers. What makes bookmaking technically illegal. Also known as the "vig" or as "juice."

Wire Rooms: What joints used to be called.

Work (pronounced "woik" by many bookies): The written record of a bookie's dealings with his customers. Done weekly and usually in code or duplicate in case of a bust. Often referred to as "the figures."